MASSIVE
PISSED
LOVE

ALSO BY RICHARD HELL

GO NOW

HOT AND COLD

GODLIKE

I DREAMED I WAS A VERY CLEAN TRAMP

MASSIVE PISSED LOVE

NONFICTION 2001-2014

RICHARD HELL

SOFT SKULL PRESS
AN IMPRINT OF COUNTERPOINT / BERKELEY

Library of Congress Cataloging-in-Publication Data
Hell, Richard.
[Essays. Selections]
Massive pissed love : nonfiction 2001-2014 / Richard Hell.
pages cm
Includes bibliographical references.
ISBN 978-1-59376-627-6 (paperback)
I. Title.
PS3558.E4752A6 2015
814'.54—dc23
2015030008

ISBN 978-1-59376-627-6

SOFT SKULL PRESS
An imprint of COUNTERPOINT
2560 Ninth Street, Suite 318
Berkeley, CA 94710
www.softskull.com

Printed in the United States of America
Distributed by Publishers Group West

10 9 8 7 6 5 4 3 2 1

CONTENTS

LOVE

LIST OF ILLUSTRATIONS

AUTHOR'S NOTE

I've always liked thinking about subjects that move me, like movies and painting and music and writing, and even life that isn't art yet, when I notice it, and I'm lucky that I've been able to write about them without a lot of interference from editors. Much of the writing in this book came from me approaching editors with subjects I wanted to apply myself to. Part of the reason I have the freedom I've had in non-fiction is that editors will think of me as a freak. I'm allowed some latitude because after all you're watching a punk write as if he's an intellectual.

The organization of the book is semi-arbitrary. It was too dull to just divide it by subject matter, so I skimmed through it in search of aspects. I saw that some pieces were lengthy, some were angry, and many were thrilled or adoring: massive, pissed, love. So I had a possible title too. (Though the subtitle is slightly inaccurate—there are three pieces from the '90s-2000 and one from 2015. Other pre-2001 nonfiction is in my book *Hot and Cold*.) Within sections, I just went with the classic flow, kind of like sequencing songs on an album, but with a few random other factors, like the technical ones affecting what and where I could color illustrate.

Writing this book was almost all fun, even though sometimes stressful. I like to do research, and to be sure anything I present as factual is. The first couple of times I took on something large, or even small (a thousand word film review), I would get annoyed with the way it's necessary to endlessly research and fact check in order to turn up the three percent which will actually be used. But pretty soon I accepted that and even reveled in it. Some of the writings are practically scholarly, or at least studious, while others are neatened notes for loose talks. For the "Mouth of Hell" columns the system was I'd set the alarm on my calendar to pop up one day before each deadline and then ask myself what I'd been thinking about, go 500 words from there, and turn it in the next morning. Foundations are hidden. I like my notes and drafts towards pieces almost more than the pieces themselves.

When I was young I made aggressive rock and roll music, but it originated in thought and analysis and artistic ambitions too, no matter how physical, emotional, and crude it might have seemed. One thing I've learned in years of thinking about people's artworks is that the interesting, useful way of looking at them is to assume that the artist knows what he or she is doing. It's profitably confusing when the artist actually is an idiot, or a punk.

MASSIVE

THE DEVIL, PROBABLY

THERE'S NOT ENOUGH TIME. There's not enough time. I remember when I was a kid in my early twenties and trying to teach myself to write I was also publishing books as a small publisher and I was doing a book of Patti Smith's. We were calling it *Merde*, and she drew some pictures for it and one of them was just the penciled words, "There's not enuf time" (she first wrote "enough" and changed it to "enuf" which was better), and I thought that was glamorous, because for me there was way too much time, way way too much time. Which brings me to *The Devil Probably*, doesn't it, because the devil makes play—wait no it's "work"— for idle hands.

But what I was really thinking when I said there's not enough time was that when I consider how I'd like to speak of Robert Bresson, there's not enough time. I don't have enough time to be brief! Because it's true I'm not who I was when I was twenty or twenty-five and I have come to the kind of existence where there's not enough time and I am ultimately glad of that, even if it brings an awareness that I can't do justice to Robert Bresson.

But what brings me to this movie this afternoon is the recognition in it of that kid who I was in the 1970s. Doubtless it's presumptuous and ignorant of me to come to the movie in such a self-centered way, but I think it's no worse than coming to it by way of picking pockets. It's a strange path I have had to take to come to Bresson.

So I want to talk a little about how this movie affected and affects me. As I say, I came to Bresson late. I don't know why. I've always loved movies and I thought I had fairly sophisticated taste and knowledge. It's true that Bresson goes against everything we're conditioned to appreciate in movies by Hollywood and modern life, but then so does Godard whom I've loved since I first saw his movies in my teens. But then Godard did start out riffing on his love for Hollywood genre movies, so he took you on this educational ride, whereas Bresson is astonishing for his fidelity to filmic values that forego all audience manipulation, all pandering for any cheap thrills. For instance, as Susan Sontag pointed out, there's no conventional suspense in his movies. His movie about a prisoner trying to get away actually reveals its denouement in its title: *Un condamné à mort s'est échappé* (literal translation: *A Man Condemned to Death Escapes*; English release title: *A Man Escaped*). In fact, it's funny, when we posted at my website in advance of this screening a little account of the story of *The Devil, Probably* I made the ending of it into a hyperlink so that the reader would have to choose if he or she wanted to know the ending. But of course later when I was looking at the movie again I saw that practically the first shot of the movie is a newspaper headline shouting out the movie's climax. (By the way, the movie's color though the stills here aren't.)

Also there's no humor in Bresson. Well, it is pretty much impossible for anything really good not to be a little funny, but there's as little humor as you can imagine. Dostoevsky seems to have been an artistic brother for him, at least in terms of themes—*Pickpocket* and *Une Femme Douce* and *Four Nights of a Dreamer* are all derived to degrees from Dostoevsky—and maybe the incidental humor in Bresson happens the way it does in Dostoevsky, rooted in grotesque pathos. Nobody ever even smiles in a Bresson movie. The only moment I noticed in *The Devil, Probably* where there was a hint of upturned lips on a character was during the most disturbing scene of the movie and happened when the main character Charles realizes the bus he's on is out of control.

I also detected exactly one joke. When Charles is in a psychiatrist's office—where he's gone at the insistence of his girlfriend who's worried about his suicidal tendencies—he relates a dream of being dead but of still being hit and trampled by his killers, and the shrink, who looks like a rabid raccoon, asks him, "Do you see yourself as being a martyr [in French: uh mar-teer]?" And Charles replies, "Only an amateur [ama-tare] . . . When I wanted to drown myself or pull the trigger, I realized it wasn't all that easy." Pun!

It's also kind of funny that later on in that psychiatrist scene, when Charles in his endearingly sincere way describes again his problem with actually being able to carry out the deed, the psychiatrist—in what doesn't seem like some kind of reverse psychology but actually just fatuous self-important pride-in-erudition—points out, "That's why the ancient Romans entrusted a servant or friend with the task." Which of course is exactly what Charles needed to hear, as the movie moves to a close . . .

Nearly all movies made are not only essentially filmed theater, but are confections contrived to elicit audience saliva, to give reflexive thrills, to play to weaknesses. They're fast food and candy. I'm not saying I don't like such movies: there are lots of them that not only give me pleasure but that I respect. For instance in the midst of my thinking about Bresson in the last couple of weeks, I was invited to a screening of a movie by Doris Wishman. She was a woman who made soft-core porn movies, mostly in the '60s and '70s, though the one I saw was from the '80s. It was called *Let Me Die a Woman* and was a shockumentary type sexploitation flick about transexuality, and it was fantastic—and I don't mean that from any kind of so-called irony or double standard—and it was great to see while I was thinking so strenuously about Bresson because it was for all practical purposes as satisfying as he, as different as its origins were. It was a demonstration and reminder that good will and a purity of spirit even when fully devoted to the pleasing of an audience can result in a very great movie.

But Bresson is in a class of his own—the film lover's filmmaker and the filmmaker's filmmaker—for his heroic insistence on fidelity to the soul and truth of film as moving pictures in sequence with sound, rather than mere filmed theater. Filmed theater being acting—people adopting facial expressions as signals of emotions, for instance. But beyond that even, Bresson doesn't want a piece of film to have any significance apart from its relationship to another piece of film. He really means that and it's radical—if you isolate a shot of his there's hardly ever any narrative information in it; if he has to tell you something happened for narrative purposes he's likely just to have someone in the film say it happened. Doubtless this is partly why it took me so long to find him: his films at first glance and in comparison to what we're barraged with in the way of audio/video can seem straight and colorless and impossibly elliptical. There are no special effects; in fact he uses only one lens ever, a fifty millimeter, the single lens that most closely approximates the view of the human eye; he uses music only very sparingly, and by the last few films, such as *Devil*, only music the source of which exists in the movie, like a record playing or a church organist; and most notoriously he never uses actors, but instead non-actors that he refers to as "models," none of whom he ever used more than once, and whom he rehearsed relentlessly to get all taint of expression out of their speech and faces. In fact he tends not to show any extreme moments, anything "dramatic" at all (for instance the way he handles the bus crash scene I referred to, which is partly what's so disturbing about it). He leaves out precisely everything that Hollywood builds movies around. He likes to shoot people's feet, he likes hands on doorknobs, he likes windows and doorways and street noises. Above all it seems to me his movies are like life. Not very much happens in life. But in life, as in Bresson's movies, that not very much that is happening is very important, in fact it's God, and after you watch Bresson for a while it's almost unbearably charged and beautiful.

Speaking of God, you have to when talking about Bresson. His movies feel spiritual, in the least cornball way possible. My personal definition of God is "the way things are" and that's what it seems to me Bresson's movies are about, as is just about all interesting art one way or another. But once you start learning about Bresson, you discover that he's a Catholic and much is made of his beliefs in that line. Of course most French people are Catholics and it's said that once they get you for your first few years they have you forever. Rimbaud used to write "God is shit" on park benches. Truffaut saw Hitchcock as a Catholic filmmaker. But apparently for at least a significant part of his life Bresson was what is called a Jansenist. I know hardly anything about Catholicism and its offshoots, though I've been doing a little research. There are two things I've found mentioned most often about Jansenism. One is the belief that all of life is predestined, and the other is that it's possible to achieve grace but the attainment of it, the gift of it, is gratuitous—grace doesn't necessarily go to the so-called "good." Personally, as perverse as Catholicism has always seemed to me, at this stage of my life I don't find those beliefs strange at all. Naturally Bresson resisted being classed as a Catholic artist in a way that purported to explain his movies. There's an interview with Paul Schrader where Bresson gets very impatient with Calvinist Schrader's presumptions about him. But Bresson doesn't make a secret of his belief that life is made of predestination and chance. At first glance to many this will seem impossibly strange, but I think it can also be seen as something simple and clear and ordinary, namely a kind of humility and mercy, a kind of forgiveness and compassion, and also as even obviously true. Look at history. Has all the talk, or rather all the doctrine, changed anything? No. People are who they are and things happen as they must. It's nobody's fault and it doesn't change. It's nobody's fault. It's God. Or the devil, probably. It's just how things are.

Another quick thing about religion and about Bresson's uncompromising casting of his movies. It's interesting that even though Bresson utterly opposes false Hollywood values, his "models" are really good looking. When I first considered this, my reasoning went, a little pettily, ah-ha—so he isn't perfectly pure—he still can't resist attractive people as his "stars" even if they aren't pre-established-commercial-draw type stars; and then, but that's not necessarily "corrupt"—he naturally wants the people who inhabit his stories to be people we care to look at; and then finally I came to the sense that what his models' appearances have in common is the same quality of the models used in medieval and renaissance religious paintings, paintings of saints and martyrs—the faces are hardly ever merely beautiful, the insipid beauty of the fashion model or porn-star type, they're oddly beautiful, they're emphatically but eccentrically beautiful (like Dominique Sanda—of *Un Femme Douce*—and Anne Wiazemsky, costar of *Au hasard, Balthazar*), but above all they feel soulful, they read as having an inner life, a depth, even when inhabiting the most deprived of characters like Mouchette in *Mouchette*. (Incidentally, many of the leads in his movies—there were thirteen features and *Devil* was the twelfth—never worked in any other films, but Dominique Sanda did, for Bertolucci, etc., and Anne Wiazemsky went on to Godard, whom she married too, and there's the odd trivia that Wiazemsky was the granddaughter of Francois Mauriac, and Antoine Monnier who plays Charles in *Devil* is the great-grandson of Matisse . . .)

But on to *The Devil Probably* . . . I wanted to speak about this particular Bresson movie for very personal reasons. I hope you will bear with me in this. I didn't see this movie until 1999, but it was made in 1977. Bresson's birthdate is half the time listed as 1901 and half the time 1907, so anyway he was at least seventy when he made the film. I was in my twenties at that time and I was writing poems and fiction but mostly writing and playing and recording music, songs. My first album was also released in 1977 and it was called *Blank Generation* after the song on it of that title. That album and the things I was doing became classed as "punk" along with a lot of other musicians and music that surfaced around then. Frankly though, I'd always felt that that album of mine, which I really see as consistent with the other things I was doing at the time including my "novelina" *The Voidoid* and the book of alienated, despairing poems I wrote in collaboration with my then friend Tom Verlaine, that we called *Wanna Go Out?* by Theresa Stern, as well as the many interviews I did, not to mention such things as the t-shirt I made which read "please kill me" on the front, were all kind of failed in a significant way, even though they got a considerable amount of attention and even respect. I felt like they were failed because I never got any indication that they were received, were "read," were interpreted in the way they were intended. That the overall view I was trying to convey, the condition I was trying to express, wasn't communicated. I remember an interview I did with one of the people most sympathetic to what I was doing and saying, Lester Bangs, and I spent the interview trying to elaborate, because he asked me to, on my take on things in songs like "Blank Generation" and "Love Comes in Spurts" and "Who Says (It's Good to be Alive)?"—songs which he was crazy about, but about which he could only willfully half-hear what I was saying in defense of their messages of doubt and hopelessness because he thought there was something immoral in that hopelessness . . . I tried to explain to him, I wasn't choosing doubt and suspicion and despair, I was taken there by reality. I wasn't affirming that condition, I was just trying to see clearly. But he couldn't hear that—in my opinion, because he was scared of those things in himself, but for whatever reason he could only reject my position as being infantile and immoral. And basically he was the only person I was aware of who'd even fully acknowledged these messages, this condition, that the work tried to convey, the only person who wanted to talk about it. All the other writers who alluded to it at all just dismissed it as solipsistic and nihilist and beneath consideration.

And then twenty-five years later, and even quite a while after falling in love with Bresson, I come to this movie and for the first time find someone—independently, of course, of any knowledge of me or my local world but in the same period when I was experiencing these things (circa 1977, when the film was made)—and he's perfectly comprehending them and presenting them with the greatest delicacy, respect, and highest artistry. So it wasn't all a dream! How amazing. I existed and Robert Bresson said it matters and is interesting. I not only existed but I was worthy of the most careful consideration. To tell you the truth I knew this, but still it is most gratifying to hear it from Bresson. It is so cool to be verified and validated by the filmmaker whom one already loved above all others! So maybe you'll laugh at me, but I'm confident of it and I don't care.

I have to admit I have no idea what the significance is supposed to be of the line in the movie that gives it its title. It occurs during that bus scene which I mentioned as being the most disturbing and ominous of the film. I don't know because I have no idea where Bresson is coming from when he brings up "the devil." In the scene, which is full of mirrors and push-buttons and levers and the tops of heads and people's midsections, Charles says to his travelling companion, "Governments are shortsighted," and suddenly everybody in the bus is chipping in. One says not to blame governments, "it's the masses who determine events . . . Obscure forces whose laws are unfathomable." A woman adds, "Yes something is driving us against our will." Someone else: "Yes you have to go along with it," and people continue until someone asks, "So who is it that makes a mockery of humanity? Who's leading us by the nose?" And the first guy who spoke goes, "The devil probably," and the bus crashes and the soundtrack degenerates into horrible honking horns . . . It's amazing the way everything about the scene builds to a crescendo of ghastliness.

There are many such scenes in the film. In fact sometimes looking at the movie I get a feeling of the world as a horrible prison, or some kind of Gnostic-type third-rate universe made by degenerate gods. The continuous sharp clicking of the footsteps and the noise of traffic, the evident poisoning of the world by money mad humans, everyone's inability to help each other in any way, the tedious deliberation with which every motion is made . . .

But at the same time it's all breathtakingly beautiful. The movie of Bresson. Though my description of *The Devil, Probably* may make it sound extreme and sensationalistic—what with suicide and predestination and political horrors, etc.—the notable thing really about it and all other Bresson films is its absolute simplicity and its commitment to ordinary moments of everyday life. It's just an everyday life that is lived with open eyes and with a desire to know reality. Bresson was a painter before he made movies and though he described true filmmaking as "writing"—just as he reconceived the people of his films as models rather than actors, he reconceived cinema as "cinematography," his term used not in the familiar meaning in English of "camera-wielding" (the job of the "camera man" on a movie), but in his own sense of "writing with a motion-picture camera"—along with this, he also referred to himself as a painter all along, with a painter's eyes and sensitivities. (In fact in a late '60s interview with Godard where the origin of Bresson's *Au hasard, Balthazar* comes up, he says, "The idea came perhaps visually. For I am a painter. The head of a donkey seems to me something admirable. Visual art, no doubt. Then all at once, I believed I saw the film.") And Bresson's filmmaking gives a dignity and tremendous power to ordinary life, the truth of life that hardly any other films acknowledge at all. Other films don't trust life or people, they have to give a false drama to everything, make a spectacle of pointless dishonest overstimulation. In Bresson, the quiet becomes excruciatingly rich. I think finally the reason the films have the spiritual feeling they do is precisely because their whole purpose is to try to avoid lying—to try to avoid being misled and to try not to mislead anyone—but rather to just see and listen and reflect. It is such an achievement to notice and consider, it actually becomes way more intense than *Star Wars* shootouts or whatever.

Believe it or not there is so much more I could say and I would like to and even intended to say about Bresson, but I should just let him speak for himself. I'll only point out that there are two wonderful books you should get too if you are interested in him. The first is his *Notes on Cinematography* which is a series of short statements which more or less encapsulate his intentions and ideas as a filmmaker; and then this real good anthology of writings about him and interviews with him, called *Robert Bresson* edited by James Quandt.

Introduction for screening in a film series curated by Poty Oliveira at YWCA Cine-Club, NYC, 2002

THE VELVETS VS. THE STONES

MY FIRST THOUGHT was that it'd be fun to crush the Beatles with Guided by Voices. But that would take too much research. Those bands were prolific. Then I thought of the Velvet Underground and the Rolling Stones. I was surprised the first time I saw the title of the Velvets bootleg called *The Psychopath's Rolling Stones*, but there was something there. And the Velvets only released four albums during their entire existence, so that'd reduce the homework. Furthermore, I only own one Beatles album and never play it, while I often play many of the large number of Velvets and Stones records I have.

(A little aside here, regarding the phrases "crush the beatles with guided by voices" and "the velvet underground and the rolling stones." I don't know if I can duplicate the experience for you by describing it, but those phrases, when I read them on the computer screen, unexpectedly took place in my brain separated from their rock and roll band applications, and it was a mental kick, like true poetry, maybe as high an instance of it as rock and roll can achieve. Never mind.)

The first order of business has to be getting our opponents into the same weight class, since the Stones have made so many more records than the Velvets. To do that, I'll restrict the albums considered to each band's output during the years that the Velvets existed, 1966-1970 (their first public appearance was actually in December 1965). This works out neatly, since not only is Lou Reed (b. March 2, 1942) practically the same age as Jagger and Richards (July 26, and December 18, 1943), but the Stones album—their fifth—that came out in mid-1966, *Aftermath*, was their first of exclusively original songs. All the Velvets' records contained only original material, and they recorded their first album in the same period as *Aftermath*, May 1966 (though it was not released, as *The Velvet Underground & Nico*, until early '67).

One band was an international megahit-making group of super stars, considered by many the greatest rock and roll band in the world; the other an abject commercial failure widely reviled, excoriated, and dismissed. The Stones records were crystal clear and crisp, no matter how driving and aggressive, while most of the Velvets' were a scratchy, fuzzy clatter of muffled screeching noises, beats, drones, and snarls. A retrospective distinction of the Velvets, though—one in a class with being regarded for a time as "the greatest rock and roll band in the world"—is that they became the first completely hitless rock and roll band to end up in everyone's short-list pantheon of all-time best groups.

The obvious things the two groups have in common are 1) instincts and skills for the construction and arrangement of catchy rock and roll songs and 2) full scary sexy worlds of attitude and style, style-auras like silvery sick-thought balloons or dim naked-limb-filled miasmas which each group emanated and in which everything they were and did took place. This phenomenon of whole extreme environments associated with specific musicians is at the center of rock and roll. People love bands and their music for the alternate worlds they betoken as much as anything else about the music. The music business promoters know it, too. Stones Manager Andrew Loog Oldham's liner notes on their very first album (1964) included the slogan, "The Rolling Stones are more than just a group, they are a way of life," while a radio ad for the Velvets' third album (1969) intoned, "[…] here are expressions of a new dimension in honesty, purity, and feeling […] not a probe, not an exploration, not an experience, but a whole complete reality: The Velvet Underground."

As for the music's roots, the Stones came out of a mix of blues and early R & B, Chuck Berry, Bo Diddley, and rockabilly, while the Velvets de-emphasized their blues and Bo and Berry in favor of the subsequent rock and roll development of largely urban, Brill building pop song-writing and doo wop (Brian Wilson was big for Lou Reed too), with the addition of the early '60s raga/modal drone John Cale had been playing with LaMonte Young, and Reed's partiality to free jazz (which had already been affected by Indian music in the '50s). In terms of song ideal, probably the meeting point of the Stones and Velvets is Phil Spector. Both bands adored the idea he formulated of the stunning pop gem, the resplendent, massive, white-lit wall of glittering sound.

Rock and roll is wallpaper, like tendrily patterns, on a wall of sound, and the wall surrounds a way of life, various ones for every great rock and roll maker, and in each of those worlds the song is like a cup, and in that cup is the lead singer's voice. Elvis's or James Brown's or Dylan's or Mick Jagger's or Lou Reed's. Sneers and swagger are almost always ingredients. Part of the Beatles' problem was that they were deficient in sneers. There are great oeuvres that are pretty wholesome—Beatles hero Buddy Holly for instance—but it's a handicap. Teeny bopper music is a weak strain of rock and roll. (Holly strutted and threatened more than it might appear at first glance. Consider the lyrics to "That'll Be the Day.")

Rock and roll is aggressive self-assertion. Full fledged front men have to be difficult, egotistical people, and, if they write the songs too, then the songs are likely to have plenty of that meanness and egotism as well. Part of the job description of the front person is to be godlike for teenagers. A rock and roll show is about the audience agreeing to surrender to the band in such a way that the band gives back that which it's received from the crowd in the form of the crowd's pleasure in itself, in the form of the crowd's ideal of itself, of its own glory (as personified by the band's front man). And teenagers need to swagger and be sarcastic and furious because they have so little power (or self-assurance either) otherwise and elsewhere, and because sex chemicals are pouring through them. The music, strictly aurally, physically, in sound waves and rhythms, embodies and unleashes power too, and emotion, but it's the human thing, the focal point presented by the front person, that's the essence of the band, and it's dirty and mean.

The lead singer is a dick. The lead singer is a cunt. When a person needs to have that power, a godlike power enabling him to confer a feeling of immortality on his audience, to perform well, needs to have that absolute self assurance which is required to satisfy audiences ravenous for the thrill of its reflection in themselves ("I'll be your mirror"), that driven self-certainty will make him a creep. (It's really not easy on the performers either, as seen not just in their level of sheer crankiness, but by their fatality rate.)

Maybe I'm just talking about my own tastes, because after all there are also Bruce Springsteen and Joey Ramone and Joe Strummer, all of whom are pretty flatly nice people. But I don't find them interesting as performers. I can't get into proletariat rock, cartoon rock, jam rock, or college kid irony rock. I believe in the idea of "no hero" rock and roll, but prefer the music of monstrously self-involved front men. I don't have to like them or admire them. Still, I'm grateful for them, and believe they deserve all the pampering they need.

My original notes for this article had the heading "The Beautiful Music of Nasty Little Shits." It just gets complicated, one's feelings towards people who make works that have made one's life better, and the difficulty of separating the talent from the character, or trying to figure out the relationship between the talent and the character. In rock and roll, the expression is so direct and personal-seeming. (What's more personal and expressive than a voice?) A soulful thing about Keith Richards (more on which later) is his tolerance for the nastiness of front-men. He has said about Jagger, "It's a hard gig, out front there. [...] You gotta be able to actually believe you're semi-divine when you're out there. Then come offstage and know that you ain't. That's the problem, that eventually the reaction times get slower and you still think you're semi-divine in the limo and semi-divine at the hotel ..."* I mean Richards let Chuck Berry hit him in the face. (About which he said, "He can hit me in the eye again anytime. [...] See, Chuck

---

* Keith Richards, quoted in Stanley Booth, *Keith* (New York: St. Martin's Press, 1995), pp. 157-8

fascinates me—he's an absolute asshole but I've had lots of experience working with them. And to me it's kind of a loveable trait. It's not a big deal that a guy is an asshole. It doesn't mean that you don't bother with him. To me, it's more intriguing than a guy who's fairly well balanced and has all the answers . . ."*)

Back to how the bands compare . . . First—despite Reed's many loving references to the term, it seems correct to call the Stones a "rock and roll" band, but not the Velvets. The Velvets *are* a rock and roll band, but one for a new age in which words have to be put in quotation marks. The Sex Pistols liked to claim to have destroyed rock and roll, but it was the Velvets who did. By comparison the Pistols were classic-rock. The VU are the original white lo-fi band, but that's not the important thing. Maybe you could say they're art rock, but that's unfairly precious sounding. What they were was meta-rock. Not a subset of rock, but a superior set, an arch to the point of over-arching set. They're the first rock and roll band to play rock and roll that's about rock and roll. They're reconsidering it. They're a step removed.

The Velvets are linear, surface, compared to the Stones, whose best records have real depths. "Surface" isn't bad though. Spector's monophonic wall of sound was surface, like a tidal wave. As Andy Warhol, the Velvets' first manager/promoter and Reed's mentor, said in 1967, "if you want to know all about Andy Warhol, just look at the surface of my paintings and films and me, and there I am. There's nothing behind it."† The Velvets are like that: without differentiation. (I remember how it blew my mind when it first really hit me that each moment of a recording is only one sound—one single sound of a given pitch, timbre, and loudness, no matter how many noises of what type went into producing it.) There had never been anything like that free jazz, Eastern, paradoxically frenzied drone that the Velvets in Cale's period (the first two albums) brought to

---

* Ibid., pp. 176-7

† Andy Warhol, quoted in Gretchen Berg, "Nothing to Lose: An Interview with Andy Warhol" in *Andy Warhol: Film Factory*, ed. Michael O' Pray (London: British Film Institute, 1989), p. 56

rock and roll. Cale's amplified viola on "Heroin" and Reed's guitar solo on "I Heard Her Call My Name" are more interesting and important and innovative than anything the Stones did musically. There hadn't been the confrontational intensity of the Velvets' sound either—this is their main contribution to "punk" style. The band reveled in offending people with decibel level and aural chaos. (Warhol encouraged this too, recommending, "Always leave them wanting less.")*

Speaking of "punk," you can find the basis of so many bands' and stars' whole sounds and styles in specific Velvets songs: The Modern Lovers came out of "Sweet Jane" and "Sister Ray" ("Roadrunner" by another name); my nomination for song most revealing of Tom Verlaine's debt to Lou Reed would be "Temptation Inside Your Heart," (recorded in 1968 though not officially released until *VU* in 1985)—Television's style is an anal version of the way that song sounds; half of Bob Quine's guitar style can be heard in "Some Kinda Love"; Sonic Youth is prefigured in the long monotonous stuttering rhythmic droney sitar-sounding distorted shrieking and feedback break on "European Son"; Patti Smith's singing style sounds ennabled by the Doug Yule of "Oh! Sweet Nuthin'" and her lyric-writing approach would appear to have taken seriously such Reed efforts as "I'm Beginning to See the Light":

I wore my teeth in my hands
so I could mess the hair of the night
baby I'm beginning to see the light
now now now now now now now
baby I'm beginning to see the light
it's coming closer
hey now baby I'm beginning to see the light
I met myself in a dream
and I just wanna tell you everything was all right
hey now baby I'm beginning to see the light.

---

* Andy Warhol, quoted in Victor Bockris, *Transformer* (New York: Simon & Schuster, 1994), p. 120

here comes two of you
which one will you chose
one is black and one is blue
don't know just what to do
well I'm beginning to see the light

The whole original alternative rock college-kid slew of bands like Pavement derived their disjunctive, non-sequitur lyrical mode from songs like "Pale Blue Eyes":

skip a life completely
stuff it in a cup
she said, money is like us in time
it lies, but can't stand up
down for you is up
linger on
your pale blue eyes

Reed's lyrics probably do come the closest to poetry of any in rock and roll. Dylan is his only competition. Dylan rules, but I'd venture that the lyrics on *The Velvet Underground* are the best as a suite, as an album set, of any in rock and roll history:

Candy says "I've come to hate my body
and all that it requires in this world"
Candy says "I'd like to know completely
what others so discreetly talk about"
("Candy Says")

put jelly on your shoulder
lie down upon on the carpet
between thought and expression
let us now kiss the culprit
("Some Kinda Love")

linger on
your pale blue eyes
("Pale Blue Eyes")

Jesus
help me find my proper place
help me in my weakness
cuz I'm falling out of grace
("Jesus")

I'm beginning to see the light.
("Beginning to See the Light")

I've been set free
and I've been bound
let me tell you people
what I found
I saw my head laughing
rolling on the ground
and now I'm set free
I'm set free
to find a new illusion
("I'm Set Free")

that's the story of my life
that's the difference between wrong and right
but Billy said both those words are dead
that's the story of my life
(which are the entire lyrics to "That's the Story of My
    Life")

Consistent with the general ironic, meta-viewpoint of Reed's Velvets music-making, though, he sings all his lyrics flippantly, sarcastically (with the rare exceptions of a breathless, monotonous, Nico-like

"Sunday Morning" or two). He mocks everything. The music supplies a sturdy foundation with its incontrovertible drive, but it too is unsentimental—rough—to the point of near-parody (though it got notably more mellow towards the end, post-Cale, especially on *Loaded*). There are pretty harmonies, but they're rec-room style too. It all has no frills and makes no concessions to pop polish. And if a song is to be sung with any innocence or sincerity it has to be sung by someone other than Reed (Maureen Tucker on "After Hours" and "I'm Sticking With You," and Doug Yule on "Who Loves The Sun," "A New Age," and "Oh! Sweet Nuthin'").

There is a weird, oblique contact-point between Jagger's and Reed's otherwise fairly dissimilar singing styles. Jagger is a mimic of the blues-roots and backwoods American singing from the small-label "race" and rockabilly records that his band grew out of. But if you listen cold to Reed's singing on "White Light / White Heat" you realize he sounds as if he were in blackface, like a parody of a vaudeville minstrel (which is already a mockery), not just down to the southern broad "a" sound in words like "mind" and "blind" (*mahnd* and *blahnd*), but in African-American idioms too: "Ooo have mercy white light have it goodness knows," "I surely do love to watch that stuff," "Hey there foxy mama," "Goin up side yo head," "goodness knows, work it!" The music sounds crazed and rabid, but, unlike the way Jagger sings in a threatening style on the more aggressive Stones songs, Reed, true to his form, just gets all the more goofy and mocking over this insanely violent speed-freak rave. The mysterious thing is how, even though Reed's singing style is one that screams with its every burlesque inflection that none of it matters, the world is fake ("I'm set free to find a new illusion"), it's the Stones who by comparison come off sounding artificial.

Gee, I didn't really intend to go this direction. During the period under consideration, the Rolling Stones released *Aftermath*, *Between the Buttons*, *Their Satanic Majesty's Request*, *Beggar's Banquet*, and *Let it Bleed*, along with such singles as "Nineteenth Nervous Breakdown," "Paint It, Black," "Mother's Little Helper," "Have You Seen Your Mother, Baby, Standing In the Shadows?," "Who's Driving Your Plane," "Let's Spend the Night Together," "Ruby Tuesday," and "Jumpin' Jack Flash." Good God. Those are some snappy recordings.

The main thing that the Stones have that the Velvets don't is Keith Richards; meaning: soul. Lou Reed has a lot going for himself, but soul isn't part of it. You have to grant that he explicitly rejected it ("no blues licks" is said to have been a rule for the Velvets), but still, soul is usually a desirable quality. What is soul? It's humane empathy that in music gets expressed as loose swing (no matter how harsh and biting the chords might be, or pumping the beat); it's the sound of musicians respecting each other and submerging their egos to create conjunctive syncopated rhythms that make the listener's body sympathize and want to play off them by moving around to them. (You could object that auteurs such as James Brown and Ike Turner were obsessively controlling egomaniacs who dictated some of the deepest, most sexily greasy soul music of all time, but that's another essay. Maybe titled "They Contained Multitudes, Each of Whom Loved Each Other and Played Separate Rhythm Parts.") Richards is a hero of that kind of musical generosity. Lou Reed is not generous.

Neither, though, do the Velvets have a Jagger or a Charlie Watts. What Jagger brings is the apotheosis of that front man function. Not only can he do a lot more with his voice than Reed, but he's the leaping monkey who serves that "appointed god to make us perfect" role for his audience in a way Reed couldn't begin to try. As for Charlie, maybe he even exceeds Keith's contribution in the battle with the Velvets. The snap, bam, and sliding virility of the way his drum kit makes Stones recordings riveting puts them in another class altogether from the VU in the percussion department. Maureen's drumming is perfect in its one dimensional way, but Charlie makes every other drummer in rock and roll sound handicapped.

The most striking difference between the Stones and the Velvets, though, is the Stones' committed commerciality. Sometimes this works in their favor and sometimes it doesn't. *Aftermath* seems the most relentless and fun catalogue of misogyny (or honesty about how boys wish they could act towards girls, but only star-level charisma enables) ever to thrill teenagers, with "Stupid Girl," "Lady Jane," "Under My Thumb," and

"High and Dry," until *Between the Buttons* comes along and ramps the level up further with "Yesterday's Papers,"

who wants yesterday's papers
who wants yesterday's girl

—"Back Street Girl"—

please don't you call me at home
please don't come knocking at night
please never ring on the phone
your manners are never quite right. [...]
don't want you part of my world.
just you be my back street girl

and "Cool, Calm & Collected," "Please Go Home," and "Miss Amanda Jones." All these tracks drive and syncopate and are thrilling and they're also all like novelty songs, pop concoctions, with lots of harmonies and echo and reverb and handclaps and—thanks to Brian Jones's versatility—exotic instruments like recorder, sitar, slide guitar, bells, and marimbas. The world they talk about is one of fashion and money and drugs, which is the world the group, Jagger especially, inhabited, even if the girls of that world are viciously mocked by the street-kid rock and roll stars. But the star is a fastidious snob too (viz. "Back Street Girl"). I don't mean to be playing superior to this stuff. I liked it then and I like it now. Contrasted to the Velvets it does seem fey, but you could interpret its pop aspirations as respect for an audience as much as some deficiency of integrity. Or at least as honest ambition. Every rock and roll band wants to be popular and rich and pursued by lust objects. These songs are timelessly exciting and charged with pleasure.

It's hard to excuse *Satanic Majesty's Request*, though. At best you could take it as endearing in a certain way: the Stones showing their true colors as determined to keep up with all trends, no matter how lame and inappropriate the results. It's only rock and roll. But unfortunately that record's not really rock and roll, and it's pretty inexcusably horrible. They did give it a good title. Changing the classic form-wording of a British royal invitation, her "Brittanic Majesty's request," to "Satanic" was more outrageous than the ten years subsequent "God save the queen, she ain't no human being."

Following this faux-*Pepper* travesty, the group tried to redeem itself by coming down to earth, raising a glass "to the hard-working people," and taking political stands on their generation's big current events. But *Beggar's Banquet* is as overwrought, in different ways, as the previous album was. It may not trick itself out in psychedelic effects, but it's boringly grandiose and bombastic, like old-fashioned bad acting—it's intended for stadiums. The songs aren't true or personal, but are roles played (most likely imitating a Beatles mode again). The superficial appearance of political radicalism is betrayed by the lyrics too. The violent "Street Fighting Man," which sounds like a topically timely call to arms, is actually the meek opposite, a variation on the Beatles' recently released "Revolution" ("But when you talk about destruction / Don't you know that you can count me out"):

> *what can a poor boy do*
> *except to sing for a rock and roll band*
> *cuz in sleepy London town*
> *there's just no place for a street fighting man*

Jagger takes on exaggerated hillbilly accents for a few hokey jokey songs ("Dear Doctor," "Prodigal Son"). The album is all poses and compromise.

Then comes *Let it Bleed*. You have to sit up for this one. You have to push everything out of the way. It's a contender for best rock and roll record ever. Brian is gone. Keith played all the guitars on two of the set's most powerful cuts—"Gimmie Shelter" and "Let It Bleed." These songs give you chills. Velvets songs don't give you chills. Not only do the tracks, with their monster guitar parts and whipping licks and fills and gospely and choral back-up singing, reach you emotionally, but the music is physical in a way the Velvets never are. It's music that commands your body. You don't feel manipulated, as on *Beggar's Banquet*, but uplifted. The lyrics and feelings are personal and plain and true to life. Even the down-home–mask adopting—"Love in Vain" and "Country Honk" ("Honky Tonk Women")—sounds genuine not just as tribute but as emotional identification, and in the case of "Honk" as actual experience. The lyrics are the Stones' best ever. Their themes come out of the intense '60s drug pain fashion money and sex underworld the group had helped create, but they don't reflexively, defensively deride the debutantes so much, and they're more detailed and juicy than ever before, while also being funny.

> *I got nasty habits, I take tea at three*
> *yes, and the meat I eat for dinner*
> *must be hung up for a week*
> *my best friend he shoots water rats*
> *and feeds them to his geese*
> *doncha think there's a place for you*
> *in between the sheets*
> ("Live With Me")

and

> *I'm a flea-bit peanut monkey*
> *all my friends are junkies*
> *that's not really true*
> *I'm a cold Italian pizza*
> *I could use a lemon squeezer*
> *how'd you do*
> ("Monkey Man")

Jagger even seems to match Richards's soulfulness with his lyrics to such as "Gimme Shelter"—which has got to be one of the top three rock and roll tracks of all time, and which doesn't say much more than

war, children, it's just a shot away, it's just a shot away
it's just a shot away, it's just a shot away
love, sister, it's just a kiss away, it's just a kiss away
it's just a kiss away, it's just a kiss away

and "You Can't Always Get What You Want"

you can't always get what you want
but if you try sometime you just might find
you get what you need

The record is scary and compassionate. You love being tossed around on it. It does that thing of taking you out of yourself into a whole ocean.

Oh, and to bring up the Stones's fruitful influence on subsequent bands . . . Their presence so permeated rock and roll culture for so long that it's almost impossible to isolate their mark—it's everywhere, especially in the countless great garage punk groups of the mid- and late '60s, as found on the Nuggets compilation albums, whose bands played fuzz-box guitar and yelled and taunted and couldn't get much satisfaction because their sex drive was relentless but all the girls were too stuck up and stupid. There are two specific great and important groups I can think of who owed a whole lot to the Rolling Stones: the New York Dolls, who of course were almost like a robust drag-queen hallucination of the Stones (to find the roots of the Dolls' style, Johansen's singing especially, check "Doncha Bother Me" from *Aftermath*); and the Stooges of *Raw Power*, showcasing James Williamson's K. Richards-besot guitar and songwriting.

I remember being surprised to notice that when Keith gets asked about first knowing and working with Mick, he always mentions how Mick came from a higher social class. Jagger's father was a physical education instructor for school kids, whereas Keith's worked in a factory. This seems like a fine distinction to me, but those minutely calibrated social classifications are still how people think in England. The Stones were the classic rock and roll story of white underclass kids who surprised themselves by becoming rich and famous playing the even more underclass music (mostly African-American) they loved, like Elvis before and Eminem later. The shock of success was further exaggerated because of the extreme British class-consciousness, combined with the amperage of youth trends in the '60s when the baby boom created the greatest number of teenagers the world had ever seen. So the Stones were these street kids thrust into the middle of a world of commercial hit-making and upper-class attentions. They kept their self-respect by defying social conventions and emphasizing their rebellious, impolite attitudes, but at the same time, as proud young players in the world of pop music—and contemporaries of the Beatles—they accepted the standard of sales figures being the measure of their achievement. (Notice for instance how whenever Keith is asked in interviews about his friend Gram Parsons he always remarks on how impressed he is by the way people are interested in Parsons even though he never made a hit record. Richards can't think of public respect for his rock and roll peers except in categories of record sales.)

The Velvets were a world away from that classic hit rock and roll scenario. The Velvets were Americans (except for Welsh John Cale), middle class—citizens of a place where, though economic class levels certainly exist, social class levels are a lot more permeable than in Britain. And the Velvets were intellectuals. Lou Reed's first mentor (or at least his fantasy mentor) was the brilliant (speed freak) American poet Delmore Shwartz, with whom he studied at Syracuse University. Musically Reed was as excited by rarified avant-garde noise-jazz and faceless white professional song writing (like Goffin and King, Barry and Greenwich) as he was by roots rock and roll. Cale was a serious modern classical musician who studied composition at the university level for years, and was influenced by avant-garde classical musician LaMonte Young, with whom he studied and played, and John Cage. Sterling Morrison started out majoring in physics at university, and, after the Velvets, returned to school and ended up being a college professor of literature.

The Velvets were a rock and roll band, but they took all of recent music, from Bo Diddley through Phil Spector through John Cage,

Ornette Coleman, and La Monte Young as their province. They were high artists, bent on making the most stimulating and aesthetically interesting music, built on the foundations of their broadly various musical preoccupations, that they could. Their world was as "outlaw" and depraved and scornful of conventional social values as the Stones' (this is built into rock and roll too, because it's the teenage view of what's desireable), but was a great deal more intellectually oriented, a new thing in rock and roll. It might sound strange that the intellectual approach has cruder results, the way the Velvets' music is so much messier sounding than the Stones, but it's not. It's comparable to the way, say, Duchamp's *Fountain*, a signed urinal, made Picasso look like a commercial artist. The Velvets made the choice of being strictly faithful to their own advanced ideas of what was most interesting to do in rock and roll, without conceding anything to less sophisticated conventional tastes that would have packaged their ideas in pop-music sheen. They wrote beautiful ballads and visceral driving rock and roll but only paid attention to their personal ideas about what were the important features of that music to present.

My expectation of which band would come out on top here has changed a few times in the course of this writing. In a way rock and roll that's not hit music is failed rock and roll. Rock and roll is pop teenage music. If masses of kids don't respond to it, then by definition it isn't good. Also a lot of what we love about rock and roll is that wallpaper quality, of a given song being pasted everywhere on the (youth) culture for a few months, so that it comes to represent that time and place forever, as well as provide alternate or idealized identities to its fans by the world of feelings and values embodied in it. The Rolling Stones have this to a degree that obliterates the Velvets.

Of course, you don't have to choose. You can like it all. When you are a kid, your identity is your favorite band. But you realize, when you know more, that you can like them all. Or not. It is interesting how preferences and interests fluctuate. So the winner has to be provisional. I was kind of looking forward to beating up the Velvets with the Stones. Lou Reed was obnoxious enough in the Velvets, but he really became insufferable in his subsequent career (which is devoid of records of Velvets caliber too). I would have liked to try to bring him down a peg. But it began to look like it wasn't going to turn out that way. Then I came to *Let It Bleed* and I started reconsidering again. That record is uniquely magnificent. But here at the moment of truth, the Velvets can't be denied. They take the crown. Lou Reed is queen for a day.

From Rock and Roll Cage Match: Music's Greatest Rivalries, Decided, *ed. Sean Manning (New York: Three Rivers Press, 2008)*

CHRISTOPHER WOOL'S PHOTOGRAPHS

CHRISTOPHER WOOL IS a prolific photographer, but his photos have always been presented in the form of artist's books. He rarely exhibits the photos or offers them to collectors and when he has, to date, it's only in the sets as compiled for the books. Ten of his twenty artist's books are comprised of his photographs. Seven of those are made of photos of his paintings, though the photos are often manipulated electronically or otherwise, and some of the books served as unconventional exhibition catalogues. Of the remaining three photo books, two comprise "street" photographs, and one is a small pamphlet of pictures

of the artist's damaged studio following a 1997 fire. This essay will discuss the two sets of street photographs, *Absent Without Leave* (1993) and *East Broadway Breakdown* (2003), and one exhibition catalogue of painting photos, *Christopher Wool* (2001).

Absent Without Leave originated as a kind of photo notebook kept during the artist's travels between1989 and 1993. He spent most of those years outside the U.S., in Rome and Berlin on fellowships, as well as on trips to Turkey and Japan and elsewhere. There's very little in the pictures to locate them though. They're often shots of visual patterning—tiles, leaves and branches, fabrics. Perhaps the building facades with their window grids fit this category too. He'd been making paintings of

patterns—stencilled or paint-rollered—at the time. Wool's word paintings, which he'd recently begun making as well, could also be seen as patterns. Many others of the photos in *AWOL* are taken from the windows of moving vehicles, which accounts for some of the smeared, blurry effects. Wool remembers thinking as he snapped the pictures from inside cars and trains that this was the way the world looks now.* There are also a number of pictures of dogs and cats (which creatures also show up in

---

* This and other background information from conversations with the artist, fall 2007.

his word paintings conspicuously often), usually on the street. There are very few people in the entire set. As in all of his books, the images are sequenced with care. (Later Wool made a short movie comprising all the pictures in *Absent Without Leave* in sequence.)

Each of the 188 photographs in *Absent Without Leave* was photo-copied before being reproduced on the 8.5" x 11" page (one photo per page, inside approximately .5" white borders). The artist has described the

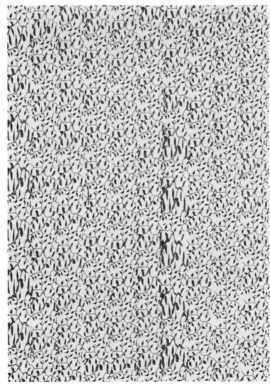

photocopying as being a way of bringing the pictures together. But one can't help thinking that the photocopying not only unites the pictures by endowing them with similar surfaces, and flattening them somewhat, but that it brings out qualities they already have in common—negatively, being those features which survive photocopying, but, positively, in the implicit assertion that the images' import is emphasized by the degradation of photocopying. And you can see how it works. The photocopying eliminates the detail and heightens the contrast while also degrading the black, so that the pictures are values of grey but full of glaring white areas. One sees them as patterns in their shared flatness and exaggerated contrast, but also as an appropriately abject catalogue of the abject corners and grid floor of the world, the ubiquitous: sagging powerlines, stray pets, highways, glaring illumination, filthy concrete, urban foliage, motel telephone, lattice of windowed facade—like the field upon which our lives take place, ubiquitous unto invisibility, or as low and low grade as common electronic static, like the static, the visual noise, imposed by old photocopy machines, now brought to the foreground, appreciated and proffered for appreciation, from out of the dim corners of one's eyes, up into appreciative contemplation from beneath contempt.

In Wool, media interchange: words are images, paintings are photographs, books are paintings. Though the Wool photos most susceptible to discussion as photographs are the "street" photographs, his "painting" photos demand attention here too.

The catalogue *Christopher Wool* (2001) for a show at Vienna's Secession Museum arrays color Polaroids (reproduced here in black and white) the artist made of his paintings. Again, the photographs were not originally intended as independent works, as "art" at all. They were taken in the course of his painting activity, 1994-2001, to help him assess ideas. He was experimenting with alterations to big paintings, often the application of narrow vertical rectangular areas of white paint which he'd try out by taping white strips of paper to the paintings' surfaces, snapping Polaroids as he went. Later he could compare possibilities by looking at the Polaroids. He first thought of publishing the Polaroids when he

realized that some of the paintings looked better in transitional stages than in their final forms.

Not only is Wool interested in the book as an artist's medium, but he's acutely conscious of the weakness of the conventional exhibition catalogue as a means for representing paintings in shows. His catalogues often make little pretense to accurately depicting paintings, but rather operate as works themselves that can be logically taken as equivalent to what's in the exhibition. The catalogues more or less say, "if a painting in this show were a book, it might look like this." He uses the catalogue as an opportunity to make a work of art, since it's futile to represent paintings in reproduction. The Polaroids in the Secession catalogue include pictures of most of the paintings in the show, but not all of them, and it contains many which aren't in the show, and many which don't exist at all, because they were passing stages in the making of paintings. And, as flash-lit Polaroids, the photos blatantly depart from their painting subjects in other ways, being not only extremely small, but often obviously faded and discolored, and including big white bursts of reflected flash-bulb in the middles of paintings.

In the book the reproductions of the Polaroids are presented edge to edge in two-photo by three-photo vertical blocks per page, for forty pages. The sequence is roughly reverse-chronological, though pages are composed for the eye. Again, he downplays the photographs-as-photo-graphs (or even photograph images as images), by jamming them together on the page, emphasizing the "artist's book" aspect over the photographs themselves. (He did eventually include 120 of the Polaroids—half the ones in the book—in a museum exhibition, but they were exhibited the same way, edge to edge, and they've never been offered for sale.) Wool tried them enlarged to fit each on an 8.5" x 11" page and that didn't look right, so he took the wall-to-wall, "actual-size," route. The book is an embarrassment of riches, considering all the levels, both conceptually and physically, on which it works. (There was also published a related book, the 300-copy edition *Maybe, Maybe Not* (2001), of black and white reproductions of photocopy enlargements of altered versions of some of the Polaroids of paintings. Wool had applied marks in Wite-Out and felt-tip marker to the Polaroids, repainting the pictures in another way.)

The pictures in *East Broadway Breakdown* were shot by Wool in 1994-95 with the idea of eventually making a book, but the book wasn't compiled and published until 2003. The 160 photos are nearly all urban exteriors and are all taken late at night. Human figures appear in only a couple of them. The largest number of them were shot in the slum, or derelict industrial, Bowery/Chinatown area of New York through which the artist traveled between his studio in the far East Village on Ninth St. between Avenues C and D and his living loft on Chatham Square in Chinatown, in those days. He often didn't use the viewfinder when he snapped the pictures, but would just hold out the camera and flash a shot in the direc-tion of a scene that interested him. The original prints were all standard 4" x 6" snapshots run off automatically by the mechanized labs to which film rolls are delivered from stationary shops and drugstore drop-off points. Wool regards the editing of the book—his choice of which pictures to include from among the 2500 or so he shot—as its crux. He scanned his selections into his computer and used Photoshop to adjust brightness and contrast to compensate for the inflexible assembly-line lab.

Especially interesting is the district of the world that is exposed in the pictures. The photographs—like the ones in *Absent Without Leave* and

even the Secession catalogue, but more so—are like obscure corners of
the world exposed by lightning, with that revelatory flash into a hidden
reality, previously invisible not only for being hidden from the light, but
by being assumed unworthy of attention, passively ignored. They're like
the ghost world only accessible to the pure of heart, or by accident, in
worldly time-and-space's interstices. It's not just the redemption of an
"ugliness" and its annexation by beauty, but a faith in the value of a certain physio-psychological means of apprehending the world, exercised
and shown worthy and effective. And that opens up into Wool's paintings, where apparent casualness, sloppiness, paucity of means, seemingly
haphazard framing and smeared and out-of-register areas also appear.
The visionary poetry of the peripheral, the poetry of peripheral vision.
And, in *East Broadway Breakdown*, the thing that makes the images

visible at all, also largely creates the distinctive way they look: the flash,
making white the web of whatever crosses space within its range, and
the exaggerated contrast created by which also serves to flatten the
image into pattern.

The pictures are eerie, are uncanny. The point of reference that always
arises in talking about them is the police crime-scene photo—Weegee
type functional, journalistic, black and white—that, because of the squalid
settings, becomes sensationalistic. The pictures are like environmental

pornography, or like passing voyeurism of the cityscape indulged, as if the streets had been caught not merely naked (as per Weegee, *Naked City*) but unconscious, and we can't help staring and relishing. This sensationalist aspect of the pictures is only a small part of what they provide though. They're stunning for the way they capture and present for our admiration a realm which had been mostly disregarded until Wool focused on it, but they share qualities with Wool's paintings, despite the paintings being not figurative, not "representational" (apart from the occasional stylized, cartoon or pattern/decorative, flower or word or other standardized 2-D

shape) or apparently journalistic at all. Looking at these photographs in the context of Wool's other work, his painting, enhances the photographs, but the photos also inform the paintings.

Some time in the late 19th century—a convenient marker could be Monet's haystacks—artists began tending to work in series and "periods" rather than in paintings or individual works. Picasso would be the prime originating examplar of the "period" mode of art making. If the viewer didn't know otherwise, it would be quite possible never to guess that the paintings of Picasso's "blue" period and his cubist paintings and his "neo-classical" paintings were all the work of the same person. But knowing it enhances one's response to each separate period. And to some extent the paintings in a given "period" can be thought of as a series, a series exploring the possibilities of the mode of that period. It's as if painters began to paint in time as well as space: exploring ideas and interests in successions of canvases, or works, rather than going for the masterpiece that would be the apotheosis of the artist's preoccupations in a given period. In a real way, often, an individual work by an artist in our time is a fragment—it needs the context of the artist's entire oeuvre, or at least the period in which it fits, to be fully appreciated. A given work by a contemporary artist is sometimes no more complete a representation of the artist's intentions than a frame-enlargement still is of the movie from which it's taken. Or, in the same way that one needs a certain quantity of text of a lost unknown language before there can be any possibility of deciphering it, it can be nearly impossible to "get" an isolated work by a present-time painter. A given artwork now is like a hint in a game of twenty questions, or a piece of evidence at a crime scene. It may or may not stimulate much response, isolated from its associated information, primarily the other works in its series/period of the artist.

Wool's paintings seem to say through the *AWOL* and *EBB* photographs, "See, I didn't just make this stuff up. It's there in the world." It's exciting. To an extent the photographs are like the paintings spoken in another language, so we get that second translation of the original text (the original text being the heiroglyphs made on the floor of Wool's interior by reality, as Proust conceived the material one is given as an artist) to help us grasp the full substance, in all its nuances, of his designations. To recast metaphors, they enable us to triangulate a previously unknown position, making them doubly revelatory (as art and as related to the paintings). Like the paintings, one realizes, the (street) photos are black and white, often feature patterns, exclude people, welcome smears and casual framing, and direct our attention to commonplace corners and underpinnings of our environment that tend to be not merely disregarded but to be assumed ugly.

The Secession Polaroids operate in a related area, as different a project as they are from *Absent Without Leave* and *East Broadway Breakdown*.

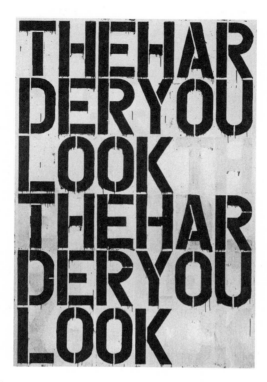

The Polaroids capture moments usually ignored—here the transitional stages of paintings, but also the look of the paintings in a moment's flash without the eye's usual adjustments and compensations. In a sense they're also a direct expression of the modern "series" mode of art-making, the departure from the outmoded ideal of the masterpiece, being inspired by Wool's realization that some of his paintings looked better at points in the process of painting them than in their final state. Needless to say, that is privileged information, unnecessary for the appreciation of the book and images, but its relevance to the discussion is another example of the way new works often require specialized information, unique to the oeuvre of the artist, to operate at their top capacity.

Wool's photographs work three ways at once: as photographs, as books, and as information that enhances one's appreciation of his paintings.

From Christopher Wool, *ed. Hans Werner Holzwarth (Cologne: Taschen, 2008)*

NATHANAEL WEST IN FIVE PARTS

1. JEWISH PROLOGUE

When Elinor Nauen called me up and asked me if I'd like to deliver a lecture on a Jewish writer, I didn't know it was because she regarded me as a Jew. I thought she liked me for myself!

But in the last few years I've been finding that more and more people are regarding me as a Jew, so part of the reason I agreed to do this talk was to investigate the issue a little. Frankly, I hadn't thought of myself as a Jew. Am I a Jew? What is a Jew? I've asked a few people. My favorite reply to that came from Cliff Fyman: "It's a great question. Why spoil it with an answer?"

Nathanael West's real, or original, name was Nathan Weinstein. His mother's maiden name was Wallenstein. Both sides of the family were Russian Jews. There was a period in his early twenties when West would sometimes represent himself as Nathan von Wallenstein Weinstein. The "von Wallenstein" was a fantasy reference to the 17th century Czech Duke and soldier about whom Schiller wrote a cycle of plays. Was West embarrassed to be a Jew? Maybe a tiny bit. Maybe not. Anyway, he didn't want to be held back by it. In America, you're supposed to be able to be whoever you want to be. Some people would think less of him for changing his name. I remember how funny it seemed and how surprised I was when I learned that Erich von Stroheim, the great and famously strict and meticulous Teutonic film director and actor, was actually the Austrian Jewish son of a hat-maker. Josef von Sternberg, the mentor of Marlene Dietrich and director of her baroque, lavish, and darkly erotic greatest films was born Jonas Sternberg in Vienna, the son of very poor Orthodox Jews. What am I getting at? I don't know exactly. I guess that it's that I'm ambivalent about my own Jewishness. I think also that West's desire to have charge of his own identity, and his rejection, to some extent at least, of his Jewish roots, played a part in his artistic sensibility.

But, this isn't really the subject of my talk. I want to bring it up, but I also want to get it out of the way and move on. Which is kind of my whole attitude towards my own Jewishness. So, what is a Jew? I've come to a conclusion about that. My father, Ernest Meyers, was an intellectual secular humanist, son of Jews. He was an atheist, or at least what they call an agnostic, behaviorist psychology professor whose parents were also professionals who didn't practice religion though they certainly regarded themselves as Jews. My best information is that their predecessors emigrated from Germany in the early nineteenth century. My mother came from poor Southern WASPS in Birmingham, Alabama, of Welsh and English ancestry, and they were Methodists. She was the first person in her family to go to college. She met my father at Columbia University. I was born and grew up in Kentucky. My father died when I was seven, and as you can see, I don't even quite know what a Jew is. Nobody ever told me anything about it. I'm fifty-five and I wore my first yarmulke at Elinor's Bat Mitzvah a couple of years ago.

But some way or another I've in recent years become publicly identified as a Jew in a way I hadn't been before. I was invited onto a Jewish-oriented radio show back in the '90s and I went on it and talked about my ethnic background a little, so maybe that was a factor. In the '70s I was the co-creator of the poet-identity Theresa Stern, whose ancestry I described as Puerto Rican and Jewish. In 1996 I named the protagonist of my first novel Bernhardt, though the subject of Judaism never arises . . . But then, four or five years ago a book called *Jews Who Rock* came out that listed me as a Jew, and I started getting regular requests for interviews and gigs that had some Jewish connection. I was kind of annoyed by that book. I thought, "Shouldn't they have talked to me before they claimed me?" I didn't really regard myself as a Jew. Anyway, it was muddy. What is a Jew?

Well, I've concluded that a Jew is anyone whom anyone else calls a Jew. I realize that I am a Jew because it's only healthy to understand that that's the case. Put plainly, Hitler was not an isolated phenomenon. We know it happened in Germany in our parents' or grandparents' lifetimes to many Jews who regarded themselves first as Germans. But the most cursory knowledge, even the history in this lecture about Nathanael West, makes it clear it can happen at any time, anywhere. That's what being a Jew means to me, because that's what I know about Jewishness. That Jews are whom other Jews can claim and whom bigots can reject and attack and seek to harm. So I realize that I qualify. Maybe someday I'll know more, but for now that's enough. On to Nathanael West.

2. WEST'S BEGINNINGS

Nathanael West's parents were Lithuanian. Both the Wallensteins and the Weinsteins were successful builders, construction-craftsmen and building contractors there in the mid-nineteenth century, when Lithuania, though technically part of Russia, was governed by Germans and suffused with German culture. Because of their bourgeois success, the families faced few anti-Semitic legal restrictions in society then. They thought of themselves as cultivated Germans. But, after 1881, Czar Alexander III's "Russification" policies altered the status of all Jews in Russian territories. The czar began to restrict Jewish travel, trade, and education, as well as force long-term military conscription of Jews. So, towards the end of the 19th century West's forebears and their immediate families immigrated to New York. They took up their trades again here and they flourished. In 1902 Mordecai Weinstein married Chana Wallenstein in a small orthodox ceremony. Mordecai would be known as

Max, and Chana, Anna. The following year Anna gave birth to Nathan Weinstein. He would have two sisters, Hinda, a year younger, and Laura, with whom he would be especially close, eight years younger. Max and Anna taught their children German and moved in circles of Litvak Jews in New York. They went to Temple twice a year, on the high holidays. They attended the Metropolitan Opera more often.

Nathan had a privileged upbringing in a family that valued education, but he was a bad student. He ended up dropping out of high school. Soon after that, when he decided he wanted to go to college, he forged his high school transcript to apply. He was accepted at Tufts University in Massachusetts, but didn't attend classes there either and lasted a semester before being expelled for failing every course he took. As it happened, though, there had been a second Nathan Weinstein registered at the school who had done well enough so that when West got ahold of his transcript and doctored it, he was able to get admitted to Brown University as a sophomore. He coasted and finessed at Brown too, but scraped through to graduation in 1924.

West loved literature, including exotic avant-garde poetry, and he valued highly his suave, pricey Brooks Brothers outfits, but he had no taste for work. Probably the most important result of his time at Brown was the making of acquaintance with the man who would be his best friend—and, promptly, brother in law—for the rest of his life, S. J. Perelman, the soon-famous writer of humor and satire, frequent contributor to *The New Yorker*, and author of Marx Brothers movies.

Following graduation, West returned to New York, where he worked at his relatives' construction sites and lived off his family for a couple of years. In 1926 his father's brothers agreed to pay his expenses for a stretch in Paris. He had gorged on Baudelaire and Rimbaud and Lautréamont and Apollinaire and was excited, too, by the contemporary generation of avant-garde writers, French and American, in Paris. Before he got his passport he legally changed his name to West. In France he burned through his bankroll in three months and had to retreat to New York. Later, he'd often lead people to believe he'd spent years in Paris as a young man.

He took up a life in Greenwich Village among young bohemian/radical novelists, poets, editors, and journalists such as Edward Dahlberg, Dashiell Hammett, Philip Wylie, and Michael Gold, as well as friends from Brown. He got acquainted with Edmund Wilson, and, through S. J. Perelman, *New Yorker* writers like A. J. Leibling and Dorothy Parker. He attended gatherings of a group of young Jewish intellectuals at George Brounoff's apartment on Central Park West, where there was a lot of intense discussion of Dostoevsky and Joyce, along with close attention to international Marxist writings.

West's first book, *The Dream Life of Balso Snell* was begun soon after college, but wouldn't be completed and published for nearly six years. *Balso Snell* shows the influence of the most anti-social of the dadaists and surrealists who had been inspiring West. In West's own (unsigned) 1931 advertisement for the newly published book, he likens it to the works of Apollinaire, Jarry, and Roussel, but in that lineage it seems most reminiscent of another of his interests, Lautréamont, author of the ferocious nineteenth century proto-surrealist masterpiece, *Maldoror*. Maybe even more significant is the book's debt to the Marx brothers' subversive style of ceaseless word play and dramatic chaos.

The novel opens with the poet Balso Snell coming upon the Trojan horse in the tall grasses outside Troy. He decides to enter it via its only convenient access, the giant horse's ass. "O Anus Mirabilis!" West exclaims, shortly before Balso adds to the valentine graffiti across the nether lips of the equine sculpture, effusing, "O Byss, O Abyss, O Anon, O Onan!"

The book is stuffed with literary allusions, scatology, sex, and mocking considerations of the nature and purpose of art. Balso wanders through the horse's guts like Gulliver or silly Dante, encountering various eccentric inhabitants, nearly all literarily inclined, until he finally escapes his *Dream Life* confinement via nocturnal emission. Or something. To stick with the theme, I'll present a few paragraphs that include a Jewish interlude. This is from the fourth or fifth page in the book. Balso is being led on his tour of the horse's innards by a professional guide.

[. . .]He let the guide do all the talking and they made great headway up the tube. But, unfortunately, coming suddenly upon a place where the intestine had burst through the stomach wall, Balso cried out in amazement:

"What a hernia! What a hernia!"

The guide began to splutter with rage and Balso tried to pacify him by making believe he had not meant the scenery. "Hernia," he said, rolling the word on his tongue. "What a pity childish associations cling to beautiful words such as hernia, making their use as names impossible.

"Hernia! What a beautiful name for a girl! Hernia Hornstein! Paresis Pearlberg! Paranoia Puntz! How much more pleasing to the ear (and what other sense should a name please?) than Faith Rabinowitz or Hope Hilkowitz."

But Balso had only blundered again. "Sirrah!" the guide cried in an enormous voice, "I am a Jew! and whenever anything Jewish is mentioned, I find it necessary to say that I am a Jew. I'm a Jew! A Jew!"

"Oh, you mistake me," Balso said, "I have nothing against the Jews. I admire the Jews; they are a thrifty race. Some of my best friends are Jews." But his protests availed him little until he thought to quote C. M. Doughty's epigram. "The semites," Balso said with great firmness, "are like to a man sitting in a cloaca to the eyes, and whose brows touch heaven."

When Balso had at last succeeded in quieting the guide, he tried to please him further by saying that the magnificent tunnel stirred him to the quick and that he would be satisfied to spend his remaining days in it with but a few pipes and a book. The guide tossed up his arms in one of those eloquent gestures the latins know so well how to perform and said: "After all, what is art? I agree with George Moore. Art is not nature, but rather nature digested. Art is a sublime excrement."

That's pretty typical. It's a young writer's warm-up: enjoying its own unleashed imagination, hoping to offend the pretentious and amuse the cognoscenti. It takes some patience to finish the book even though it's barely fifty pages long.

In 1927 West got a job through family connections managing a hotel, the Kenmore Hall, on East Twenty-third Street in New York. Later he would manage The Sutton on East Fifty-sixth. This was lucky, as the Depression loomed. It was also handy for some of West's hard-up friends like Dashiell Hammett and his lover Lillian Hellman, Edmund Wilson, Quentin Reynolds, James T. Farrell, and Erskine Caldwell, who were allowed to move in free of charge when they needed.

In 1929 West finished writing *Balso Snell*, the stock market collapsed, Perelman married West's sister, Laura, and West commenced work on his second novel. One night Perelman had invited West to dinner with a friend named Susan Chester who'd taken a job handling an advice-to-the-lovelorn column in the *Brooklyn Eagle*. She wanted to show Perelman some of the letters she'd been receiving there because she thought they might make good material for him. They weren't right for his style, but West was amazed by them and began to conceive a novel about an advice columnist.

3. WEST'S ARRIVAL, PT. 1

West later described *Miss Lonelyhearts* as being the kind of novel suited to modern America by likening it to Poe's definition of a lyric poem, one that's short enough that a very high level of intensity can be maintained from beginning to end. West wrote, "Forget the epic, the master work. In America, fortunes do not accumulate, the soil does not grow, families have no history. Leave slow growth to the book reviewers, you only have time to explode."

Miss Lonelyhearts is like that, a captured explosion, as if you could film one the way you could film a building, entering and tracking around in it, going in for close-ups, pulling back out. It's a novel of about seventy-five pages that starts in cold, bloody ferocity and stays there. It was written, and painstakingly rewritten multiple times, 1929-32, and published in 1933. Here's the opening:

The Miss Lonelyhearts of The New York *Post-Dispatch* (Are-you-in-trouble?—Do-you-need-advice?—Write-to-Miss-Lonely-hearts-and-she-will-help-you) sat at his desk and stared at a piece of white cardboard. On it a prayer had been printed by Shrike, the feature editor.

"Soul of Miss L, glorify me.
Body of Miss L, nourish me
Blood of Miss L, intoxicate me.
Tears of Miss L, wash me.
Oh good Miss L, excuse my plea,
And hide me in your heart,
And defend me from mine enemies.
Help me, Miss L, help me, help me.
In saecula saeculorum. Amen."

Although the deadline was less than a quarter of an hour away, he was still working on his leader. He had gone as far as: "Life is worth while, for it is full of dreams and peace, gentleness and ecstasy, and faith that burns like a clear white flame on a grim dark altar." But he found it impossible to continue. The letters were no longer funny. He could not go on finding the same joke funny thirty times a day for months on end. And on most days he received more than thirty letters, all of them alike, stamped from the dough of suffering with a heart-shaped cookie knife.

On his desk were piled those he had received this morning. He started through them again, searching for some clue to a sincere answer.

Dear Miss Lonelyhearts—
I am in such pain I dont know what to do sometimes I think I
will kill myself my kidneys hurt so much. My husband thinks no
woman can be a good catholic and not have children irregardless
of the pain. I was married honorable from our church but I never
knew what married life meant as I never was told about man and

wife. My grandmother never told me and she was the only mother I had but made a big mistake by not telling me as it dont pay to be innocent and is only a big disappointment. I have 7 children in 12 yrs and ever since the last 2 I have been so sick. I was operated on twice and my husband promised no more children on the doctors advice as he said I might die but when I got back from the hospital he broke his promise and now I am going to have a baby and I dont think I can stand it my kidneys hurt so much. I am so sick and scared because I cant have an abortion on account of being a catholic and my husband so religious. I cry all the time it hurts so much and I dont know what to do.

Yours respectfully,
Sick-of-it-all

Miss Lonelyhearts threw the letter into an open drawer and lit a cigarette.

Dear Miss Lonelyhearts—

I am sixteen years old now and I dont know what to do and would appreciate it if you could tell me what to do. When I was a little girl it was not so bad because I got used to the kids on the block makeing fun of me, but now I would like to have boy friends like the other girls and go out on Saturday nites, but no boy will take me because I was born without a nose—although I am a good dancer and have a nice shape and my father buys me pretty clothes.

I sit and look at myself all day and cry. I have a big hole in the middle of my face that scares people even myself so I cant blame the boys for not wanting to take me out. My mother loves me, but she crys terrible when she looks at me.

What did I do to deserve such a terrible bad fate? Even if I did do some bad things I didnt do any before I was a year old and I was born this way. I asked Papa and he says he doesnt know, but that maybe I did something in the other world before I was born or that

maybe I was being punished for his sins. I dont believe that because
he is a very nice man. Ought I commit suicide?
  Sincerely yours,
  Desperate

The cigarette was imperfect and refused to draw. Miss Lonelyhearts took it out of his mouth and stared at it furiously. He fought
himself quiet, then lit another one.

Dear Miss Lonelyhearts—
  I am writing to you for my little sister Grace because something
awfull hapened to her, and I am afraid to tell mother about it. I am
15 years old and Gracie is 13 and we live in Brooklyn. Gracie is deaf
and dumb and biger than me but not very smart on account of being
deaf and dumb. She plays on the roof of our house and dont go to
school except to deaf and dumb school twice a week on tuesdays and
thursdays. Mother makes her play on the roof because we dont want
her to get run over as she aint very smart. Last week a man came
on the roof and did something dirty to her. She told me about it and
I dont know what to do as I am afraid to tell mother on account of
her being liable to beat Gracie up. I am afraid that Gracie is going to
have a baby and I listened to her stomack last night for a long time
to see if I could hear the baby but I couldn't. If I tell mother she will
beat Gracie up awfull because I am the only one who loves her and
last time when she tore her dress they loked her in the closet for 2 days
and if the boys on the blok hear about it they will say dirty things like
they did on Peewee Conors sister the time she got caught in the lots.
So please what would you do if the same hapened in your family.
  Yours truly,
  Harold S.

He stopped reading. Christ was the answer, but, if he did not want
to get sick, he had to stay away from the Christ business. Besides,

Christ was Shrike's particular joke. "Soul of Miss L, glorify me. Body of Miss L, save me. Blood of . . ." He turned to his typewriter.

Although his cheap clothes had too much style, he still looked like the son of a Baptist minister. A beard would become him, would accent his Old-Testament look. But even without a beard no one could fail to recognize the New England puritan. His forehead was high and narrow. His nose was long and fleshless. His bony chin was shaped and cleft like a hoof. On seeing him for the first time, Shrike had smiled and said, "The Susan Chesters, the Beatrice Fairfaxes and the Miss Lonelyhearts are the priests of twentieth-century America."

A copy boy came up to tell him that Shrike wanted to know if the stuff was ready. He bent over the typewriter and began pounding its keys.

But before he had written a dozen words, Shrike leaned over his shoulder. "The same old stuff," Shrike said. "Why don't you give them something new and hopeful? Tell them about art. Here, I'll dictate:

"*Art Is a Way Out.*

"Do not let life overwhelm you. When the old paths are choked with the debris of failure, look for newer and fresher paths. Art is just such a path. Art is distilled from suffering. As Mr. Polnikoff exclaimed through his fine Russian beard, when, at the age of eighty-six, he gave up his business to learn Chinese, 'We are, as yet, only at the beginning . . .'

"*Art Is One of Life's Richest Offerings.*

"For those who have not the talent to create, there is appreciation. For those . . .

"Go on from there."

It's a book of despairing exhaustion, hard bitten toughness, and homely fanaticism, like the offspring of a threesome involving T.S. Eliot, Raymond Chandler, and Flannery O'Connor. The advice-columnist main character, a man, is never identified by any other name than "Miss Lonelyhearts." He is a reader of Dostoevsky and the son of a Baptist minister and his frightening futile leapings and graspings at Christianity batter from within, like someone trying to punch himself out of a potato sack. The book's horror is a kind of cartoon horror, with deep feelings being mocked for their unreality in a language and imagery so striking that the intensity of the language itself becomes what's funny. West, in fact, claims to have originally considered doing the book as a comic strip. If he had, he would have been a good forty years ahead of his time, but as it is, there was no book much like this one before it appeared.

Near the end, Miss Lonelyhearts has a religious experience:

After a long night and morning, towards noon, Miss Lonelyhearts welcomed the arrival of fever. It promised heat and mentally unmotivated violence. The promise was soon fulfilled; the rock became a furnace.

He fastened his eyes on the Christ that hung on the wall opposite his bed. As he stared at it, it became a bright fly, spinning with quick grace on a background of blood velvet sprinkled with tiny nerve stars.

Everything else in the room was dead—chairs, table, pencils, clothes, books. He thought of this black world of things as a fish. And he was right, for it suddenly rose to the bright bait on the wall. It rose with a splash of music and he saw its shining silver belly.

Christ is life and light.

"Christ! Christ!" This shout echoed through the innermost cells of his body.

He moved his head to a cooler spot on the pillow and the vein in his forehead became less swollen. He felt clean and fresh. His heart was a rose and in his skull another rose bloomed.

The room was full of grace. A sweet, clean grace, not washed clean, but clean as the inner sides of the inner petals of a newly forced rosebud.

Delight was also in the room. It was like a gentle wind, and his nerves rippled under it like small blue flowers in a pasture.

He was conscious of two rhythms that were slowly becoming one. When they became one, his identification with God was complete. His heart was the one heart, the heart of God. And his brain was likewise God's.

God said, "Will you accept it, now?"

And he replied, "I accept, I accept."

He immediately began to plan a new life and his future conduct as Miss Lonelyhearts. He submitted drafts of his column to God and God approved them. God approved his every thought.

Suddenly the door bell rang.

You'll have to read the book to find out what happens next.

The novel impressed a lot of poets. William Carlos Williams, Philippe Soupault, and W. H. Auden all published admiring discussions of it. F. Scott Fitzgerald championed the book in print more than once in the year following its publication.

West had become friends with William Carlos Williams. They'd met after the editors of the small literary press Contact Editions, to whom West had submitted *Balso Snell*, sent the ms. to Williams for an appraisal. Williams was impressed by *Balso*, recommended publication, and Contact had brought it out in 1931 in an edition of five-hundred copies. Later that year, when Williams took on the editorship of a revival of the literary magazine extension of Contact Editions, *Contact*—the original incarnation of which Williams'd edited with Robert McAalmon in Paris in the '20s—Williams asked West to be his associate editor. West signed on, honored. The magazine lasted three issues in 1932, publishing, among others, e. e. cummings, S. J. Perelman, Erskine Caldwell, Charles Reznikoff, Marsden Hartley, Nancy Cunard, James T. Farrell, and the editors.

Neither *Balso Snell* nor *Miss Lonelyhearts* was profitable. In West's entire career he would make less than $1,500 from his fiction.

3. WEST'S ARRIVAL, PT. 2

In the 1930s many of America's best writers spent time in Hollywood as contract workers on movie scripts for the studios. The money was spectacular, especially considering it was the Depression. S. J. Perelman was living there. In 1933 he'd already written *Horse Feathers* and *Monkey Business* for the Marx Brothers. That summer of 1933 West joined Laura and Perelman, taking a job as a junior writer at Columbia Studios. He'd already begun his third novel, *A Cool Million*. He would finish it that fall. It would be published in the summer of 1934 by Covici-Friede in an edition of 3,000.

A Cool Million's style is different from either of West's previous books. It's a very broad satire of American shysterism and money worship—a parody of Horatio Alger stories, something like *Candide*, a picaresque, the hero of which, Lemuel Pitkin, never loses his innocence, even as, in his pursuit of the American dream, he loses his teeth, an eye, a leg, his scalp, and finally his life. It features politicians as frauds, capitalists as thieves, revolutionaries as dupes and vice versa and interchangeably, but also portrays their idealistic constituents/cell-members/customers as fools. It gets a lot of mileage out of silly names. It's a vaudeville show of the spectacle of modern America, "the business of which," as Calvin Coolidge had recently put it, "is business."

It's not a work on the level of *Miss Lonelyhearts*. The book's humor feels strained pretty quickly—the writer's performance is something you "get" right away, and after that it doesn't hold your interest. But its message is pertinent still. I'll show a passage from near the end of the book. Lemuel and the former U.S. president he considers his friend, but who is actually his main exploiter, Shagpoke Whipple, have been working for a traveling carnival/medicine show when Shagpoke decides he must dispose of the show's proprietor, Sylvanus Snodgrasse. Speaking of Snodgrasse, Whipple tells Lemuel,

> "[...] Rather must we bide our time until a good opportunity presents itself, then denounce him for what he is, and his show

likewise. Here, in Detroit, there are too many Jews, Catholics and members of unions. Unless I am greatly mistaken, however, we will shortly turn south. When we get to some really American town, we will act."

Mr. Whipple was right in his surmise. After playing a few more Midwestern cities, Snodgrasse headed his company south along the Mississippi River, finally arriving in the town of Beulah for a one-night stand.

"Now is the time for us to act," announced Mr. Whipple in a hoarse whisper to Lem, when he had obtained a good look at the inhabitants of Beulah. "Follow me."

Our hero accompanied Shagpoke to the town barber shop, which was run by one Keely Jefferson, a fervent Southerner of the old school. Mr. Whipple took the master barber to one side. After a whispered colloquy, he agreed to arrange a meeting of the town's citizens for Shagpoke to address.

By five o'clock that same evening, all the inhabitants of Beulah who were not colored, Jewish or Catholic assembled under a famous tree from whose every branch a Negro had dangled at one time or other. They stood together, almost a thousand strong, drinking Coca-Colas and joking with their friends. Although every third citizen carried either a rope or a gun, their cheerful manner belied the seriousness of the occasion.

Mr. Jefferson mounted a box to introduce Mr. Whipple.

"Fellow townsmen, Southerners, Protestants, Americans," he began. "You have been called here to listen to the words of Shagpoke Whipple, one of the few Yanks whom we of the South can trust and respect. He ain't no nigger-lover, he don't give a damn for Jewish culture, and he knows the fine Italian hand of the Pope when he sees it. Mr. Whipple . . ."

Shagpoke mounted the box which Mr. Jefferson vacated and waited for the cheering to subside. He began by placing his hand on his heart. "I love the South," he announced. "I love her because her women are beautiful and chaste, her men brave and gallant, and her fields warm and fruitful. But there is one thing that I love more than the South . . . my country, these United States."

The cheers which greeted this avowal were even wilder and hoarser than those that had gone before it. Mr. Whipple held up his hand for silence, but it was fully five minutes before his audience would let him continue.

"Thank you," he cried happily, much moved by the enthusiasm of his hearers. "I know that your shouts rise from the bottom of your honest, fearless hearts. And I am grateful because I also know that you are cheering, not me, but the land we love so well.

"However, this is not a time or place for flowery speeches, this is a time for action. There is an enemy in our midst, who, by boring from within, undermines our institutions and threatens our freedom. Neither hot lead nor cold steel are his weapons, but insidious propaganda. He strives by it to set brother against brother, those who have not against those who have.

"You stand here now, under this heroic tree, like the free men that you are, but tomorrow you will become the slaves of Socialists and Bolsheviks. Your sweethearts and wives will become the common property of foreigners to maul and mouth at their leisure. Your shops will be torn from you and you will be driven from your farms. In return you will be thrown a stinking, slave's crust with Russian labels.

"Is the spirit of Jubal Early and Francis Marion then so dead that you can only crouch and howl like hound dogs? Have you forgotten Jefferson Davis?

"No?

"Then let those of you who remember your ancestors strike down Sylvanus Snodgrasse, that foul conspirator, that viper in the bosom of the body politic. Let those . . ."

Before Mr. Whipple had quite finished his little talk, the crowd ran off in all directions, shouting "Lynch him! Lynch him!" although a good three-quarters of its members did not know whom it was they were supposed to lynch. This fact did not bother them, however. They considered their lack of knowledge an advantage rather than a hindrance, for it gave them a great deal of leeway in their choice of a victim.

Yes, this stuff tries a little too hard. West's writing at its best doesn't try to be funny, but is funny for the surprises of its merciless revelations of specific American grotesqueries, instances isolated by him that would be hard to perceive otherwise, camouflaged as they are in the flow of hype and misrepresentation which half-comprises us. His fourth book would be a return to finest form.

West went back east after his first job in Hollywood ended in the fall of 1933, but eighteen months later, in March of 1935, after *A Cool Million* had tanked commercially, and he'd also failed at making a couple of attempts at playwrighting pay off, he returned to Los Angeles. He couldn't find work at first and had to live on loans from the Perelmans. He stayed in the industry town's seedier hotels, alongside bit players, stuntmen, low-level crew-people, and those he would describe in *The Day of the Locust* as having "come to California to die." He loitered at Stanley Rose's bookstore on Hollywood Boulevard, meeting place for many of the city's more literarily ambitious writers, like John Fante, John O'Hara, Horace McCoy, William Saroyan, Scott Fitzgerald, William Faulkner, Budd Schulberg, Erskine Caldwell, and Hammett. Some of these were already his friends; he would become friends with most of the rest of them. Rose himself was a colorful character, a sometime con man who introduced West to the world of the area's smalltime crime, from brothels to cockfights.

In January of 1936, West got a screenwriting contract with Republic Pictures. Unlike most of his Hollywood writer friends, he didn't feel compromised or diminished by working for hire at the studios. He accepted the job for what it was—exploiting for profit the mass market's dreams and fantasies—and didn't confuse it with his work as a novelist, but unresentfully took up the challenge of trying to do it as well as he could. He succeeded pretty quickly, steadily rising in income and prestige as a screenwriter of innocuous but profitable theater filler. In the meantime he was writing a novel about what he saw around him in Hollywood.

The Day of the Locust is West's best book, as well as the best novel of the many that have been written about Hollywood. The only one that might have outdone it is Fitzgerald's unfinished *The Last Tycoon*, which may well have been influenced by it. *The Day of the Locust* treats mass culture and modern American life with all the focused, cold insight of *Miss Lonelyhearts*, but is less melodramatic and more complex. It's the most incisive, and one of the first, depictions of American culture as a series of facades, fantasies, dreams, and advertisements without end, like a haunted house of mirrors. Everybody in it is trying to be or acquire an idea they've been sold of what it would be exciting to be or have.

The central, as well as most self-aware and perceptive, character in the book is Tod Hackett, a painter who was hired out of the "Yale School of Fine Arts" to come design sets and costumes for National Films. Tod is obsessed with Faye Greener, a seventeen year old aspirant to stardom who takes what work she can get as an extra and sometime prostitute in the meantime, and who is composed entirely of affectations—

[...] His interest in her grew despite the things she said and he continued to find her very exciting. Had any other girl been so affected, he would have thought her intolerable. Faye's affectations, however, were so completely artificial that he found them charming.

Being with her was like being backstage during an amateurish, ridiculous play. From in front, the stupid lines and grotesque situations would have made him squirm with annoyance, but because he saw the perspiring stagehands and the wires that held up the tawdry summerhouse with its tangle of paper flowers, he accepted everything and was anxious for it to succeed.

—but she rebuffs Tod because, as she explains to him, she "could only love a handsome man and would only let a wealthy man love her." "She wasn't hard-boiled. It was just that she put love on a special plane, where a man without money or looks couldn't move." Faye has a number of admirers in the book. The most devoted of them is the book's example of a typical California immigrant who has come there to die, and his name is, funnily, Homer Simpson. Homer is a bookkeeper from Wayneville, Iowa, who has moved with his life savings to Hollywood. The better part of his days there are spent lying dimly in his ugly yard watching flies tempt the resident lizard. Homer is afraid of many things, including the way Faye attracts him. "He thought her extremely beautiful, but what affected him still more was her vitality. She was taut and vibrant. She was as shiny as a new spoon." But, alone on his broken deck chair, such thoughts "frightened him and he bolted into the house, hoping to leave them behind like a hat."

Here's a section describing what happens when Tod in his office at the studio lot spots Faye outside costumed for an historical epic in which she's an extra. He runs downstairs to catch her. . . .

[. . .] He shouted for her to wait. She waved, but when he got downstairs she was gone.

From her dress, he was sure that she was working in the picture called "Waterloo." He asked a studio policeman where the company was shooting and was told on the back lot. He started toward it at once. A platoon of cuirassiers, big men mounted on gigantic horses, went by. He knew that they must be headed for the same set and followed them. They broke into a gallop and he was soon outdistanced.

The sun was very hot. His eyes and throat were choked with the dust thrown up by the horses' hooves and his head throbbed. The only bit of shade he could find was under an ocean liner made of painted canvas with real lifeboats hanging from its davits. He stood in its narrow shadow for a while, then went on toward a great forty-foot papier mâché sphinx that loomed up in the distance. He had to cross a desert to reach it, a desert that was continually being made larger by a fleet of trucks dumping white sand. He had gone only a few feet when a man with a megaphone ordered him off.

He skirted the desert, making a wide turn to the right, and came to a Western street with a plank sidewalk. On the porch of the

"Last Chance Saloon" was a rocking chair. He sat down on it and lit a cigarette.

From there he could see a jungle compound with a water buffalo tethered to the side of a conical grass hut. Every few seconds the animal groaned musically. Suddenly an Arab charged by on a white stallion. He shouted at the man, but got no answer. A little while later he saw a truck with a load of snow and several malamute dogs. He shouted again. The driver shouted something back, but didn't stop.

Throwing away his cigarette, he went through the swinging doors of the saloon. There was no back to the building and he found himself in a Paris street. He followed it to its end, coming out in a Romanesque courtyard. He heard voices a short distance away and went toward them. On a lawn of fiber, a group of men and women in riding costume were picnicking. They were eating cardboard food in front of a cellophane waterfall. He started toward them to ask his way, but was stopped by a man who scowled and held up a sign— "Quiet, Please, We're Shooting." When Tod took another step forward, the man shook his fist threateningly.

Next he came to a small pond with large celluloid swans floating on it. Across one end was a bridge with a sign that read, "To Kamp Komfit." He crossed the bridge and followed a little path that ended at a Greek temple dedicated to Eros. The god himself lay face downward in a pile of old newspapers and bottles.

From the steps of the temple, he could see in the distance a road lined with Lombardy poplars. It was the one on which he had lost the cuirassiers. He pushed his way through a tangle of briars, old flats and iron junk, skirting the skeleton of a Zeppelin, a bamboo stockade, an adobe fort, the wooden horse of Troy, a flight of baroque palace stairs that started in a bed of weeds and ended against the branches of an oak, part of the Fourteenth Street elevated station, a Dutch windmill, the bones of a dinosaur, the upper half of the Merrimac, a corner of a Mayan temple, until he finally reached the road.

He was out of breath. He sat down under one of the poplars on a rock made of brown plaster and took off his jacket. There was a cool breeze blowing and he soon felt more comfortable.

He had lately begun to think not only of Goya and Daumier but also of certain Italian artists of the seventeenth and eighteenth centuries, of Salvator Rosa, Francesco Guardi and Monsu Desiderio, the painters of Decay and Mystery. Looking downhill now, he could see compositions that might have actually been arranged from the Calabrian work of Rosa. There were partially demolished buildings and broken monuments, half-hidden by great, tortured trees, whose exposed roots writhed dramatically in the arid ground, and by shrubs that carried, not flowers or berries, but armories of spikes, hooks and swords.

For Guardi and Desiderio there were bridges which bridged nothing, sculpture in trees, palaces that seemed of marble until a whole stone portico began to flap in the light breeze. And there were figures as well. A hundred yards from where Tod was sitting a man in a derby hat leaned drowsily against the gilded poop of a Venetian barque and peeled an apple. Still farther on, a charwoman on a stepladder was scrubbing with soap and water the face of a Buddha thirty feet high.

He left the road and climbed across the spine of the hill to look down on the other side. From there he could see a ten-acre field of cockleburs spotted with clumps of sunflowers and wild gum. In the center of the field was a gigantic pile of sets, flats and props. While he watched, a ten-ton truck added another load to it. This was the final dumping ground. He thought of Janvier's "Sargasso Sea." Just as that imaginary body of water was a history of civilization in the form of a marine junkyard, the studio lot was one in the form of a dream dump. A Sargasso of the imagination! And the dump grew continually, for there wasn't a dream afloat somewhere which wouldn't sooner or later turn up on it, having first been made photographic by plaster, canvas, lath and paint. Many boats sink and never reach the Sargasso, but no dream ever entirely disappears.

Somewhere it troubles some unfortunate person and some day, when that person has been sufficiently troubled, it will be reproduced on the lot.

A little later he hears cannons and realizes he's found Waterloo:

Neither Napoleon nor Wellington was to be seen. In Wellington's absence, one of the assistant directors, a Mr. Crane, was in command of the allies. He reinforced his center with one of Chasse's brigades and one of Wincke's. He supported these with infantry from Brunswick, Welsh foot, Devon yeomanry and Hanoverian light horse with oblong leather caps and flowing plumes of horsehair.

For the French, a man in a checked cap ordered Milhaud's cuirassiers to carry Mont St. Jean. With their sabers in their teeth and their pistols in their hands, they charged. It was a fearful sight.

The man in the checked cap was making a fatal error. Mont St. Jean was unfinished. The paint was not yet dry and all the struts were not in place. Because of the thickness of the cannon smoke, he had failed to see that the hill was still being worked on by property men, grips and carpenters.

It was the classic mistake, Tod realized, the same one Napoleon had made. Then it had been wrong for a different reason. The Emperor had ordered the cuirassiers to charge Mont St. Jean not knowing that a deep ditch was hidden at its foot to trap his heavy cavalry. The result had been disaster for the French; the beginning of the end.

This time the same mistake had a different outcome. Waterloo, instead of being the end of the Grand Army, resulted in a draw. Neither side won, and it would have to be fought over again the next day. Big losses, however, were sustained by the insurance company in workmen's compensation. The man in the checked cap was sent to the dog house by Mr. Grotenstein just as Napoleon was sent to St. Helena.

When the front rank of Milhaud's heavy division started up the slope of Mont St. Jean, the hill collapsed. The noise was terrific.

Nails screamed with agony as they pulled out of joists. The sound of ripping canvas was like that of little children whimpering. Lath and scantling snapped as though they were brittle bones. The whole hill folded like an enormous umbrella and covered Napoleon's army with painted cloth.

It turned into a rout. The victors of Bersina, Leipsic, Austerlitz, fled like schoolboys who had broken a pane of glass. "Sauve qui peut!" they cried, or, rather, "Scram!"

The armies of England and her allies were too deep in scenery to flee. They had to wait for the carpenters and ambulances to come up. The men of the gallant Seventy-Fifth Highlanders were lifted out of the wreck with block and tackle. They were carted off by the stretcher-bearers, still clinging bravely to their claymores.

History is Hollywood dreams. Is there such a thing as history? Maybe not. Is there such a thing as reality? No.

The book ends apocalyptically, with the riot and stampede of a crowd that'd formed to ogle the stars at a film premiere. West had deduced that many of the fans most crazy about movie stars were as jealous of them as they were devoted, and were apt to turn on them with the slightest excuse.

The Day of the Locusts was published by Random House in 1939 and sold fewer than 1500 copies.

4. WEST'S DEPARTURE

West had become successful as a contract film writer though, and his life took an especially dramatic turn for the better, too, in 1939, when he met Eileen McKenney. She'd been the subject of her sister Ruth's book *My Sister Eileen*, which had originally been published in *The New Yorker*, and she'd moved in the circle of that magazine's writers, which had been familiar to West in New York. Neither of the couple had had much luck in romantic relationships prior to this, but by all accounts they were a great match and very happy. They got married six months after meeting, in April of 1940. In December of that year, returning from a trip to Mexico together, West, thirty-seven, ran a stop sign and crashed into another car and both he and his bride were killed.

5. SUMMATION

Seventy or so years ago Nathanael West wrote two short books that remain thrilling and revelatory. I prefer his writing to that of Fitzgerald, Hemingway, and Faulkner. West and Fitzgerald have things in common: a clear, simple style in the service of flashing lyricism; great depth of perception into their characters, as well as into those characters' positions in relation to each other in the American landscape. But West wasn't hampered by Fitzgerald's eager prep-school romanticism. Fitzgerald was the more ambitious of the two, though. West's intense virtues are also limitations: his books are not multi-leveled. They're genre works, perhaps better compared to the great detective novels of Raymond Chandler than those more ambitious guys. He's not really going after what it's like to be alive, "how things are" on every scale, or, you could say, aiming to make works that correspond to life, which is what the very most interesting art does. But who succeeds at that? Three or four people a century . . .

One other, anecdotal, but striking, thing about West is that the qualities, the features, of American life that he exposes in his books are reflections of things he felt in himself. Which partly explains the horror they evoked in him. He was aghast at the absence of any solid identity, any deep foundation in inherited values, of modern Americans, and the way that that makes us vulnerable to all kinds of exploitation, manipulation, delusions, despair, and impulses to violence. He himself was an example of a free-floating citizen of the New World, for whom the parental function of anchoring one's identity in values evolved by a culture for generation upon generation had been replaced by the substitute-parent of the mass media and the corporate promulgation of what it serves the corporations' profit-line to make seem attractive, all resulting in the reduction of any ideal of personal fulfillment to three main things: money, fame, and sex appeal. Or maybe I'm just talking about myself again.

Talk given for lecture series "By the Waters of Manhattan," "by/on Jewish poets" curated by Elinor Nauen for Jewish Below 14th and the Committee on Poetry, at Poets & Writers, NYC, 2005

DREAMING

THERE ARE A LOT of obvious things about dreams that come to mind instantly. First, that dreams with rare exceptions are boring to everyone but the dreamer. Second, that, first hand, dreams are indistinguishable from waking "reality." Third, that, supposedly even "scientifically" (with the advent of psychoanalysis), dreams can reveal information about a person that would otherwise be hidden. And, for me, fourth is that they're a source for a lot of art, including some of the best. The instance which surprised me the most was that Jasper Johns got the idea for his flag paintings from a dream. Maybe the most impressive example is Coleridge's "Kubla Khan," which ravishing, timeless fifty-four lines he brought back with him from a laudanum nod. Speaking of nods, William Burroughs also scavenged a huge proportion of his fiction from his dreams. I don't know if a distinction should be made between narcotic nodding and conventional dreams. I think possibly—my impression is that a nod is a light doze that permits easier access to detail than a full-fledged R.E.M. dream normally does.

I've had a lot of perceptions and conceptions of dreams in a long appreciative relationship with them. Though, in fact, that relationship has been exhaustive enough that recently I've sometimes found myself tired of dreaming. I awaken multiple times a night in such a way that I almost always recall my dream of the moment, and they start seeming annoying, like brain gutter runoff, nagging.

I also recently had the experience of perceiving, in situ, the generative process of dreams. I've for a long time, basically ignorantly, been skeptical of Freud, not trusting any science of psychoanalysis (penis envy, Oedipal complex, what have you), but I've found Jung's approach to dream interpretation useful. Namely to regard all the characters in a dream as being aspects of oneself and to immediately, while the dream is fresh, ask oneself what personal psychological activity is suggested by the relationships and activities of the people (all oneself) in the dream. In my experience, an answer will immediately suggest itself, which often is revelatory. But the experience of getting an unimpeded front-row view of the process that forms dreams has given me a new respect for Freud, since it seemed to support his method of dream interpretation . . .

Over the years I've compiled a small collection of phrases and sentences brought back from dreams, for example, "All you have to do is pick up that front door and write 'Charles Brodley' on it," or, ". . . spilled by the biggest airtime images in the Carbonville pap." The other day I had the fluke luck to retain observation of the process by which such sentences are formed, which was self-evidently the same process, on a different scale, that generates dreams themselves. You start with a unit of meaning—a word (in the case of sentence-forming), an image, or what have you, and instantly that unit spins off an array of associations that could have been suggested by any quality of the object—its shape, its sound, its color, its utility, anything. Largely by chance, one of these associations (all of which are inherently psychologically relevant or revealing to some degree because they're limited to one's personal repertoire) falls into the slot (like a reverse roulette wheel—many balls and one slot), and it's that new object in the string (now two units long) that sets off the next array of associations, and the dream proceeds like that. The combinations are largely chance, but not only are they limited to one's stock of associations, but the number of related associations will increase according to one's preoccupations, so the dream is personal.

* * *

Over the years, I have exploited into works a number of dream images, words, and narrative threads. Maybe a third of them came from my drug days. In a way it's a disservice to the works to identify them as rooted in dreams, because it risks inclining readers to trivialize them and class them as forms of anecdote, but what the hell. How much can I lose, and I'll give you the benefit of the doubt. Real appreciators of art know that the "source" is irrelevant, it's the execution that matters. My favorite is a poem (from after I'd stopped using drugs) that takes for its title a phrase from a dream, and then describes in a kind of indirect, carefully composed and annotated way, an experience of succumbing to sleep and dreaming:

THAT TO THE SIDES OF THE DARK SHINE THE THEORIES

Yesterday, late in the evening, I started feeling thick and heavy as if I were being pulled down, as if something deep underground had started to exert a new kind of gravity that was sucking my body and senses towards it, while my floating mind stayed above. I could hardly keep my eyelids raised and I had to lie down. Once I did that, my body hollowed and lightened, like a drawing of itself. My mind seemed to float loose while leaking into my body like molecules: sex, sax, six, socks, sucks . . . It was like my body liquefied, then evaporated, the whole prehistoric breathing, and my mind was a rudderless little boat that drifted in it. I seeped and haltingly flowed according to the permeability and slant. In the puddles at the bottom of the boat was a tumbled messy litter of everything imaginable that had happened or could happen to me. How could it be so small? My senses seemed to have returned, but were caught in the contents of the boat, as if perception were engendered by those objects.* It seemed that if I looked at one item—a tan-colored life-size hobby shop model of a robin, for instance—everything else in the strew became possible, so that when my attention left the glued-together plastic bird, the items around it had become something other than what they'd been before. Oh, it was too beautiful, this surrender. It is the secret standard of worthiness. All who do it are good! My mind** opened and the boat, being one, the only, wasn't a boat.***

---

* Later I heard "that to the sides of the dark shine the theories."†

** If the brain-neurons are buzzing, are individual, can choose, aren't they all of life and history? Each person is God and the brain's neurons are all the people of the history of the world. We are the neurons in God's brain. (Is God asleep? Will God awake? And then what happens to us? God's wakefulness the laws, God's sleep the activity . . .)

*** Somewhere in the ocean I started getting an erection. Marilyn Monroe had a penis. The boat sprang a leak. I "woke up"§ with come all over me.

---

† If you want to be an artist, go to sleep.

§ Falling, going to, then coming, up . . .

Another, the earliest one, was also drug-free. I was about twenty-one when I wrote this poem that was a pretty faithful rendering of a nightmare I had:

OOPS

jokes
bad jokes
I broke down a wall to find
another wall! further and further
until I came to my heart!

and it was dead Oh no
and bristling with knife points
of the people who'd tried
to cut their way out when it died.

I held my heart.
What do I do???
I asked of
all the old ladies I knew.
Then I realized I had to eat it
to get it back inside.
How do I prepare it,
I despaired,
fried with butter???

I started picking out the knives
and there was Bernadette
and she was alive.
She said, Now that you've found me
you don't need it anyway.
Beautiful Bernadette
I thought she must be right. So I
threw it away. But
Bernadette
you *lied*.

One of my favorite of my drawings came from something I saw in a
dream. It was a fountain made of iron, the design components of which
were a simple pipe, maybe three inches in diameter, gushing water
straight up from near the top of the contraption, and a couple of feet
below that, maybe seven feet off the ground, a set of riveted slats in the
crude shape of the outline of a horse's head that mechanically swiveled
back and forth in an arc of maybe 100 degrees, with one extreme of the

arc ending at the spot most convenient to turn itself upwards and open its jaw as if drinking from the fountain. All the mechanics of the machine were exposed (though I didn't try to show them in the drawing, but rather just sketched a large cone instead):

Another poem I like was a slightly reframed but fully faithful dream transcription. It happened after I quit drugs too.

TROPHY

The two men in their formal clothes handed me a plate, inches thick, that separated about in half at an almost invisible careening line which opened to reveal the gorgeous strata of its materials. The outer layer of the giant coin had been designed to look worn—it was dented and smudged, loose-seeming, simulating the effects of years of handling. I accepted my award, turned, shook my head accidentally, reflexively, in consideration of my situation, and began back to my seat embarrassed a little for having done that. I held a half-section in each hand. I didn't want to stare at them but I couldn't resist lingering in my peripheral vision as I tried to watch where I was going at the same time. The thing was just so charged with its own image—such an odd mixture of intentions resulting in a (double) object of extreme pleasure to the eye and utter incomprehensibility. One of those breathtaking serendipitous conjunctions the humor and meanings of which, intended and not, are as seductive as its ravishing sensory, formal qualities. The weight of it seemed like destiny. And now I had one! It was like owning an original Mickey Mouse cel. And better even because I didn't give a fuck in hell for the prize or the people who voted me worthy of it. In fact I felt a little dirty for carrying it, but it's always like that here. I sat down next to my wife.

The most amazing experience I had in these lines does come from a period of heavy drug use. I was a heroin addict and one morning after a long night of supplementary cocaine consumption, I woke up from a delirious sleep in the late morning alone on the floor mattress in my girlfriend's loft, with an entire novelistically complex, or film-ready, plot, complete in my consciousness. Nothing like that had ever happened before and nothing like it since. It was all there, a detailed narrative (grand guignol, noir, pulp) from beginning to end:

LOWEST COMMON DOMINATOR (synopsis)
A Psychological Horror Story

This is the story of a group of six unexceptional lower middle class Americans and their relationship with a rich and famous sensationalist gossip columnist.

The group of six all live in New York City. Their jobs are: secretary, bank teller, taxi driver, department store clerk, newsstand operator, and factory worker. But, more pertinently, they are all of a type not usually given much attention in art or storytelling, being dull, mildly suspicious, and resentful souls, even in their negative qualities small and undistinguished. They've been casually neglected and mistreated enough their whole lives so as to end up mildly dim and mean. The type of the petty bureaucrat.

Chance has finally brought this crew some good luck though. Two of them become friends. Then another is accepted into the group, until, one by one, they become a circle of mutual support. They all feel similarly cynical about the world, but their relationships with each other warm and relax them. They get together at each others' apartments to watch TV and they go to movies together and meet for pizza.

A particular thing they have in common is admiration for mass-media legend Arthur Lyman. He's a tabloid entertainment gossip columnist and TV interviewer who is malicious towards his celebrity subjects, but in a subtle, insinuating way, and from a stance of moral indignation. His forté is the cunningly cutting, guardedly sarcastic interview with a major star of the moment. He strikes a gracious pose in these confrontations, while alternating innuendo with disengenuous bluntness to exploit every suggestion of a nasty rumor or suspicion about each subject. He thrives as beneficiary and exploiter of the resentment of the famous by those who've made them that.

Some of his victims handle it better than others. The comedians usually do best. But hardly anyone refuses an invitation to his table, because to be invited for an interview by Arthur Lyman is the ultimate celebrity achievement, equivalent to an Academy Award.

One night, Herb, the taxi driving member of the six, is complaining to the cohort about how cabbies with the fanciest cars get the best tips. He's always wished he had tinted windows. Joan, who is a practical, self-reliant corporate secretary in her early fifties, suggests he might be able to find some kind of spray-on. But no, there isn't such a thing. The group gets inspired. Over the course of a few weeks of investigation and research, and then consultation with a lawyer, the group comes up with a plan to market cans of three different shades of spray-on windshield tint.

They advertise mail order in motor magazines. Sales are slow. They place some spray-cans in hardware and auto-parts stores. Sales start to increase a bit. After a few months they begin getting mail that leads them to realize that people are using their product to tint prescription eyeglasses. They change the cans' labels and advertising and sales start to take off. They add new colors. Sales rocket. It's a huge fad. Within a year the six are all millionaires.

Their success becomes national news. They're covered by the popular media, are guests on TV talk shows. People are charmed by their frankness and lack of affectation. It's a fantasy story—six ordinary, uneducated, feisty, grumpy people become self-made corporate millionaires.

The six are invited to be interviewed by Arthur Lyman.

Lyman's legend is complicated. He's a devout Catholic who comes from an old-money wealthy family. He was born with withered legs and is confined to a wheelchair. This all contributes to his populist appeal: he's viewed by his public as a man with their bedrock values, who has overcome adversity, including the temptations of snobbery, to become the handsomely cultivated representative of their sceptical, honest, salty spirit.

Lyman's faculties have also ended up taking a particular aesthetic and religious turn. His Catholic devotion is part of his legend—he collects paintings of the crucifixion—but its full flowering is personal. He regards certain artists and religious figures as being his only true equals (while at the same time he earns himself his own spiritual congratulations for acknowledging that all men are of equal value in the eyes of God).

There is a whole protocol and drill to the Lyman interview. He lives in a townhouse in Chicago and his subjects must visit him there for the interview weekend, every hour of which is strictly scheduled.

He has a famous personal chef (who actually despises him, as do Lyman's other servants).

One aspect of his household is secret: Lyman has had all the living quarters in it bugged with hidden microphones. He uses them to eavesdrop on his subjects in hopes of turning up dirt he can use to his advantage. By listening in on such things as the conversations of his subjects with their entourages, or to what they say in phone calls, he acquires information with which to discomfort them.

When Lyman's six guests arrive on a Friday afternoon, he electronically eavesdrops on their chatter and is surprised by how innocent it seems and at how genuinely excited they appear and how much they admire and respect him.

In the evening, when drinks are served, Lyman is confused and disarmed. He's like the classic grumpy old man unable to adjust to the innocence and warmth of the cheerful orphan he's inherited. This makes him even more icy and formal, which begins to disconcert and alienate his guests.

Things continue to deteriorate at dinner. Lyman can't find anything about the six that he can profit from slyly deriding. They are perfect representations of his audience itself, so how could he please that audience by ridiculing them? Lyman is stiff and the six are confused. They're becoming disillusioned, suspecting that Lyman feels himself to be above them. Lyman can see what they are thinking and it disturbs him further. He really does consider himself to be at soul a man of the people and he can't adjust to this contrary evidence. His mind is spinning without being able to engage. He's like a laboratory animal which has suddenly had the reward lever begin delivering punishment.

By the time they all retire that evening, the guests to their second floor rooms, and Lyman to his bedroom on the top floor, one above, Lyman's desire to sarcastically expose them in some hypocrisy is hopelessly struggling with the inexplicable craving he feels to be worthy of their respect. He twists and squirms inside, groping for a way of framing his situation. Why did he feel inferior to his guests? Finally a door opens in his mind and he realizes there's a way that he can safely accept his guests and free himself from this mental maze. His guests must be proof of the holiness of all humans, and this real-life illumination is his welcome from God into the ranks of His elect on earth. Lyman spends the deepest hours of the night reflecting and embroidering on the revelation. He doesn't exactly acknowledge to himself his certainty that perceiving the perfection of his guests is his coronation by God, but rather assumes so deeply that the one must follow the other that he can't realize it consciously.

At breakfast the next morning he frightens his guests even more. He is unshaven and incongruous. He speaks in a strange soft murmer, and insists on placing one of them at the head of the table, and that they make up their own menu. His obsequiousness continues to outrage them. Lyman can tell how they are misinterpreting his humility as mockery, but, being new to this line of undiluted honesty, he can only compound the problem with more earnest sincerity. He's bothered by their scepticism, but, after all, what else but suffering and misunderstanding can be the fate of a holy initiate on earth?

Lyman has stopped using his secret tape snoop apparatus. Not only is he preoccupied with this new spiritual era, but the recording system is a bleak vestige of his old, petty self.

The six, meanwhile, have been provoked to defensive action. They don't have to take anybody acting like he thinks he is God towards them anymore, no matter who he is.

The house's chef, Lyman's only confidante, enlists to conspire with the six in a scheme for revenge. The six will pursue the prank with the same determination and care as they'd advanced the inspiration that had made them famous. They have one more day and night, Sunday, to carry out their plan, and they go to sleep satisfied.

The next day Lyman's erratic state makes it easy to keep him distracted with flattery, which, in a feedback effect, reinforces his delusions, in turn strengthening the resolve of the guests to carry out their elaborate revenge. The interview is scheduled to take place after dinner. When cocktail hour arrives, they have gotten privacy, even from the servants, with their host. They give him a doctored drink which knocks him out.

Lyman is unconscious for about three hours. When he first comes to, he is facing the mirror in his bedroom, naked. The mirror hangs on the wall above a small table opposite the foot of his bed. He is groggy, confused, and can't turn his head, but in the mirror he stares in dawning shock as he realizes that he has been crucified, naked, except for the binding straps around his head, upside-down, on the wall opposite his bedroom mirror.

Realizing this tears him away in layers of terror and humiliation. His short and withered legs have been pulled sideways and his arms allowed to hang downwards where they are nailed together against the wall. This gives him the look of a crucified homunculus with genitalia in place of a head and vice versa. He vomits, spilling his stomach into his eyes and down his forehead

He aches all over and sees a lot of blood on himself, especially around his feet and hands. He realizes that, despite all his failings he has finally gotten himself right up to heaven's doorstep. He can't possibly survive more than a few hours.

This event is the fulfillment of the ambitions of all its participants—ridding the six of their only remaining obstacle to bliss, and bestowing on Lyman confirmation of his analysis of the meaning of human life, which is death. Perfection. That's how it is interpreted by him anyway, until the next morning, after his visitors have left, and his servants have unstrapped him from where he dozes under the continued influence of the sedative. He awakes to grasp that he's only been bound harmlessly to the wall and given a few shallow razor slices in a joke on his weakness for the crucifixion motif.

His unassailable egotism and snobbery have been used against him more successfully than even the perpetrators can have imagined. This knowledge reaches him, finally, where he really lives and from that morning forward he is clinically catatonic.

That was a dream I had.

Finally, another visual image. This is a painting that I actually saw myself painting in a dream. I had to go buy paint and try to reproduce it. I didn't succeed. My painting is superficially true to the dream, but (though you can't really tell here, where there's not a sense of scale) the

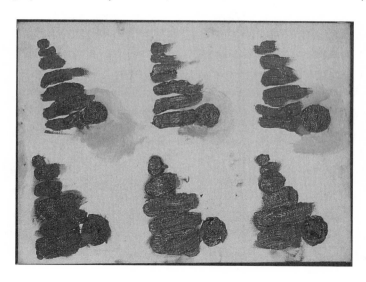

one in the dream was much larger, maybe five feet tall, and the paint application in the dream was more painterly, dense and rich, and the whole painting was an integrated image, not merely rows of items against a ground. (Also, as can't be seen in this black and white reproduction, the stripes are crimson and the disks in the lower right corners of them are black/deep grey.) Some day I'd like to try to get it right. In the dream it was a good painting.

I used a computer-graphics wallpaper version of it for the back cover of the the red and black and grey dust-jacket (here shown in black and white) for the first ("preliminary") version of my book *Hot and Cold*:

From This Long Century, *thislongcentury.com, eds. Stefan Pietsch and Jason Evans, 2010*

GODLIKE SUPPLEMENT
shadow info regarding my novel *Godlike*

QUOTES COPPED

[None of these are attributed in the book. Those in quotation marks here have them in the novel; those without don't. "Slight misquote" = negligible error, insignificantly mis-recollected.]

p. 13
"God made everything from nothing, but the nothing shows through."
   —Paul Valéry

p. 23
"Scent of garbage and patchouli and carbon monoxide . . ."
      —slight misquote of John Ashbery from his intro to *Collected Poems of Frank O'Hara*

p. 24
"Tomorrow is another day. But then, so was yesterday."
      — James Schuyler, from "Bleeding Gums," *Hymn to Life*

p. 24 (also p. 37)
"teeth to hurt"
      —Ted Berrigan, from "Poop," *So Going Around Cities* ["Nature makes my teeth 'to hurt'"]

p. 28-29:

the untitled poem, "Most of all I meant to come to you."

> —translation by R. Hell of Frank O'Hara's "To the Harbormaster,"
> *Meditations in an Emergency*

p. 33 (also p. 37)

"I lift my voice in song."

> —Ted Berrigan, from documentary film *Poetry in Motion*, as quoted
> by Ron Padgett in his *Ted* ["The gods demand of the system that
> a certain number of people sing, like the birds do, and it somehow
> was given to me to be one of those people—and I mean I did
> have a choice—I could have decided not to, to be a truck driver
> or a filmmaker. But I like doing that, and I feel that probably the
> major reason I write is because the gods might destroy . . . the
> whole thing could fall apart. I lift my voice in song. I lift my voice
> in song."]

p. 33

"And I'm just like that bird, singing just for you."

> —Bob Dylan, from "You're a Big Girl Now"

p. 35

the candor of his odor

> —modified from Paul Verlaine, "To Clymène," (in the book *Fêtes
> Galantes) Selected Poems*, trans. C. F. MacIntyre ["the candor / of
> your odor"]

p. 36

But the snow is sand in this tedium.

> —modified from Paul Verlaine, "Dans l'interminable . . ." (or "VIII"
> of "Ariettes Oubliées" in *Romances Sans Paroles*), *Penguin Book of
> French Verse*, "plain prose" translation by Anthony Hartley ["In
> the interminable tedium of the plain the shifting snow shines like
> sand."]

p. 41

'The sound of an apple broken in half.'

> —modified from Bill Knott, "Poem (I am the only one who can say)," *Auto-Necrophelia* ["Your nakedness: the sound when I break an apple in half"]

p. 57

"Wouldn't it be booful if we could juth run together into one gwate big bwob?"

> —slight misquote of William Burroughs, as quoted in Ted Morgan's *Literary Outlaw*

p. 57

"your lips are indeed a disaster of alienated star-knots"

> —Frank O'Hara, from *Second Avenue*

p. 63

"Johnny's in the basement mixing up the medicine / I'm on the pavement thinking about the government"

> —slight misquote of Bob Dylan, from "Subterranean Homesick Blues"

p. 63

"My arms are warm."

> —Aram Saroyan, [untitled], *Aram Saroyan*

> My arms are warm
> Aram Saroyan

---

p. 84

"That gutter drain [in Paris at the end of the 19th century], slobbering mud and rubies, is the mouth of a tomb, buried church, a subterranean temple (as in Egypt): the flickering muzzle of the god-jackal Anubis, guide to the underworld. While, above, the flame—inverted pubic-hair triangle—of the oil-lamp street-light rises from the wick which gathers as a storm, as a storm gathers, the insults which comprise it, and the flame still always reaches upward, perversely, no matter how the lamp sways: poetry of Baudelaire. Baudelaire. Not funeral wreaths dried in cities without evenings could serve as offerings to him when the very city's shimmering reality is the ghost, the soul, of Baudelaire, like an atmospheric element we must breathe even if it kills us."

—Mallarmé, "The Tomb of Charles Baudelaire," (a sonnet) in prose translation by R. Hell

p. 85
mint-condition can of Rumford's Baking Powder, celluloid earring, Speedy Gonzales, the latest from Helen Topping Miller's fertile escritoire, a sheaf of suggestive pix on greige, deckle-edged stock

—slight misquote of John Ashbery, from "Daffy Duck in Hollywood," *Houseboat Days*

p. 89
"Let the dead bury the dead," and let the young fuck the young (but as for you, go and proclaim the kingdom of God).

—*Luke* 9:57-60, New Revised Standard Version ["As they were going along the road, someone said to Jesus, 'I will follow you wherever you go.' And Jesus said to him, 'Foxes have holes, and birds of the air have nests; but the Son of Man has nowhere to lay his head.' To another he said, 'Follow me.' But he said, 'Lord, first let me go and bury my father.' But Jesus said to him, 'Let the dead bury their own dead; but as for you, go and proclaim the kingdom of God.'"]

p. 90
Also, he let language have its way with him.

—asseverated by Frank O'Hara, talking at a Club panel, 1952, as quoted in Brad Gooch's *City Poet* ["Poetry which liberates certain forces in language, permits them to emerge upon the void of silence, not poetry which seeks merely to express most effectively or most beautifully or most musically some preconceived idea or perception."]

p. 90

It's all appearances, and what is art but playing with appearances, etc., etc.

—asseverated by Jorge Luis Borges, preface to the 1954 edition of his 1935 first book, *A Universal History of Iniquity* ["The learned doctors of the Great Vehicle teach us that the essential characteristic of the universe is its emptiness. They are certainly correct with respect to the tiny part of the universe that is this book.... It is all just appearance, a surface of images—which is why readers may, perhaps, enjoy it. The man who made it was a pitiable sort of creature, but he found amusement in writing it; it is to be hoped that some echo of that pleasure may reach its readers."], and Jim Thompson's suggestion that "there is only one plot—things are not as they seem," as quoted in Robert Polito's *Savage Art.*

p. 112

the untitled poem, "The skywriting of all things was"

—translation by R. Hell of Frank O'Hara's "Poem" ("The eager note on my door said 'call me,'"), *Meditations in an Emergency*

p. 118-119

He kept drinking malted milk. Malted milk kept rushing to his head. His doorknob kept turning. It must have been spooks. The hair rising on his head: a warm old feeling.

—modified from Robert Johnson, "Malted Milk"

I keep drinking malted milk, trying to drive my blues away.
I keep drinking malted milk, trying to drive my blues away.
Baby you just as welcome to my loving as the flowers is in May.

Malted milk, malted milk, keep rushing to my head.
Malted milk, malted milk, keep rushing to my head.
And I have a funny, funny feeling and I'm talking all out my head.

Baby, fix me one more drink and hug your daddy one more time.
Baby, fix me one more drink and hug your daddy one more time.
Keep on stirring in my malted milk, mama, until I change my mind.

My doorknob keeps on turning, it must be spooks around my bed.
My doorknob keeps on turning, must be spooks around my bed.
I have a warm old feeling, and the hair rising on my head.

p. 120
"We live as we dream—alone."
　　—slight misquote of Joseph Conrad, *Heart of Darkness*

p. 122-123
the poem, "Evening Prayer"
　　—translation by R. Hell of Arthur Rimbaud's "Oraison du soir"

p. 121-124
Paul said to T., "I understand you." T. just shrugged his shoulders.

* * *

While I'd thought we were two happy children free to wander in a
Paradise of sadness.

* * *

The world turns and we become sick. He defined vertigos. I do believe
that true life is elsewhere.
　　—These and a scattering of other phrases and lines on those four pages
　　modified from A. Rimbaud's "Delirium (I & II)," *A Season in Hell*

p. 124
"Poetry is making a comeback." But why is it always bad poetry, or a false
idea of poetry, that is making a comeback? I don't think good poetry has
ever made a comeback, or ever will. That's one reason it's necessary to
keep on writing it.
　　—Kenneth Koch, "My Olivetti Speaks," *Straits*

p. 126

God said the world. In the beginning was the Word. Later, the Word was made flesh, and dwelt among us (and we beheld His glory, the glory as of the only begotten of the Father), full of grace and truth.

> — *John* 1:1, 12-14, King James Version [In the beginning was the Word, and the Word was with God, and the Word was God / The same was in the beginning with God. / All things were made by him; and without him was not any thing made that was made. / . . . / And the Word was made flesh, and dwelt among us, (and we beheld his glory, the glory as of the only begotten of the Father,) full of grace and truth.]

p. 128

"The external world is only a manifestation of the activities of the mind"

> —"Lankavatara Sutra," trans. Suzuki and Goddard

TITLES

Everything Is Its Opposite
[Everything is true, but very little is permitted.]
Diamond Dusted
Demonic Clarity
Pink and Blue Smear
Fasm
Licked
The Magic of Intensest POETRY-SNOT Penetrating Literature
So-Called
[Godlike [[Thorax . . .]]]
The Compassion of the Poets
Nipple Rouge
Cheap Hotel Room
Emergency
Know Secret
Static

The Morning of the Poem
The Way Things Are
He and I
Phenomena Make You a Joke
Things Are
Lilac Sky-Flow [Lilac Sky-Floe]
2-D Beckoning [and name T. a double D. name instead, like
   Dermot something]
Love Is Real
Werd
Excitement
A Paradise of Sadness
Paradise of Sadness
Sad Heaven
Heavens of Sadness
Paradise of Sad
Sad Paradise
Mortal Heaven
Heavenly Sadness
Broken
Broken Open
Broke
Haw
Mistakes
Ism
Most Completely
Atrocious

EPIGRAPH IDEAS

- "One recognizes the truth by its efficacy [, by its power]."
  —Bresson, *Notes on Cinematography* [the same as T.'s "the
  truth is what works"]

- "I want to write a poem about an old person dying of loneliness. I want to write a poem about an old person, alone in a room, dying of hunger and loneliness. No one has ever written a poem about an old person dying in the cold, of hunger and loneliness. Except of course Ava Gardner, who is always our master." —John Weiners in 1984 interview with Raymond Foye, from Weiners's *Cultural Affairs in Boston*

- "... No, it is impossible; it is impossible to convey the life-sensation of any given epoch of one's existence—that which makes its truth, its meaning—its subtle and penetrating essence. It is impossible. We live, as we dream—alone ..." —Conrad, *Heart of Darkness*

- "Off bending down the thrown gulp / In funny threes" —Padgett, from "Detach, Invading"

- "None of the famous landscapes that we saw / equalled the mysterious allure / of those that Chance arranges in the clouds ..." —Baudelaire, "Le Voyage," *Les Fleurs du Mal*, trans. Richard Howard

- "It seemed to me that everyone should have had several *other* lives as well. This gentleman doesn't know what he's doing; he's an angel. That family is a litter of puppy dogs. With some men, I often talked out loud with a moment from one of their other lives—that's how I happened to love a pig." —Rimbaud, "Delirium II: The Alchemy of Words" *A Season in Hell*, trans. Paul Schmidt

- People aren't real; they are just books.

From handout printed for West Coast Godlike *promotional reading tour, 2006; published in* Flesh World *magazine (Norway), ed. Kier Cooke Sandvik, 2008*

PISSED

LESTER BANGS'S *MAINLINES, BLOOD Feasts, and Bad Taste: A Lester Bangs Reader*

IT'S GOTTEN TO WHERE just the name does it: Lester Bangs. It makes me happy. It's like raindrops on roses and whiskers on kittens. Of course, even apart from the guy it signified, its perfection of pure form is stunning, but the person who came with it was even better. I think of his innocence and good will first, and his compulsion to talk about whatever was going on and to figure out what mattered, starting from music, and it makes me sorry I can't call him up. It's strange. I didn't even like being around him that much when he was alive. Just five or six years ago when his biographer was asking for stories about him I told him that when I knew Lester I didn't take him very seriously or pay very much attention to him. That, though doubtless my distaste was partly that of the junkie for the lush, I mostly thought he was a buffoon. Lester was this big, swaying, cross-eyed, reeking drooler, smiling and smiling through his crummy stained mustache, trying to corner me with incessant babble somewhere in the dark at CBGB's, 1976 or so. He was sweet like a big clumsy puppy, but he was always drunk and the sincerity level was pretty near intolerable.

Now I miss him.

Of course it's easier to like a good-hearted, hard-working dead person, the extremely edited Lester, than the obliviously intrusive physically present one, but Lester has made way more friends than most

since he died. Posthumously, he's become the non-charismatic Elvis of
rock writers: obscene provocateur and polite mama's boy, vulnerable and
egotistic, trashily prolific and artistically transcendent, anti-drug and
full-time addict (who died young that way); but most of all forgiven
everything and adored by his fans while being the most popular model
for those who would essay his trade. Well maybe that's a little strained;
probably Jack Kerouac would be a better comparison, if not as much
fun. Because Kerouac actually did influence Bangs a lot and the appeal
of Lester shares a lot with Kerouac's: that innocence and good will and
drive to describe and be true to what matters in life. People like a writer's
writing because they like the writer's company. Writing is intimate and
finally what draws you to an author's work is the shape of the mind and
quality of feeling you find there, and Lester, like Kerouac, reads like a
real good friend to a lot of people.

   I have to interrupt and confess how I'm struggling to resist taking
revenge on rock critics. I was a musician and I've thought a few times
of rating the critics the way they do the artists. But I'm really really
going to try to restrain myself. How petty would that be, if I were to
go after them? Not only have they generally been good to me, but my
life is more fun than theirs. I must try to be large I must try to be large.
I don't want to be a jerk. I'll just say that I believe Lester deserves his
supreme popularity (he was the critic who liked me more than any of
the others did).

   But I've got to go after the self-importance of the best-known worst
of them a little. The rock writers, naturally, want to believe that their
genre, like say the movie criticism of the *Cahiers du Cinema* writers such
as Godard and Rivette, is sometimes actually the work of important
artists. In fact Greil Marcus, in the introduction to Bangs's previous
collection of rock journalism, *Psychotic Reactions and Carburetor Dung*,
wrote, "Perhaps what this book demands from a reader is a willingness
to accept that the best writer in America could write almost nothing
but record reviews." (That line is typical of the way Marcus ruins good
things by laying the burden of his pretentiousness on them.) And it's
true that writers as good as Patti Smith and Nick Tosches wrote about

pop music seriously, with full respect, and really well. But I don't see much justification for a line like Marcus's about Lester. Lester was lovable and perceptive, but the writing is wired thinking-aloud; it's pure process, and my feeling is that Lester had too many blind spots and neuroses for writing that depends so much for its value on the shapeliness of his mind and reasoning. As with Kerouac, you go to Bangs's work to be refreshed with your pleasure in the characteristic beauty of his mission and mind, to be reminded of the presence of a certain being that inspires and provokes. But it hardly matters what pages you read—all the appeal is in the tone and ethical/aesthetic values, and you get them immediately, so a little goes a long way.

Nevertheless, of all the most highly regarded rock journalists of his time (say Tosches, Christgau, Marcus and the execrable and excremental Richard Meltzer) Lester was the only one who valued self-doubt and who actually seemed to like the music more than he liked himself. Lester was a critic who reserved the right to be wrong, which seems to me admirable. Like many rock writers Lester took extreme stances, but unlike the other most flamboyantly contrary of them, he didn't paint himself into a miniscule corner of supported music, and he didn't go sour with cynicism and resentment (or maybe he did a little towards the end—which was 1982 for Lester—when punk seemed to end up genuinely, fatally, hopeless). Lester was large and he was interested in doing what was right—which sometimes entailed willfully offending those whose values he opposed—not merely being right in his taste and musical standards. He wanted to learn. What's appealing about him is the same thing that he valued in the music he wrote about: the life in it—engagement with and responsiveness to the world. To put a positive spin on the spew and rant factor, he didn't care about beauty except as flow. He wanted everything included. He was confrontational but it came from good will, from his belief that feelings—sensitivity to what's going on—are what matter and that if you're going to really notice things, really perceive, there's going to be a lot of sadness and horror and filth as well, so to some extent they're a necessary part of beauty. Basically Lester always wanted people to *care* more. That could be really tedious, but when the examples of things due more loving regard are such as *White Light/White Heat* and *Raw Power* and *Pangaea*, it gets interesting.

If you like Lester, you'll like this new book. It's a lot like *Psychotic Reactions* but it has more Miles Davis and Rolling Stones than the Lou Reed and Iggy of that first collection, along with some big chunks of autobiographical writing.

From the Village Voice, *2003*

JOEY RAMONE MEMORIAL BIRTHDAY BASH

HE WAS SO SHY AND STRANGE. I remember him best looking across the room at something and whispering in my ear, "It's really sick y'know." It's so great that people like the Ramones could be stars. It makes me proud to be an American. That and the Simpsons.

They were one of the strangest groups in the history of rock and roll. Like Roy Orbison with the Stooges doing Chuck Berry.

A lot of rock and roll's been about uncool guys, people who are not accepted, *willing* themselves to be cool. Like dirt-poor truck-driving Elvis dressing like a pimp. He giggled at himself too, like the Ramones did. Elvis wanted to be a comic book super hero and I think the Ramones kind of did as well. They all made it. What the hell were the Ramones trying to do? How much of it was calculated, how much could they just not help themselves? What possessed them to use that name? I know they wanted to be a kind of Bay City Rollers, a kind of hard boy-group, and that's how come they all took the group name as a last name (or vice versa), and they dressed the same, but then what were they thinking with songs like "Now I Wanna Sniff Some Glue"? . . . The pinhead fixation, "Gabba Gabba Hey."

Joey was the big-hearted Ramone. He supported young groups, opposed oppressive Reagan type rich-people's politics . . .

"That which is not slightly distorted lacks sensible appeal." [Baudelaire]

I never sniffed any glue but thanks to the Ramones I feel like I have.

I don't believe Joey died, I think he went back to ramone where everything is completely ramone in all ramone all the ramone ramone ramone . . .

Spoken at posthumous Joey Ramone Birthday Bash, 2001

ROBERT QUINE OBITUARY

ROCK AND ROLL COGNOSCENTI and Robert Quine's friends
were angry and torn up last week to hear that on Saturday, June 5, his
body had been discovered in his loft on Grand Street, a suicide. Quine
never injected drugs, but this was an injection and one containing way
too many bags of heroin to have been accidental. By his own avowal,
he'd survived a similar try this past winter. He didn't want to live after
the completely unexpected death by heart attack of his wife Alice last
August. They'd been together since the mid-'70s.

I won't presume to try and analyze the factors contributing to his
ceaseless, abysmal despair of recent months, but he'd never been exactly
a cheerful person, though he was always one who had something funny
to say. In fact, if you're not crying, it's hard to think of him without
smiling. Or possibly you could do both at once. Then again, he wasn't
averse to provoking anger, and he was an angry person himself. It contributed to his magnificent guitar playing.

Like Miles Davis and Lou Reed—probably the two instrumentalists
he most admired—Quine brought new ways of playing to improvised
music. Quine had many influences, and he loved perpetuating them (all
of his friends have compilation tapes made for them from his gigantic
record collection), but anyone who cares can recognize one of his solos
immediately, and even those who don't care are likely to perk up when

exposed to what he'd wring from a guitar for the twenty or thirty seconds of one of his perfectly structured but outrageously wild expositions in the middle of a song by Reed or me (or Tom Waits, Lloyd Cole, Matthew Sweet, or John Zorn). His command of technique came from endless hours of studying the records that moved him—but it was the combination of rage and delicacy, and the pure monstrosity of invention, that set him apart.

Quine grew up in a fairly privileged family in Akron, Ohio. His father owned a car-parts factory. His uncle was the Harvard philosopher W.V.O. Quine. Bob himself had passed the bar in Missouri, though he never practiced law. He also attended the Berklee College of Music. Part of his legend was the way that, though a member of one of the first "punk" bands, the Voidoids, in 1976, he was already thirty-three when the band began, and he dressed like an office clerk, in jeans, innocuous sport coat, and open-collared button-down shirt. Underneath though was the connoisseur of moronic rapture who thrived on such material as the Blue Echoes' "Cool Guitar," Ronnie Speeks and the Elrods doing "What is Your Technique," Al Sweat's "I Hate Myself," Jimmy Copeland's "Satellite Rock," and Floyd Mack's "I Like to Go."

He was still playing guitar for hours every day, alone, up to the end. All his friends wanted to help and called him often and got him out to eat, but he couldn't stop crying. He would tell you how he'd gotten the crying down to two hours a day from four. He was still almost always funny, though. Ivan Julian, who played with him in the Voidoids, told me about a wisecrack Quine made when they recently went out to eat. When the check came, Ivan reached for it, but Bob snatched it away, snarling, "No, I got it. It's my way of saying good-bye."

From New York *magazine, 2004*

PICTURING PUNK

PUNK IS PRETTY FUNNY. It's like reality itself, as exemplified by the statement, "This sentence is a lie." It's hard to be authentic.

The first thing I noticed about this picture book is that it's one in a series the main purpose of which is to have the widest possible public appeal. The twenty or so prior volumes have subjects like baseball, Star Wars, golf courses, the Civil War, and gardens. So far there are three pop music collections in the series: the *The Beatles*, *The Rolling Stones*, and now *Punk*. It's weird that punk could be classified with the Beatles and the Rolling Stones, not to mention golf and gardens. The original punks did intend to conquer the world, but right away everybody failed and flamed out, and soon it was accepted as logical and inevitable that all those musical propagators of subversion, chaos, poetry, and destruction (frequently the "self" variety) were doomed to be appreciated strictly by connoisseurs. Thirty years later, punk is everybody's aspiration.

Unlike the subjects of those two previous band photo books, though, "punk" may have gotten big, but it's as an idea, an ideal, that no one band, or even ten bands, can fully embody. Or at least that no one band was successful and long-lived enough in pursuing to provide 365 good pictures. The English Invasion and '60s rock really did spring from the Beatles and the Rolling Stones. Rockabilly came from Elvis. Funk came from James Brown. But "punk" has a much muddier, grungier, more various pool of sources and archetypal exemplars. (Though a good case could be made that it all sprang from the Stooges and the Velvet Underground, bands that I'd argue made the best records of any of the groups in this book. But the word "punk" was adopted to describe a genre that arose after those groups . . .)

The Sex Pistols came closest to embodying the ideal, but even they fell short of dream-punk perfection in a few major ways: for instance, much of their style was manufactured by their boutique-owning image-making manager (so much for "do it yourself"), and their famous tunes were written mainly by a guy—Glen Matlock, their original bass player—who was soon fired because the group decided he was too straight and unthreatening to be a Sex Pistol (so much for community and disdain for "public image"). His replacement, Sid Vicious, was suitably "anarchic," but pretty soon the band ran out of material, and, as everybody knows, they broke up after one album. But ultimately such failings themselves are "punk" virtues too.

Yeah, in a way, punk is about failure. "There's no success like failure," as one wiseass pre-punk put it. Take the Ramones. They failed miserably year after year. They weren't especially highly respected or popular even at CBGB's, in the days of the original five or six core bands. They were a self-conscious cartoon concept of rock and roll, like the Stooges mixed with surf music. Talk about "managed style"—they conceived of themselves as a boy band and a brand, like the Bay City Rollers, more than anything else. They wanted to create as reliable an experience as McDonald's and as funny a one as Huey, Dewey, and Louie Duck, in the personae of bored kids from the projects on glue. And they did, but still they never had a hit song or album, and it took them over twenty years of failed bidding for mass attention via brutal touring, culminating in the ultimate failure—of Joey Ramone's pulse—before they finally broke through to the general public. How punk is that? I mean exactly how punk? If all that's punk, what is punk?

Punk is an idea, not a band. It's a good idea. It's about subversion, but in the service of youthful pleasure. It's opposed to everything adult. It's against not just success, but good manners, good grooming, and any education or skill. But no definition of "punk" is true. It's poetic that way ("This sentence is a lie."). Maybe it's about failure because it's the ultimate kids' music and nobody can remain a kid, except maybe by deciding to die early enough, which was the route taken by more than one (Sid Vicious, Ian Curtis, Darby Crash). It's about honesty, anger, frustration, obnoxiousness, and chaos, but it's also about funniness, shared values, artistic control, personal appearance, and, in a surprisingly secret way for "rock and roll," sex. Maybe sadistic sex, drug sex, infantile cuddly sex, stripper sex. Not much "love," anyway. But there's always a punk band to which some, or even most, of these definitions don't apply. Because a good band wants to be quick enough not to get pinned down. Taking a picture just takes a split second, though, so here are some pictures of it.

Foreword to Punk 365, *ed. Holly George-Warren (New York: Harry Abrams, 2007) [365 photographs of punk musicians and punk scenes]*

FILM COLUMN:
Don't Come Knocking /
Battle in Heaven / L'Enfant

Don't Come Knocking director: Wim Wenders; script: Sam Shepard, story by Shepard and Wenders; cinematography: Franz Lustig; cast: Sam Shepard, Jessica Lange, Tim Roth, Gabriel Mann, Sarah Polley, Fairuza Balk, Eva Marie Saint

Battle in Heaven director: Carlos Reygadas; script: Carlos Reygadas; cinematography: Diego Martinez Vignatti; cast: Marcos Hernandez, Anapola Mushkadiz, David Bornstein, Berta Ruiz

L'Enfant (The Child) director: Jean-Pierre Dardenne, Luc Dardenne; script: Jean-Pierre Dardenne, Luc Dardenne; cinematography: Alain Marcoen; cast: Jérémie Renier, Déborah François, Jérémie Segard, Fabrizio Rongione, Olivier Gourmet

AS A RULE, I don't write about movies I don't like, just because it seems like a waste of space. I didn't see any I liked for this issue, though, so I'm writing some straight pans. There were three movies that were bad for similar reasons, having to do with how they tarted themselves up in art drag when really all they were was the drag part. One was simply disappointing, one I hated, and one was frustrating in a complicated way. After all that, I'll lighten up with some good news at the end.

The plain disappointment was the new Wim Wenders film, *Don't Come Knocking*, written by and starring Sam Shepard. Wenders has always been an over-romantic Americanophile, the kind of European who wants to make western road movies with a lot of motels and desert, fronting an electric guitar soundtrack. At the same time, I appreciate his casual, eye-oriented style. I've liked some of his documentaries and re-member being susceptible to *Wings of Desire* too, though I haven't seen it for a long time. *Paris, Texas*, his earlier movie written by Shepard, was too ploddingly portentous for me. Shepard, before he was a movie star, was the playwright hero of the 1970s and has continued to be that for two or three generations of rock and roll cowboys of the theater, reeling off drama into the dawn the way most people go to sleep. He's successfully worked his radiotronic rabbit tooth or his silver dog smell on me more than once over the years. I liked a lot of those plays, and I also respect, as I do in Wenders, Shepard's anti-Hollywood priorities. But this movie is so bad and bad in such a way as to make me wonder if I could have been wrong about the earlier Shepard. This shit is too fucking macho, faux-mysterioso, and much a mental mess, like a blind cut-up of Sam's and Wim's own faded old material. It's strange to see these guys, who so conspicuously reject Hollywood formulas, making works as formulaic as the stuff they oppose. There are a lot of good looking shots in this movie, of western desert, of the big-skied beat-up streets of downtown Butte, Montana, of outrageous disco-squared Nevada casinos, of the star's vintage Packard wheeling down the two-lane, etc. But that all is as tired by now as teeth-gnashing mega-pixel dinosaurs. More tired. And who cares about another jacked-in cowboy having an existential crisis all over his family? He should do that on his own time. Eva Marie Saint as Shepard's mom is really great though. I wish they'd stayed at her house and let her be the movie.

If *Don't Come Knocking* is derivative of its own filmmakers, the other two movies here are counterfeits of interesting recent trends. Apparently, there are enough art movies succeeding these days that what at first was fresh gets immediately degraded by imitators. (The one film I've walked out on in these two years of movie reviewing was *Napoleon Dynamite*, a moronic and mean-spirited psuedo-type of Todd Solondz's great *Welcome to the Dollhouse*.) The movie I hated is called *Battle in Heaven*. It's from Mexico and is the second feature by director Carlos Reygadas. The techniques that Reygadas exploits here are those originally used sensitively and organically by directors like Abbas Kiarostami (Iran), Bruno Dumont (France), Pedro Costa (Portugal), and their cinematic godfather Bresson, employing non-actors in stories about ordinary, usually poor, people in mostly everyday scenes—though the everyday scenes often include violent death, frequently suicide. Lately, explicit acts of sex have joined the real life detail of some of them, too. *Battle in Heaven* opens with a shot travelling slowly, from a mushy face, down the full-frontal flesh of a very fat and homely naked guy whom you eventually see, in unforgiving close-up, is getting his purplish penis sucked by a pretty young woman. The imagery—the camera work, lighting, angles and material subject—definitely get your attention. You want to trust this director because he's showing you strong stuff. You want to find out where he's going to go with it, what he's going to indicate to you about its importance. Unfortunately, he goes nowhere and means nothing. The movie is pure exploitation masquerading as art. It's degrading to watch. It's all strategic smoke-blowing, the smoke being filmic techniques that we've learned from the director's betters to read as signifying insight and intelligence, but which here are used in the service of emptiness and vanity, emptiness made to further keep your attention with explicit sex and extreme violence. It's pure Hollywood pretending to be its opposite. I'll take *Get Rich or Die Tryin'*.

The frustrating film is *L'Enfant* (*The Child*). Isolated from its models and influences, the movie would seem more than worthwhile: it's smart, well-acted, shot well, and compelling. It actually won the Dardenne brothers, who produced, wrote, and directed it, their second Palme d'Or—the first was for *Rosetta* in 1999—at Cannes. Like *Battle in Heaven*, it shows underclass folk (and fully credible ones, in contrast to the freaks predicated by Reygadas), carrying out their daily routine. The story is of a dim and luckless twenty-three-year old petty thief and beggar, his eighteen-year-old girlfriend, and their new baby, on the streets of an industrial city of Belgium. In *L'Enfant* the roles are played by actors, though they're good enough and the film is shot in such a way—hand-held camera, natural light—as to make it feel uncannily real. As in Bresson, there is no soundtrack music. By the time it's over, you're moved, though for me it was against my will, because it all wasn't enough. We've seen it before, in Italian neo-realism, in Bresson. . . . The climactic scene, which defines the film, is a shameless appropriation from Bresson's *Pickpocket*. I don't know, this sort of thing isn't unprecedented. Brian DePalma made a lot of enjoyable movies that were homages derived from Hitchcock. But DePalma's movies were intended half as goofy film freak larks, not intense depictions of our condition, like the Dardennes' film. There's certainly a lot to be usefully learned from Bresson—Kiarastami and Dumont and Costa prove that—but this film too narrowly imitates him. It's like if you hadn't heard Little Richard doing "Long Tall Sally," you might think the Beatles' version was great. If you've seen *Pickpocket*, *L'Enfant* is kid stuff.

To conclude on an up note, I'll point out that DVDs have recently been released of two really good films that you might have missed in theaters in 2005: Miranda July's *Me and You and Everyone We Know*, and Arnaud Desplechin's *Kings and Queen*. Both are strikingly original (!), intelligent, and entertaining, the former a whimsical, spooky tale of the quest for romance of a video/performance artist in nowheresville Southern California; and the latter a novelistically complex look at crises in the life of a thirty-five year old French woman (played by the tremendous Emmanuelle Devos). While being very different from each other, they also have a kind of poetic imagination in common, which, in mixing the real with the hallucinatory, makes everything more real (and funny). There's not space to say more, but I think you wouldn't regret renting either.

BlackBook *Film Column #11, March 2006*

FILM COLUMN:
Travel Issue: The Criterion Collection

I LIKE THE THEME of this issue. As William Burroughs paraphrased Pompey, "It is necessary to travel. It is not necessary to live." Hollywood has become horrible. In our films, America presents pretty much the same identity to the world as it does politically: smug, arrogant money and power, sans inspiration, insight, or beauty. (I'm really baffled by "patriotism" as exploited by politicians. What kind of value is patriotism? Obviously we don't want to betray each other, but why do we have to claim America is superior to everyone else? What's up with that?) Whereas, as Mark Twain put it, "Travel is fatal to prejudice, bigotry, and narrow-mindedness, and many of our people need it sorely on these accounts. Broad, wholesome, charitable views of men and things cannot be acquired by vegetating in one little corner of the earth all one's lifetime." Of course the kind of travel we're talking about is not first class travel to luxury hotels in order to regard the foreign culture as a weird curiosity. I didn't like *Lost in Translation*. S. Coppola's world view is that of a bright, highly-entitled, sentimental-in-the-world-weary-way-of-a-fifteen-year-old, preppy girl. The flick was cute but I think a few weeks in Detroit without credit cards or phone privileges would have had a more enlightening effect on her.

Don't get me wrong. I love a good escapist movie and there are plenty of commercial American directors that make me happy: Sophia's father, for one, and Ang Lee (actually, or originally, Chinese), and John Woo (ditto), and such less crowd-pleasing ones as David Cronenberg (originally Canadian) and recent David Lynch; as well as a lot of American independents whose films I wouldn't miss, like Todd Solondz (*Welcome to the Dollhouse*), Todd Haynes, David O. Russell (*Three Kings*). The American I know of who's really making genius movies now is Harmony Korine (*Gummo* and *Julien Donkey Boy*). I hope he can keep his head above water.

The problem with typical Hollywood movies is not that they're empty, but that they're cynically, and often even ineptly, false and manipulative. It's like the difference between good and bad recreational sex. There's nothing wrong with having sex strictly for fun, but at minimum you should be good at it, and, more importantly, you shouldn't mislead your partner about what your purposes are, or else it might not just be "empty" but evil (like David Fincher). That would be known as fucking someone over. The worst Hollywood movies are the ones that aren't honestly inviting us in for a shared good time (thrills perhaps), but are sleazily pretending to, i.e., telling us how smart and sexy we are while they're actually picking our pockets.

The living great director whose values are most opposed to Hollywood is French: the notorious Jean-Luc Godard. Ironically, he first made his name—as a critic—in the 1950s with his brilliant film-zine prose-poems of praise for such semi-anonymous American studio directors as Frank Tashlin, Nicholas Ray, and Sam Fuller. But times have changed. The battles Godard, Truffaut, Rivette, and co., fought back then to gain respect for the artistry of American genre directors have been won, and the result is, as Truffaut pointed out, that now "more often it happens that though the ambitions of filmmakers are very high their execution can't keep up with them." Yes, the directors are all supposed to be artists now, and the result is horrors like *Schindler's List* and the propensity of critics to call a false movie like *Mystic River* a masterpiece, just because it's about another serious social subject (child abuse in that case), shot in grimy working class locations (Spielberg's equivalent was to go black and white), and rigged with plenty of opportunities for actors to emote. People don't emote in Godard movies. They talk and kiss and recite and read and often die, in the service of the director and the framed image, but they don't "act." And there are no special effects and no blood (there's "blood" in Godard, but, as he famously pointed out, it's not blood but "red"), and no sets, only locations. His films are alive, rather than being contrived to elicit the viewer's bodily fluids, the way junk food's sugar and fat seduce you into fatal obesity. As Colin McCabe points out in his useful new bio, *Godard: A Portrait of the Artist at Seventy*, Godard's insistence on reality in what he shoots renders him "excluded from the greatest achievements of narrative cinema. But if he is not a novelist, he is the greatest essayist, and one of the greatest poets that the cinema has known."

I don't have the space to go into detail regarding the marvels of Godard, not to mention those of other, younger, genius directors from distant places, such as, say, Hou Hsiao-hsien (Chinese, *Flowers of Shanghai*), Bela Tarr (Hungarian, the astounding *Satantango*), or Abbas Kiarostami (Iranian, *A Taste of Cherry*), and anyway there are few cities in the United States where these movies can be seen in theaters. That's where DVDs come in. DVDs have made such a difference in watching movies at home, especially when the transfers from film are done conscientiously, in the correct aspect ratio, and carefully restored if necessary. The inclusion of supplementary material (interviews, commentary, trailers, etc.) is great too. The Criterion Collection pioneered in all these areas, and Criterion's selection of films on DVD is near impeccable. They carry a beautiful handful of Godards (the new *Contempt* is a bonanza), Kiarostami, Tarkovsky, the ineffable Robert Bresson, and many other such non-American masters. Tarr's *Satantango* hasn't been released on DVD (others of his films are out from Artificial Eye, a British company). There's a highly regarded new set of four early Hou Hsiao-hsien flicks from Sino-Movie (Taiwanese but supplying English subtitles).

I want to add a small disclaimer list: 1) I'm grateful to be an American; 2) I love Bill Murray; 3) Clint Eastwood has probably starred in more great movies than anyone alive and he directed quite a few of them.

BlackBook *film column #2, Summer 2004*

MOUTH OF HELL COLUMN:
The Michael Jackson Trial

THIS MORNING I SEE that the judge in the Michael Jackson trial admitted into evidence two books of photographs of adolescent boys that Jackson had stashed in a locked file cabinet in a closet (!) at Neverland (!!). The report in the *New York Times* describes how one of them, *Boys Will Be Boys*, "contains the following note on the flyleaf: 'Look at the true spirit of happiness and joy in these boys' faces, this is the spirit of Boyhood. A life I never had and will always dream of. This is the life I want for my children.' The note is signed 'MJ' in what appears to be Mr. Jackson's hand." Of course the books were introduced contrary to the wishes of the defense, but isn't that note poignant? Doesn't it give you a little sympathy for Michael? This sticky trial with all its strangenesses and implications almost seems like a nocturnal emission of the collective unconscious. I wish there was a "non-fiction novelist" to really cover it the way Norman Mailer did Gary Gilmore, or Truman Capote the Clutter murders. Who could do that now? Dave Chapelle? But he's really a sketch guy. Art Spiegelman? It's not his type of material. I wish someone would pay me enough to do it like they did Peter Guralnik to do Michael's teen-virgin-loving poignant fat father-in-law who OD'd on the toilet at Graceland.

When someone asks me what I think of the trial all I can say is that I haven't kept up. I don't think it's possible to have any idea what's going on from news reports anyway. Though I'll admit that the righteous fury about child "abuse" creeps me out. It's like patriotism, or the Republicans pouncing on the Schiavo case—a last refuge for scoundrels. What's wrong with a child being initiated into sex by his favorite celebrity? The people who most violently vilify those who have sex with minors as the scum of scum are protesting too much (witness how prison convicts, being the most patriotic of Americans—the white ones anyway—famously ostracize their pedophiles) ... And, come on, any parent who left her child alone with Michael Jackson knew what she was getting into. Imagine him at your door, come to interview for the babysit spot. But I'd propose that Jackson's probably made a lot higher percentage of his child-associates (and their guardians) happy than any of those predatory Catholic priests did. As ironic and weird as it is on the bleached face of it, I reckon there is some racism involved in the way this's played out.

It's all theater and concealed ulterior motives and hypocrisy and pandering anyway. It's impossible to view it in any way but as metaphor, because none of it is actually what it seems. It's all symbolic. But then what isn't? The world is weird. I hope I never get accidentally drawn into reality any deeper than writing a column like this.

Monthly column for Noel Black's Colorado Springs, CO news tabloid, Toilet Paper, *published 2004-2006*

EDMUND WHITE'S *RIMBAUD:*
The Double Life of a Rebel

MORE ASPECTS OF RIMBAUD are known than can be assimilated: his vastly various, influential and innovative poetry itself; his expressive letters; his scornful and unhesitating abandonment of poetry at the age of twenty; the anecdotes of his contemporaries showing him as a drunken, filthy, amoral homosexual teenager who becomes a reserved, hard-working, responsible and respectable—if misanthropic and disgust-ridden—adult merchant and explorer. One would have to be a genius oneself to grasp the full significance of Arthur Rimbaud, or at least have the ability to hold many opposed ideas in one's mind at the same time and still function fully. Numerous writers have sought to demonstrate their qualifications along these lines by publishing studies of him.

This biography by Edmund White is the digest version. If you're casually curious about the fuss made over Rimbaud and want the lowdown from someone literate, it will do. This approach seems to be the plan behind the series of brief biographies, each written by a distinguished author (often a novelist or scholar, not usually a professional biographer) and edited by James Atlas, first for Penguin, now for Atlas & Company, of which *Rimbaud* is the latest entry. Seems like a worthy idea; there are a lot of famous artists and thinkers one wouldn't mind getting a convenient little handle on.

Still, this book irritates a bit with some of its complacent assertions, such as that Rimbaud's famous declaration (in a letter written at age sixteen), "Je est un autre" ("I is someone else"), "meant that in the act of introspection we objectify the self, we experience our self as if it belongs to another person," which takes banality to the point of distortion. It's self-evident that examining oneself predicates a pair. But "I is another" is exhilarating, a revelation, which, at the very least, acknowledges one's undifferentiated human substance or collectivity, as for a child . . .

On a blue summer evening I shall go down the path
And, brushed by wheat, walk on the fine grass.
Dreaming along, I'll feel the coolness under my feet
And bathe my bare head in the poetic wind.
I won't speak, I will not even think,
But infinite love will geyser up in my soul,
And I'll go far, far away, like a Gypsy
Into the wilds—as happy as if I were with a woman.

. . . who is present at his own invention as an actor in life (in more ways than two: the above is Rimbaud's second known post-schoolwork poem, written at the age of fifteen, and it foresees his life—if in an innocent, far more lush and joyous light than it would actually be played out), like "the wood that becomes a violin" and "tough luck" to it for that fate (same letter), or, as Rimbaud adds, "I am present at the explosion of my thought. I watch and I listen to it. I wave the baton; the symphony murmurs from its depths or comes leaping onto the stage" (letter two days later). One witnesses one's invention by life, while one plays oneself like a symphonic conductor, in the meantime dreaming a million dreams. . . . The statement of it is thrilling, is uncanny, and it's words. This is what Rimbaud gives us. There is no limit to his reach, or his grasp.

The best full-scale English-language biography of Rimbaud is Graham Robb's (published in 2000), as White agrees in his book, incorporating such Robb insights and researches as the tally of time the vagabond rebel-boy spent at home with his mother (actually almost five of the approximately nine years between his first escape from her farm at fifteen and his eventual departure from Europe in 1880), and that, contrary to legend, Rimbaud ultimately did quite well as a merchant and weapons salesman, accumulating a small fortune (the equivalent of well over $100,000, according to Robb) in the course of his approximately eleven years in Africa.

White uses his own translations to demonstrate Rimbaud's poetry. They will do in context, but, for the interested, I'd recommend Wyatt Mason's two-volume Modern Library edition of Rimbaud's complete writings (works and letters). Any translation requires special focus from a reader. Of the large-scale Rimbaud efforts, the Mason is the most alive.

Because that's what distinguishes Rimbaud: of all poets, his writing is the most alive, even now and here, in another language more than a hundred years later. He learned a lot from Baudelaire, and in many ways Baudelaire remains his master, but Baudelaire was a poet of ennui (and dreams), while Rimbaud reels with the most robust—if often contemptuous—vitality (and dreams). This is a function of his peasant, punkish, ultra-confidence in the value of his pure (unegotistic) honesty, as an adolescent seeing through the adult hypocrisy and convention veiling the sensual, unsane world; a boy to whom language was understood as inextricable (to the seer) from reality, and who knew how to wield those words, existence itself. He didn't have to try to translate his perceptions into language; he understood that he must see in language, and he saw with the supreme, paradoxically unformed, fluid ego of an adolescent. His honesty and insight never waned—he just grew up and lost interest in the unrewarding expression of the visions.

From the New York Times Book Review, *2008*

MY DOWNTOWN SIDEBAR

WHAT I WAS DOING in the way of art in downtown New York City 1974-1984 was conceiving and playing in bands. In fact that period pretty well encompasses my career as an active musician and to my mind music was also at the center of what was going on in art then, in downtown New York and elsewhere. It was the bands that were the exciting, innovative, inspiring things. The Velvet Underground learned from Andy Warhol, but I think the "Neo-Expressionists" of the '80s learned from Patti Smith and Television and the Voidoids and the Ramones (and the Talking Heads and the Heartbreakers and the Dead Boys and Blondie), as did Richard Kern and Nan Goldin and Jim Jarmusch and David Wojnarowicz, etc.—and so did the Clash and the Sex Pistols, in fact.

I came to music from poetry, from writing and publishing poems—"publishing" not only in the sense of being published but also as a small scale publisher—and when I started playing music I had no technical music skills whatsoever. I was also interested in treating everything about my band(s) and me—the clothes we wore, our haircuts, our interviews, our posters, even our names—as vehicles of information, as conveying messages. Our approach could be thought of as a kind of advertising concept except that we wanted to subvert (and maybe inspire) by doing this rather than comfort and flatter. Most importantly we wanted to do it ourselves, rather than have it imposed on us as packaging by corporations whose only motivation was profit.

I got some of these ideas from the poetry scene (as well as from the Velvet Underground and the New York Dolls). When I came to New York as a teenage aspiring poet in the late '60s, it was at the peak time of one of the most exciting developments in the history of American poetry: the "Second Generation New York School" of young street poets—who were also sophisticated—centered around the St. Mark's Church Poetry Project. These were wild, brainy, drug-fueled kids who took back the means of production from the universities and the big commercial publishers and made the typewriter-typeset, mimeoed, staple-bound pamphlet into greater art in every respect—from their design to their graphic component to the poems themselves—than what was being offered through the conventional channels. The poets just bypassed the boring self-satisfied standard publishers and *did it themselves*. When the corporations eventually came around the books they produced were done on the poets' terms.

They called our music "punk." There are certain stylistic traits that are associated with that appellation: loud, crude, raw, angry. With all the movement's rejection of the values of the giant media purveyors that thrive by cynically exploiting people's vanity and sentimentality, maybe the thing that separates punk from previous anti-establishment youth movements is that punks were a little cynical themselves from the very beginning, or at least wary of underestimating even their own self-serving impulses. What they valued most was honesty, but they recognized the complexity of that. The punk scream was one of frustration as much as it was of anger. This is why the real pure thing tends to burn out and shut down. It doesn't survive in captivity, which is also why you won't find it in these five hundred words. You've got to do it yourself you stupid monkey.

From The Downtown Book: The New York Arts Scene, 1974-1984, *ed. Marvin J. Taylor (Princeton: The Princeton University Press, 2005)*

"PUNK" COUTURE: INSIDES OUT

THE CLICHÉ IS that the original American version of "punk" was about art while the British was about politics. There's truth to that. In New York, in 1974, we did want to make art. Even the blasting Ramones, deliberately two-dimensional and cartoony, were more like Andy Warhol than like Mikhail Bakunin.

In New York at that time, the feeling I had was of wandering around, all lyrically cold, if laugh-prone, in the ruins. The love-and-peace '60s had failed (Vietnam, Altamont, Manson), while the mass cultural atmosphere, including music, was still a thin, hazy emanation of those years. Everything was a lie or dead. In a way it was liberating. We had no attachments, nothing to lose. We could make ourselves up from scratch.

And that was the essence of what became punk: acts of consciously making yourself up from nothing but your real insides. Punk was about succeeding without any skills except honesty. Honesty isn't easy though. That's where the art, unironically, comes in. It was all poetry. Even the Sex Pistols were poetry, the purest achievement of it in the whole era, little as they'd admit it. Because there's not a dichotomy between poetry and real life. The best bands, the finest moments, were that reconciliation.

And, though songs had to be its core, part of what was interesting about starting a band was that it entailed so many other means of communication, including clothes. There were also posters, press releases, interviews, performance behavior, and names and hair and facial expressions.

That realization was especially interesting to me. When Tom Verlaine and I made a band at that time I wanted all evidence of the group to be consistent, and to mean things. I wanted to reconceive everything we did and were as what the band had to say. The idea was to take everything we were inside, including our perceptions of the world, and put it on the outside, project it, using all means.

We might not have been heavily politically oriented, but there were political implications to what we did, the primary one being to do things yourself rather than submitting to the conventional authorities who tried to further their interests by manipulating us and exploiting our insecurities and ignorance. Those authorities included fashion purveyors.

Which makes me remember how, walking in Herald Square a couple of years later—1976 or '77—I saw torn t-shirts, indirectly descended from the ones our band had originally flaunted, on mannequins in Macy's windows. It was gratifying in a way, but the point of those styles had been that they were created by who wore them. The windows were a lesson that anything associated with a desired state gets appropriated by profiteers. That's just nature. Part of the challenge is to stay a step ahead of them. The exercise is healthy.

I've been credited with originating, back in 1973-74, the practice of deliberately wearing ripped clothes, sometimes further transformed with safety pins and drawing and words; with naming myself something negative on purpose; and with inventing the haircut that got identified with punk. All that's basically true, though Malcolm McLaren and the Sex Pistols took those styles much further than I did, and Malcolm added a lot of other ingredients, and it was primarily his clothes that inspired high fashion designers. I also was inspired by others I liked and admired. I'd seen Patti Smith wear a great Triumph motorcycles t-shirt (a nod to Bob Dylan on the cover of *Highway 61 Revisited*?) that was dramatically coming apart at the seams, and Tom had been known to draw wavery shapes on his t-shirt in felt-tipped pen. Similarly to how Malcolm picked up on aspects of my wardrobe, like conspicuous safety

pins, that weren't heavily emphasized by me, I made a calculated sys-
tematic practice of wearing versions and extensions of those things that
Tom and Patti (and I—my street wear was already tattered) had done
casually, the most notorious example being the ripped t-shirt on which
I stenciled "PLEASE KILL ME" in 1974.

Without a doubt, though, the single most influential thing I've done
was my haircut. Funny fate. It's not clothing, but it's personal appearance, and I'm still amazed at its ubiquity and longevity. You don't see
middle-aged movie stars on talk shows wearing torn clothes or violently
asserting their general indifference, but you see them in some version of
that coiffure. It's sometimes said I based it on Rimbaud, but that's not
true. It came from analyzing what made the two prior main rock and
roll haircuts—Elvis's and the Beatles'—work. That line of thought led
me to recall the boy's do typical of my childhood, which was a short,
stiff "butch" or "crew" cut that had gone to seed because kids don't like
going to barbers. When that patchy raggedness was exaggerated the way
I exaggerated it, it looked defiant, even criminal. A guy with a haircut
like that couldn't have an office job. And no barber could even conceive
of it. It was something you had to do yourself.

There were two main differences between Malcolm's project and
mine. One was that Malcolm was a pure provocateur who liked creating chaos just to disrupt the status quo, and the other was that he
was also acting as a clothing merchant, as the couture houses whose
collections he inspired do, of course, as well. I have mixed feelings about
that. High fashion largely happens as conspicuous consumption among
the arrogant, smug wealthy. On the other hand, clothes are interesting
(Martin Margiella is a genius), couture often beautiful. People shouldn't
be denied manmade beauty just because they haven't the inclination
or resources to make it themselves. It's futile to fight the reality that
even the best art will be a status symbol. People pay fortunes for great
paintings that they intend not just as emblems of their success but as
self-presentation, the same as clothes. That's always been true and it
always will be, and artists often benefit from it. But clothes themselves,
no matter how beautiful or interesting, are not great art; they remain

decoration, unless they're actually worn, vivified into soul plumage, by an artiste of personal appearance. There's something inherently sad about clothes in themselves, and fashion, no matter how lovely or effective. Clothes are empty.

From Punk: Chaos to Couture *exhibition catalogue, ed. Andrew Bolton (New York: Metrolpolitan Museum of Art, 2013)*

FILM COLUMN:
The Night Listener

director: Patrick Stettner; script: Armistead Maupin, Terry Anderson, and Patrick Stettner, from a novel by Armistead Maupin; cinematography: Lisa Rinzler; cast: Robin Williams, Toni Collette, Rory Culkin, Sandra Oh

THE NIGHT LISTENER is the second feature film directed by Patrick Stettner. The first was *The Business of Strangers*, a sleekly made independent film, set in an icy corporate milieu, that was raised a few levels by the acting of Stockard Channing and Julia Stiles and Fred Weller. Both that movie and the new one are psychodramas—about extreme experience leading to self-revelation—that involve the hoaxing of their main characters by ordinary-seeming psychopaths.

Unfortunately, *The Night Listener* is pretty well unwatchable. I was compulsively yawning halfway through it. It's based on the novel of the same name by Armistead Maupin, the popular author of the cozy *Tales of the City* books from which the PBS series was made. I have to say I found the novel, despite billing as a "*New York Times* bestseller," unreadable too. The subject treated is interesting though. The story is Maupin's mildly fictionalized account of an experience he had a decade ago. In 1993, he was sent the galley proofs of a thirteen-year-old boy's memoir of the horrendous abuse—and consequent HIV infection—the kid had suffered at the hands of his parents and their friends. Maupin was moved and impressed by the writing. He not only supplied a blurb for the book but instigated a phone relationship with the author, Anthony Godby Johnson, then fifteen years old, that lasted for six years. He came to regard Tony Johnson as one of his closest friends, practically a family member.

Maybe you can guess what's coming. You're right: the kid didn't exist. He was a hoax perpetrated by a grown woman. Everybody knows who JT LeRoy is, right (or who he used to be)? This isn't him. It's another excitingly sex-traumatized youngster who suckered a lot of celebrities into saying he was a good writer, while actually being a thirty-something woman with some kind of larger agenda. Each of the two con-women successfully built a literary career for her plucky tortured dream-boy by engaging in years and years of celebrity-cultivating phone calls in the guise of the imaginary kid. The celebrities the women tricked talked, in many cases, for hours and hours, month after month, year after year, to the "child." In Johnson's case, as the years passed, she (a woman named Vicki Fraginals), claimed "his" phone voice wasn't maturing because AIDS had prolonged puberty, in LeRoy's case, she (Laura Albert) explained that hormone shots meant "he" was no longer "male identified."

Maupin, it must be conceded, leaves room for doubt about whether the boy is faked, trying to make of the story a Vertigo-like mystery about reality, illusion, and imagination in the realm of love. In interviews Maupin specifically names the Hitchcock movie as an inspiration for the novel. (Maupin co-wrote *The Night Listener* script, and it is a straightforward retelling of his book.) Not that he loved the kid as anything other than a son, but he did love him, as he repeatedly emphasizes. And, as he said in an interview about the movie, "Does it matter if we feel something strongly in our heart whether the facts are borne out?" This is the most fun thing about these cases: watching the spin that the hoaxed put on things once the truth comes out. You know it's painful and they're all trying to recover as gracefully as they can. But then, if one is really trying to understand the phenomenon, the question becomes, What if it happened to oneself? Personally, I once succumbed to a couple of hands of three card monte on the street in New York. I also bought a shrink-wrapped brick on St. Mark's Place for $100 when VCRs were really expensive. Everybody knows cons require larcenous, or at least foolish, victims. But everybody is also susceptible to the right pitch.

Intellectual—art, literary—type hoaxes are entertaining for exposing the falsity of the pretensions of cultural big shots. I can't deny I do have an urge to sneer at the writers and movie stars and journalists who promoted JT LeRoy, at the same time that I also have to admit that I felt kind of left out that "he" never tried to cultivate me too. What do Dennis Cooper and Mary Gaitskill and Marilyn Manson and Winona Ryder have that I don't have? Well, they're more famous for one thing, and by that token, if not others, more chic. Which hurts a little. But I do remember first hearing about *Sarah*, and being told it was by this kid who'd originally called himself Terminator, who was a cross-dressing former child prostitute at West Virginia truck stops, a teenager when he wrote the novel, and how all these famous writers were endorsing it. . . . I went and bought it that week. It was cute and chirpy about being a twelve-year-old whore at mom's behest; but the writing was affected-sounding and mediocre. Yes, there were arresting hillbilly/lowlife references, but it all just felt like schtick, and I read the buzz as slumming-type gutter glamour, like graffiti in galleries, or chic fundamentalist Christian outsider art, or Norman Mailer promoting literary hard case murder convicts.

Tony Johnson's book, *A Rock and a Hard Place*, has the same chirpy spirit as *Sarah* without LeRoy's shred of literary merit, but LeRoy is more interesting as a hoax than as a writer for sure. If somebody could really get to the bottom of the experience of his creator, Laura Albert, the obscure rock musician and fan of Dennis Cooper (another freak for the cultural cutting-edge, but who's an actual genius writer), it would be fascinating. But it'll never happen, any more than, say, anyone will ever be able to do justice to Michael Jackson's trials. If Albert were really savvy she'd give some first-rate writer access to herself and all the data, and share the non-fiction book contract. But judging from the way she's handled things since the story broke, basically just staying coy and continuing to spin, like Bill Clinton or something, she isn't savvy enough. But then I suppose probably it's impossible, anyway, as it is with Jackson: too many reputations are at stake. By all reports "JT'"s celebrity network confided their most intimate secrets to the irresistible, bitchy, worldly, little waif. And in Hollywood, they hire pretty hard-nosed enforcers. I could definitely see Courtney Love (one of JT's sup-porters) and Anthony Pellicano (the movie business detective hit man) doing business. . . .

It's the phenomenon of the hoax that's interesting, not the experi-ence of the hoaxed, and that's where the *The Night Listener* falls short. The question "What is real" is interesting, the answer "Who Armistead Maupin loves" is not. It's also not interesting to watch Robin Williams be sincere. He spends way too much of the movie in miniature Maup-mode, with a little catch in his voice to indicate how emotionally stressed out he is. And the corniness is not reduced, as intended, but rather in-creased, by the way the character cornily acknowledges how corny he is. Maupin wants to appear to make the con the subplot by making a big deal about how vulnerable he (Maupin) is because his long-time boyfriend just left him. As if Maupin is just so full of under-utilized love that it doesn't matter how flimsy is the pretext for its expression. An imaginary abused child will do. Yawn. The greatness of *Vertigo* was neither the psychology of Stewart's character, nor even the mechanics of the "deception," but the sublime physical correspondence of the imagery to the boundless mystery of the story it told. Yes, it was a story about the shifting and elusive identity of a person's object of love, but it didn't have a moral (like "Does it matter if we feel something strongly in our heart whether the facts are borne out?"). It had no mess and no message. *The Night Listener* is all message and mess.

BlackBook *film column #14, August/September 2006*

WEIRD, WHAT REVIEWERS CALL ME

I PUBLISHED AN autobiography last year (*I Dreamed I Was a Very Clean Tramp*, it was called) and the reception it got had me turned around for a while.

I've written a few books and I'm always fascinated by the reviews. I read them all, some of them repeatedly. I like the attention, especially certain kinds of attention, but also a book's readers play a part in creating the book. I want to know what I wrote. You learn some of that by seeing how people react to it, and all the reactions have validity even if they say as much about the reader as they say about the work. It's interesting, if sometimes complicated and confusing.

Even apart from the opinions of the reviewers, the response to this book was different than to my others. First, there were a lot more reviews than there were of my novels ("punk" "memoirs" are popular) and also because the reviews were more personal since the subject was my life story.

After seeing a lot of reviews, one thing that jumped out at me was that reviewers thought I was weird. That specific word appeared a couple of times, "weird." I hadn't thought of myself as weird. It's funny, a lot of my motivation in writing the book was to try to see what the result would be if I just told the truth about the things I'd done and experienced. I was curious. Who would this person be? Once or twice it occurred to me that maybe the natural and interesting upshot would be to kill myself: that would be a great story, the person whose autobiography drove him to suicide. But there's a limit to my artistic ambition.

I know I've rejected some of the conventionally respectable ways of doing things and looking at things, but I have always thought of it as seeing clearly, not seeing weirdly. But maybe I am weird. It's confusing. I don't even like the look of that sentence, "I am weird." But I guess it has to be true. The thing I probably most dislike about it is that it's dismissive. It allows you to discount the person you call weird.

In a way I'd rather not be weird. If it could be possible to be perfectly integrated with life and not suffer mental weaknesses but be wise and always certain of what's the right thing to do I'd love that. Who are examples? Maybe Lucretius or Montaigne. Duchamp? He seems like a good candidate. Karen Blixen? Susan Sontag? Picasso? Lucretius and Montaigne seem pretty elevated, but they're the ones I know least about. The others I know appeared weird to a lot of people. They're all artists, but that's the mode I'm into. Maybe that's weird in itself.

My feeling is that nobody is "normal," (though some are "good" for their humility and compassion and I do wish I were more like them) and all ways of being matter. That's what allows me to work. I know there are "better" artists than me, but I think what I have to say is important. Proust thought that books were more important than friends. He thought that only through reading books could we emerge from ourselves and know new worlds, namely existence as undergone by another person, the author of the work. (While at the same time, "In reality, every reader is, while he is reading, the reader of his own self. The writer's work is merely a kind of optical instrument which he offers to the reader to enable him to discern what, without this book, he would perhaps never have experienced in himself.") To him, conversation with friends was trivial and boring compared to reading a book by a decent artist. The whole point was that you got to see another world, that the artist was weird.

I didn't really set out to defend weirdness. I didn't mean to be self-serving in that way. I'm not weird! All right, I'm weird. It was strange to learn about it from book reviews.

From Filter *magazine, 2014*

JIM CARROLL'S *THE PETTING ZOO*

JIM CARROLL DIED at the age of sixty a year ago. Rumor has it that his death had something to do with liver damage due to substance abuse. If that is incorrect, repeating it here is no more or less unfair than the way he himself massaged the facts of his life for public consumption. Carroll was a product of his imagination, like many of the best poets (Guillaume Apollinaire, Josef von Sternberg, the wizard of Oz), and he was one of the best poets. There's a parallel time and world inhabited by those who understand that all information is legend, that experience is show business. That's why Hollywood is the dream factory and Carroll's first commercial poetry collection was *Living at the Movies* (and perhaps why his *Selected Poems* is called *Fear of Dreaming*). He lived in his head. Doesn't everyone? The difference is that he knew it.

Carroll was famous for his *Basketball Diaries*. The first publication of that book, an obscure small-press edition that came out when he was twenty-eight (though he claimed to be a year or two younger), contained a disclaimer that said the diaries were "as much fiction as biography. They were as much made up as they were lived out. It all happened. None of it happened. It was me. Now it's you. 'Nothing is true; everything is permitted.'" When the book was brought out by a commercial publisher two years later, that admission had been removed. The Penguin edition I have states on the back cover that he wrote the diaries between the ages of twelve and fifteen and that Jim, during those years, "chronicled his experiences, and the result is a diary of unparalleled candor that conveys his alternately hilarious and terrifying teenage existence." As John Ford put it (in *The Man Who Shot Liberty Valance*), "Print the legend."

Carroll was a continuous generator of entertaining anecdotes featuring himself. It beat working. The stories paid for his drugs, and the drugs helped underwrite the poetry. The central matter is that Carroll could tell a story as well as anybody around, no matter how he arrived at his repertoire, and furthermore, even more important, he could write a poem. He lived among the poets of history, of life, not the accountants or the police officers. He was a con man, but all artists know that, significantly, they are bedazzlers, masters of illusion. Beautiful poetry isn't life, but it's pretty to think so, and once you do, it is. Carroll wanted to be pure, and poetry is the definition of purity. He made it. His poetry is ultra-distilled, 200 proof. The ultimate proof. The proof of everything. He proved it.

Apparently, Carroll was working on this new book for more than twenty years; he presented a passage from what he called a novel in progress at a reading in 1987, and its main character had the same name, Billy, as this one's. Those pages brought thrilled gasps and happy laughs from the adoring crowd. It seemed he might well make the transition from poetry and "diaries" to great novels.

In some ways *The Petting Zoo* is "poet's fiction," like that of Rilke or Nerval—the genre of a poet's shift to prose in passionate, often elegiac, quasi autobiography. Carroll is, like Nerval, attractively a magpie of shiny poetical scraps of mythology and historical anecdote. Nerval cites Swedenborg, Apuleius, and Dante on the first page of "Aurélia" as precedent guides to the dreams and spirit world that underlie ordinary life. Billy's guide is an immortal talking crow, and Carroll, 20th-century boy, arrays his novel with gleamings like "l'appel du vide" ("the call of the void," that allure of the abyss surrounding each skyscraper); John Garfield's death "under shadowy circumstances, in a whorehouse in France"; and "milky quartz" (the composition of crystalline boulder formations found exclusively, according to Jim, on the slopes of northern Manhattan).

In comparison with the run of literary novels, though, this one is clumsy. It feels formless, as if the writer were following every association that occurs as he proceeds. The characters seem like puppets, and the sentences are often lumpy and strained. Its strongest discernible structure is in its correspondence to Carroll's being, to his history and sensibility and psychology. That's irrelevant and unfair as literary assessment, but it seems more meaningful to read the novel that way than from any critical standpoint. The book is a mess, but moving and poignant as insight into its author. You feel the autodidact trying to measure up, to alchemize his hard-earned experience and knowledge into fiction. The book's about an unschooled young New York artist whose talent gains him early fame, but who dies in a crisis of fear that he's betrayed himself spiritually.

The beautiful excerpt that Carroll presented in 1987 is the strongest example of his novel at the New York raconteur's set-piece best, but it doesn't appear in the novel as published (Carroll was still "putting the finishing touches" on the book when he died, an editor's note says). It told of Billy on a bus in the rain. The young stranger sitting next to him boasts of being a writer. Billy turns "his head to the window to completely seal himself off," and then turns back, asking, "How many people have you disappointed?" The kid fumblingly calculates on his fingers before replying: "I'll say eight. Eight people."

"He faced Billy. Billy was right there waiting.

"'I've disappointed thousands.' Billy spoke firmly, slowly, right at the kid, who seemed suddenly so much younger in every feature, but in his lips especially. 'Literally thousands.'"

From the New York Times Book Review, *2010*

NEW YORK THREE MONTHS LATER:
After 9/11

IT'S QUIET HERE NOW. Things have settled down a lot. It's rare that you can smell the fumes from the site any more. I live about two miles from it and for the first couple of weeks you could smell it most of the time. It seemed like burning plastic, like the insulation of electric wires melting, but just the other day I walked past a man jack-hammering concrete and I recognized it. Of course—it's burning stone. Though my girlfriend insists it's flesh. For weeks she wouldn't ride on the subway that skirted the area because the smell scared her too much. Then a month afterwards you only picked it up when the wind was blowing in just the right direction. It's funny, I almost liked the smell at first. It's hard to say why. Was it because it was confirmation of the physical reality, rather than all the talk and TV? But also it had the drama of the war zone. I felt it myself in the first days. It's like that Samuel Johnson line about imminent death wonderfully concentrating the mind. And there's the way that when you're made to feel like a potential object of deadly attack, everything else about you falls away. It's simultaneously degrading and relieving. Pettiness evaporates. I saw an old war hand on TV say the world's best parties happen in terrorist target-areas.

But as the weeks passed I started getting sick of the smell. It got stale, just a nagging reminder of the smoldering incinerator of body parts down there. I remember this realization I had on the first day. I'd set my

VCR to record the news (for days all stations ran nothing but continuous attack-related reportage, without commercials), and gone outside
to see what it was like and go to the bank and buy groceries. I remember
the way one car driving on Fourteenth Street both looked ghostly and
glaringly vivid for being thickly dusted with grey ash from having been
near the scene. The people inside it were grey too. But what I'm getting
at is what it was like when I got to Union Square and I looked downtown towards where the impossibly giant fluffs of dark smoke arose (I
hadn't consciously realized until then that this was the location in my
daily routine where the towers had stood). It chilled me in a new way, and
I realized what it means for a place to be "haunted." Only an hour earlier,
while watching TV I'd thought, "This is so antiseptic!" There was no reference at all to what it must be like inside on the upper floors. There were
a couple of mentions of people jumping from high windows but that was
avoided too. Then I saw some specks that were people falling through the
air and I realized I didn't want to see any more of it. I realized it was only
sane to seal off your mind at a certain point and not deliberately torture
yourself with identification with the victims. It was enough to know that
it'd happened without adding to the quotient of pain by cultivating it in
yourself. But those sealed off spaces in one's mind hold the screams that
are evoked by all reminders of the event, the strongest reminder being the
site itself where the gone rooms there correspond to the closed off rooms
in your brain, and it's haunted.

But, as I say, it's much quieter now. The war in Afghanistan is being
reported as successful for deposing the Taliban with minimal American
losses and there hasn't been any eruption of anthrax news in a while, so
things are pretty calm. People want calm. People don't want to be bothered. It's understandable! The terrorists sure did succeed, though, not only
in their mission of destruction, but in delivering the message, "You think
you're on solid ground. You're not," and in getting our attention. And everyone wants to divert that attention into pure fervor of retaliation, which
is what Bush encourages. It's been said that the terrorists killed the irony
that's been a sign of the prematurely-tired generation here, but there's
something ironic in how the hijackers stirred the mindless "fatherland"

patriotic military fervor of our politicians and their constituents exactly as the bombers must have intended. I myself have felt that impulse to lash back blindly, too, I can't deny it. For me it came some days after the attack, following the first reports of anthrax, and a death, in Florida. I was on my way out of the house—no time to go to CNN for details—when I checked my phone messages and there was one that said, "You must have heard about the anthrax discovered in New York." Outside, adrenalin poured through my system, surging, "OK let's blow them to hell," raze Afghanistan, they've got to be stopped . . .

My primary political response to the attack though has been fear of how Bush and his administration would react, and of course that fear has been justified. What I didn't expect was how all of congress (except one woman) and ninety percent of Americans would give Bush carte blanche to make war wherever by whatever means he wants. And you'd never know there had been any opposition to it at all from what the major news media report. I was shocked—I guess that's how innocent I am—to see Dan Rather, CBS TV's figurehead journalist, the man who anchors their nightly reports and who was a reporter in Vietnam in the '60s, go on the major CBS talk show, "David Letterman," a week after the attack and say, "George Bush is the President. He makes the decisions, and, you know . . . wherever he wants me to line up, just tell me where. And he'll make the call."

So I was forced to think about that too. Can I and my friends and ten powerless percent of the population be the only people with any sense? Well, first of all, as I say above, I viscerally understand that impulse to wildly lash back, though I believe the worthy thing to do is to resist that impulse. But it's all so complicated it makes my brain hurt. Thinking about it and trying to understand how this situation can be, a few things occurred to me. People really do know how sleazy politicians are, and furthermore people aren't much interested in government. Making decisions about international (and national) policy and relations is distant from most people's real concerns, and not only are such matters complex but half the relevant information is obscure when not secret. That's why we elect others to figure it out and act on our behalf. So when a crisis comes we get behind them because that's what they're there for, that's what democratic government *is*. So this is the generous—but also reasonable—interpretation of how America is behaving now.

On the other hand, these politicians aren't "leaders." They're entrepreneurs advertising themselves to the public by means of funds that they then repay to their investors with legislation and by decree. I believe a real leader would not only have explained to the country after September 11 that war really is different now—as Bush did—but then go on to actually fight the war against terrorists differently, rather than by the same, tired, failed means of bombing a third world country until its government falls (at which point, we've seen over and over again, it's replaced by a similar government—if frequently one more friendly to U.S. business interests). But what do I know? It all hurts the brain. I know I trust my readings of people and their levels of intelligence, wisdom, and decency, and it doesn't take much exposure to be certain beyond a doubt that I have far more faith in what I hear from Noam Chomsky or Susan Sontag than what I hear from George Bush or John Ashcroft (or Dan Rather). So I will continue, day to day, to oppose Bush's policies and try to sort out to the best of my abilities what's really going on, and what I can reasonably do to nudge things in a better direction. Still, I don't really trust people who are driven by certainty about how others should behave. It's almost always the worst who are full of passionate intensity when it's directed at dictating to others what's right. And I also believe that the best intentions have unpredictably horrendous consequences. And I believe that everything is curved and circles back and that anything is right next to the thing furthest from it. So, that, as far as I can see, is what things are like here now.

From Libération *(France), 2001*

STATEMENT OPPOSING
Bush's Iraq War, 2003

HI. I AM A WRITER and sometime musician who's against the war and who has taken action to oppose Bush's warmaking since the first week after 9/11. What I've done to oppose it is, at the very beginning, attend meetings to plan demonstrations and other organizing in opposition to Bush policies. I didn't keep going to those meetings very long because they made me too impatient, but I marched on many weekends—every possible weekend—those first few months and I've gone to both big Washington marches. The other thing I've done is express my reactions and beliefs in many interviews and by writing. The writing I've done has mostly been at my website, but the website has fairly good traffic for one of its type, and the things I've said have gotten some circulation, including turning up in newspapers and magazines.

When I was asked to participate in this day of discussion I understood it to be the first in a planned ongoing schedule of anti-Bush's-war activities by a new organization of writers and artists opposed to the Bush administration's aggressive policies.

I have to say that when I got the announcement for the event I was a little taken aback. It said:

"In addition to everything we do as citizens, we now call for action within the sphere of all public cultural activities as it becomes increasingly embarrassing and painful to attend events that don't even 'reference' the current reality. The false dichotomies between politics and aesthetics can only be put to rest when history is made present and resistance enacted."

I don't really agree with that, support that attitude. I love Godard, if Lenin less, and appreciate what I know of Brecht, but I don't believe that aesthetics are ethics (and I'm not looking forward to a future where they are) in the sense that artists should ever need to feel obliged to include overt statements of ethics or morals or a political stance in their works. I don't like being told what I must do in my work no matter the political views of the person telling me. I do believe that aesthetic values and choices pretty much inevitably, automatically, have a moral import, that all works can be validly interpreted for the shading of their moral implications, but that's something else. Sure—when a situation gets bad enough a good case can be made that any other activity but strenuous opposition to the cause of the problem is frivolous. But I don't want to dictate for people when that moment arrives, when that line is crossed.

Frankly I'm not even sure I'm right in my political stance. I wouldn't try to intimidate other people into behaving as I do. But at the same time part of my motivation for expressing myself about the warmaking is that as a writer I do have a certain audience of people who presumably are interested in what I say. So that is part of my motivation, and though I may be inclined to express my views in some contexts I may not be in others and I trust my instincts about it. Because what else can you do? Some people devote their lives to helping others. But on the whole I think most problems are caused by people who are sure they know how other people should behave.

When I think about it there are probably two main things that drove me to be more active, to give more time and energy to political action after 9/11. The first was the "Not in my name" reaction, that turned out to be pretty widely felt. I saw Bush encouraging the worst in people by tapping their reflexive vengeful impulses to strike out after the attack— encouraging the cheapest type of blind jingoistic patriotism, when, since people feel like traitors if they don't back the president in wartime, it seemed probably more than coincidental that that was the sure route to popularity and power for the president, whose opponent in the election just one year previous had actually gotten more votes than he had. As it did many, it made me sick and angry to hear the manipulative, arrogant, threatening, bullying things he was saying as our nominal spokesman and I had to challenge them if I didn't want to be tainted by them.

The other spur to action was even more basic. I didn't feel like I could bitch about him in private as intensely as I needed to if I didn't try to do something about him. Otherwise the complaining lacked a dimension.

To me most of the process of political activism is boring. Sometimes it's even psychologically annoying. For instance I feel the same "not in my name" reflex often enough when I listen to the speeches at the anti-war rallies. The speakers are always throwing in their personal causes which I may or may not agree with if I even know what they're referring to and I end up feeling implicated the same way I do when President Bush talks as if he's speaking for me. I want to shout out "stick to the subject" or "boo" but I waited till now.

Even the writing, like this, though it's always an interesting challenge, and easier than taking a bus to Washington, uses time I'd rather spend writing other things. But we do live in the richest, most powerful, country in the world and it's reasonable that that would carry a little responsibility to rein in our self-indulgence and greed. And of course there are also the completely real and large rewards in self-respect that can't be gotten any other way than by trying to do the right thing. I don't really believe in "self-sacrifice" anyway. People do what they're inclined to. But I would encourage people by example to get the rewards they will by opposing Bush.

Organizing like-minded activists to show their opposition en bloc is the most efficient way, short of bribery, to have an effect on politicians, so that's why I'm here, which is what I have to say. Thanks.

For "Acting in Public: Expanding Cultural Space" panel at St. Mark's Church, 2003

NEW YORK CITY DIARY 2008:
Economic Crash

WE'RE ALL POISED to see if New York will go to seed again. I've lived in the East Village since my first year in New York, 1967, when I was seventeen. I've lived in the same apartment on East Twelfth Street since 1975. I'm always being asked about the '70s and early '80s, which was both the last time that New York was really poor, and the last time it was really exciting artistically. The art form where the most action was in that go-round was music. "Punk," they ended up calling it. Is there a relationship between the squalor and the fertility? Yes, for the obvious reason that we had nothing to lose.

On the other hand, America was the great world power still. If we'd been poor in Borneo, I doubt if the music we were making would have had much impact, no matter what it was. The relationship between money and art is interesting. I like to go to galleries and museums. There has been a boom here in contemporary Chinese art in the past decade. Is the increasing interest proportionate to the increasing level of quality of recent Chinese art? I don't think so. It's that the culture gets more respect because of the country's growing economic power. As China becomes the international economic standard it becomes the aesthetic standard. Of course it's more complicated than that. There's a self-fulfilling prophecy. The money buys Chinese artists more resources for improvement in every department. It flat increases their numbers for one thing, which puts statistics on their side. But throughout history it's undeniable that the art that's most highly regarded is produced by the cultures of the greatest wealth and power. Artists take orders from the rich, and material success validates aesthetics. Quite often the greatest art is the most expensive to produce—movies in the twentieth century, for example. This whole dependence of art on wealth is one of the dirty little secrets—or "purloined letters," hiding in plain sight—of society. (Another is the inevitability of war.)

But I've gotten off the subject. Back in the '70s I didn't understand that I was living in an economic downturn. I lived in the slums because I chose to. There were other safe, quiet places I could have gone to in the U.S. I knew that my tenement apartment would get burglarized every couple of years and that a pedestrian here had better travel in company and look as penniless and hard as possible, but it was also where the best bookstores and movies and drugs and people and music were, and all of it was cheaper than anywhere else in town. Being young, I thought that the way things were was the way they are. You have to live for forty or fifty years to see that, locally, nothing stays the same. The main thing age teaches is that you have to start all over again over and over. It's interesting. On the large scale, in the long run, things never change, they happen in cycles. And there will always be people who feel like they missed out on the good times, just as there will always be people who take the initiative to make their time good.

But I've gotten off the subject again. What is the subject? My New York diary. The days of a New Yorker. I'm almost old now. I remember in the '70s being offended by the elderly on the streets of the Lower East Side. They were ludicrous, incongruous, pathetic. They were asking for trouble and it made you angry. These days the chances are smaller that aged means purse-snatched, but all these college kids make old people still look out of place. I don't have much reason to be on the streets now anyway. I don't go to bars any more and the bookstores are long gone from Fourth Avenue. All the restaurants deliver.

A common thing to do when you get older is to write your autobiography and I'm taking that route. It's quiet work. To me, all the discussion of current events, the second-guessing of governmental policies and actions, debates about international affairs, are like static, noise, or, at best, entertainment, like sports. Not only do we really not know what's going on, but there's no way to judge, to predict, the consequences of any given act. I wrote a song once called "_____ Generation" (or "Blank Generation"). I thought I was pretty clever to come up with that way of describing myself and my imagined peers. I still think so, though some of the bloom has been rubbed off by its man-handling from a few pop-culture aficionados and rock and roll scholars. I wrote it to describe the state of mind of youth who'd lived through the intense, incomprehensible tangle of America's 1960's, and come out of it buzzed-out, disgusted, angry, suspicious, and somewhat removed. Really, I feel the same way now. There isn't any justice. One can only hope one doesn't find oneself in the path of huge violent events. To the Blank Generation, the world is like the TV show *The Wire*. The good guys and the bad guys are alike.

Actually I have no patience for micro-dividing "generations." I'd almost rather be classified by my astrological sign. An age group worthy to be called a generation needs to have shared a massive experience, like a world war or Bart Simpson. In cold statistics, I, having been born in late 1949, am smack in the middle of the "baby boom"—which generation earned the title by sheer proliferation. There were so many of us that when we were young, the world was young. Now the world is getting old.

It's interesting to get old. You start to realize that opinions are boring and that all of intellectual life is basically recreation. Everything that seemed so important, the right and wrong of everything, starts to seem silly. One can see how the tendency is to get more conservative with age. It's because long experience shows how people fight from self-interest. It's not that the enemy is wrong, it's that the enemy has interests that conflict with one's own. I don't think that I myself have become more conservative—I still believe in respect for all, but I just understand the basis of that respect differently (that's the intellectual game).

I'm neutral [undecided] about whether it'd be an improvement if the East Village becomes a slum again now.

Unpublished—commissioned by the New York Observer, *2008*

MOUTH OF HELL COLUMN:
Spirituality Issue

THE ONLY INTERESTING THING about "spirituality" is what it means about how people behave with each other, and the foremost principle in that department would have to be the ever useful, "Do unto others as you would have them do unto you." Of course a lot of battered children follow from that principle, but what can you do? Life is complicated. Me, I hate God. Actually, I'm the only person I know who refers much to "God." I like to think about "God" the way other people like to think about what they're having for dinner, or how they might improve their career path, or whatever. The God I hate is the God of religions. I don't really believe in the concept of evil (it's a religious concept), but if I were to call anything evil it would be "God." (That being the God of monotheism—Judaism, Christianity, Islam . . . The old time gods of the "pagans," such as in Greek mythology, for instance, were a lot more healthy, but that's not my subject . . .) When I talk about God (my God as opposed to the God of religions), it's just a way of referring to "the big picture." It's interesting to consider what the big picture looks like, and what one's place in it might be. They do say, "God is in the details," and I can't argue with that, but what that means is it doesn't pay to make generalizations or wave around absolutes: if you want to find God, you'd best pay attention to the local mechanics of things. It's the same idea as all politics being local (it doesn't matter how much you care about "human rights" if you oppress your family). The only talk that matters is talk that refers to the real, the concrete, what's actually at hand. By saying God is "the big picture" I mean "the way things are." That's God: it's all the laws, the past and the present, what made you, and where you'll go when you die. That doesn't mean "God is good." God doesn't give a shit. God is just what is happening, and what's more interesting or important than that? By definition, it's bigger than oneself, and so is impossible to ever really know. One can only hope, and do one's best to assure (as God has willed), that one's brain is consistent with it. But then since one's brain has been created by it, presumably the two are somewhat similar. And, by the same token, so is every other brain (similar to God), so better give them respect . . . You can see where this is going. In circles. Multiplied. But isn't that the shape of the universe? "God is an intelligible sphere whose center is everywhere and whose circumference is nowhere." There you go. And what does that God command? Absolutely everything. The Infinite Commandments have you in their sway.

Monthly column for Noel Black's Colorado Springs, CO news tabloid, Toilet Paper, *published 2004-2006*

ORSON WELLES:
Rich and Rare and Strange

IT'S HARD TO KNOW where to start talking about Orson Welles. He was so good at so many things and he was so famous that there's both too much to say and hardly anything left that hasn't been said. But most of all, he knew himself, and it's all been said in his movies.

I have to admit, though, that watching *Lady From Shanghai* again this week I got mad at him. I felt like it was his fault that we were deprived of the movie as it was shot and meant to be seen. I thought he didn't have to be that way, the way he was that got all his movies but the first one either hampered by nasty constraints on their making or mangled by the moneymen in post-production.

Lady from Shanghai is one of the latter. It's a Hollywood movie— meaning that Welles had a budget—and he pretty much got to make the movie as he'd like, but his version was two and a half hours long. What we'll see is eighty-seven minutes. The studio removed an hour. That's the reason the movie has a voice-over narration, to try and help cover over the rough spots. I don't know if the film would have made more sense if we could see the whole thing—probably, but this thriller, noir, type of film often had plenty of plot holes. [It's like the famous story about the Hawks/Faulkner/Bogart *The Big Sleep* version of Raymond Chandler's detective novel (actually made the same year as *Lady*, 1946) where Hawks and Faulkner found the plot so incomprehensible they called up Chandler to set them straight and he told them he didn't know what was going on either . . .] But it makes me mad that there are the kind of patched together spots here where the sound falls out for dubbed dialogue, and a haphazard, sloppy, elided feel to the story even though doubtless it seems that way to me partly because I know how much is missing. Don't get me wrong, it's a fantastic movie, but why did he have to be like that? How the hell could he let it happen that he could work as a filmmaker from the ages of twenty-five to seventy and only have the one film, the first, *Citizen Kane* be the perfect genius movie he intended it to be? I want more and he's a bastard for not having found a way to do better!

Then again, in a way his whole body of work is an examination of this matter, this issue, and you could say that every horrible studio reshoot of a scene and every clipped sequence is really a kind of magical witty despairing Wellesian self-reference. Yeah, that's it. It's all exactly as it should be. If you follow your nature, you will retain your original nature in the end.

It's often been said that movies are like dreams. Jung's approach to dream interpretation was that everyone in the dream was the person dreaming and if you looked at it that way you could learn a lot about your inner life. Welles's dreams about the conflict within himself of the driven, cynical, mesmerizing manipulator for personal gain versus the idealistic, innocent, more serene humanist—most Welles movies follow that pattern*—and . . . They cancel each other out. That's why his films are all in shreds, that all that's left at the end are fields of broken infinity, grotesque and beautiful style. By the end, when he made *"F" for Fake*, he was acknowledging it outright: that what matters, what remains is theater, fakery, chiaroscuro sound and fury. In that movie he literally declares that real life is empty, like "The toothbrush waiting for you in a glass, a bus ticket, or the grave," and that the one certainty is that everything passes, and the central truth of life is that "we're going to die."

---

* A pattern described as a political tension typical of Welles's movies by James Naremore in his *The Magic World of Orson Welles* (Oxford University Press, 1985)

Citizen Kane was perfect and endlessly satisfying because even though it was about unsolvable mysteries, the discovery that it was about unsolvable mysteries was the solution to the mystery! But as always it was mostly about style and magic and wit and drama in the telling of the parable of its story. It is so delicious and exhilarating to be transported like that and no one could do it like Welles and that was really the point itself, to get everything intensified with meaning and beauty, to be taken through the gates of Xanadu and slid and dipped through time and the lives of strangers in the form of the most fascinating pictures where there's singing in one corner and little gleaming outbreaks of memory in another and a gargoyle's head protruding while someone gives an accidentally false confession to the sound of delicate music . . . As Nicholas Ray said, "I never think of a film as doing anything except providing a heightened sense of being." And what a worthy purpose that is, a humble and worthy one for an artist. But Welles is not really humble and I think the awestruck, but finally cheated, or at least chilled, feeling with which one sometimes leaves his movies is also significant. His movies are gothic but they're not cathedrals. Just as he said about the "Rosebud" revelation, "It's a gimmick, really, and rather dollar-book Freud." All messages and narratives and ideas for artists are finally interesting only as they reveal possibilities of the medium itself. The so-called content is just a pretext, which is the positive way of saying the story is a lie and empty, as Welles said in those lines from *"F" for Fake.*

One tends to leave a Welles film stimulated but sad, sad at some kind of failure or loss. In *Kane,* maybe you feel it along with the director, in a cathartic, pretty well resolved way. Check Borges about *Kane* in this general regard. In a short review of the movie upon its release, Borges called *Kane* the most frightening thing there is, a labyrinth with no center, and he says, "We all know that a party, a palace, a great undertaking, a lunch for writers and journalists, an atmosphere of cordial and spontaneous cameraderie, are essentially horrendous. *Citizen Kane* is the first film to show such things with an awareness of this truth." But with his subsequent movies, you feel it as a failure or loss deeper than anything he did in the movie.

Welles is one of those artists, like Rimbaud or Van Gogh, whose work you can't talk about without talking about his life.

He was born in the midwest—Kenosha, Wisconsin—in 1915 to a bon vivant of an industrialist/inventor father and a concert pianist mother. They read him Shakespeare as an infant, and he was treated as an adult, and more specifically as a genius, as soon as he could speak. His mother died when he was nine, and his father took him on a trip around the world. When they returned, Welles senior bought an Illinois hotel that was a kind of retirement home for vaudevillians, and the pair of them moved in. There Orson learned the first of the stage magic that would be a hobby for the rest of his life. He entered a progressive country boy's school called Todd where he directed and acted Shakespeare and wrote plays. His father was an alcoholic and died when Orson was fifteen whereupon he became the ward of the highly cultured opera patron, physician, and womanizer, close family friend Dr. Bernstein. Welles graduated Todd at sixteen and from there travelled alone to Ireland ostensibly on a walking and painting tour. Dr. Bernstein was encouraging him as a painter. In Dublin he bluffed his way into an audition at the famous Gate theater and won a major role that ended up getting him a gushing review in the *New York Times*. By the age of nineteen he was acting on the New York Broadway stage. At twenty he directed his first New York production, for the W.P.A.: an all-black version of *Macbeth* set in Haiti. It was so big a success that the government gave him and his producer-partner John Houseman a theater of their own. I'm not making this up! Pretty soon he marries Rita Hayworth!

To sum it up, nearly every production he staged was not only a success but made big news twice more over: for both creative innovation and topical content (Welles was a committed leftist). He was on the cover of *Time* magazine and was the voice of *The Shadow* on the radio even before the notorious broadcast of *The War of the Worlds*, which caused many listeners who tuned in late to believe the world was being attacked by Martians, when he was twenty-three. A year after that he had a movie-making contract with RKO that gave him unprecedented creative control. Famously, upon arriving in Hollywood to learn his way around the soundstages, he described them as "the biggest electric train set a boy ever had."

A year later he made *Citizen Kane*, which is still thought of by many as the greatest sound film ever made. It would ruin him. As charming and brilliant as he was it was inevitable that his success would create a resentment in Hollywood. Furthermore, his film was based on the career of a particular, living, powerful man, newspaper tycoon William Randolph Hearst. Hearst was something like Rupert Murdoch now in his politically conservative, sensationalist style as a news publisher and his stupendous reach as a media magnate. He used all his influence to try to destroy *Kane* and Welles, and many in Hollywood were not too broken up to see the spoiled kid get his comeuppance.

As Welles himself put it, he started at the top and worked his way down.

Lady from Shanghai was made in 1946, four years after *Kane*. In the interim he'd made *The Magnificent Ambersons* (1942) which was a poignant masterpiece that the studio removed from his control after shooting and then mutilated by cutting about forty-five minutes from what Welles intended while also filming new material unapproved by the director, including a more cheerful ending. Then came *Journey into Fear* (1943) a good but relatively conventional thriller the direction of which Welles influenced, and in which he acted, but that's credited to Norman Foster; and after that *The Stranger* (1946), also a relatively unambitious thriller that's full of wonderful touches. *The Stranger* took a lot of ideas from Hitchcock's 1942 *Shadow of a Doubt*. Both films are about psychotic murderers posing as benevolent charmers to win the confidence of the warm small-town American families with whom they hope to hide. Welles said later he made the movie to demonstrate his practical competence to the studios: "I did it to prove I could put out a movie as well as anyone else. I did not do it with cynicism however," and it did make money and was more than hackwork, as was everything Welles ever did (as filmmaker—he was capable of raising money for his movies with some atrocious acting stints or trash writing).

He'd married Rita Hayworth in 1943, but by now, 1946, the marriage was failing. *Lady From Shanghai* came about when Welles had to borrow money from Harry Cohn, the head of Columbia Pictures, to finance a theater production. Cohn wanted a movie in return. Welles hadn't planned to use his estranged wife in the movie, but she was a star at Columbia and Cohn insisted.*

Welles wasn't entirely blameless for the way *Lady* was shredded by the studio. The movie went three months over schedule—double the planned shooting time—and more than $400,000 over budget. Cohn said of him, "Well, it's taught me one lesson. Never have a leading man who's the director, because you can't fire the director!" Cohn panicked after audience previews, and cut Welles's two and a half hour version by an hour while adding a corny music score. The studio's confidence in the movie remained so low they didn't release it for two more years.

Still it's a spectacular film and a fair representation of Welles's abilities. Probably Welles's most striking knack was for making stories look the way they mean. That's a definition of filmmaking, but it's surprising how little it's done or with how little imagination by modern directors. Hitchcock was maybe the only other in America since silent days to work this way by policy. Kubrick comes to mind too. But Welles is the master. Possibly the most famous and most dramatic example of it in all his films is in this one: the climactic gun battle between Rita Hayworth and Everett Sloane in a funhouse mirror maze. The point about it is not just how thrilling it is to watch but the way in which it presents the meaning of what is going on between this husband and wife as they frantically lunge and grope in every direction to find with bullets the "real" spouse among the fake ones as they literally shatter their whole grotesque world (and ours since it's our dream too). What could you compare it to? Maybe the shower scene in *Psycho*. They're about in the same class. (Though god damn it a big difference is that we'll never know how good Welles's really is because it was recut by the studio . . .)

---

* Cohn was the guy whose funeral turn-out was so massive it prompted the quip, "Well, give the people what they want . . ."

Lady has many such marvelous sequences. I want to describe one other that I only just fully got as I re-watched the film this week. It uses completely different means than the mirror maze montage and only one cut to get its effect. The means are ones Welles is famous for: a long take shot in deep focus. Deep focus is a way of shooting that gets both an especially wide field of view in the frame and keeps things in focus at nearly all distances. It's an unusual way of shooting for a couple of reasons: one is that filmmakers are more often interested in directing the viewer's attention to one particular thing in the image by way of focusing on it; the other is that the wide angle distorts the shape of objects near the edge of the frame. But Welles liked to use it to be able to clearly show us things happening at more than one distance from the lens to give us the most information possible—he'll sometimes make three different points in three different planes of the shot—while the distortion actually contributes interestingly to the atmosphere of his strange and ominous stories. The sequence in *Lady* I'm talking about features Welles, as Michael O'Hara, the idealistic Irish sailor in the movie, sitting, smoking nervously in the dark decoration-cluttered office of the sleazy salesman of a lawyer who's making him a proposition. The lawyer is mesmerizing Welles into a stupor of agreement to commit a crime that Welles hopes will earn him enough to tempt Rita into leaving her rich husband. The shot lasts a full two minutes without cutting, which is very long for a shot in a movie, and the camera glides and halts and rises and falls, following the nasal, fast-talking lawyer from one chair to a wall-safe to another chair and then in circles around the sweating, frowning, mystified O'Hara, until the sailor is completely dizzy and beaten, at which point the lawyer snorts in his snide pig-squeal of a voice, "But you're not a murderer unless I'm dead . . . Silly isn't it?" And the picture finally cuts—to the huge waving tentacles of an octopus in the aquarium where O'Hara is rendezvousing with Hayworth.

But, yes, the movie is flimsy as a story—it's mostly mood and atmosphere and conflict and even that is inconsistent and we are forced to mix our pleasure in Welles's wit and invention with our pleasure in typical Hollywood reveling in the pin-up gorgeousness of Rita, probably pushed on the movie by the studio. At one point she comes out in a bottomless sailor suit that's some kind of more outrageous than a marriage of Michael Jackson and Madonna. Another example of the half-assed side of it is the repeated proverb that's supposed to say something meaningful to the story but that I find completely baffling. It goes something like, "If you follow your nature, you'll retain your original nature in the end." Huh? OK, what does that mean? Do whatever you feel like because then you're yourself even if you don't think so? OK. There is also one moment in all the fancy footwork that's actually affecting, and that's the chilling final view of a wounded Rita screaming, "Michael come back. I don't want to die!" He barely pauses. The movie is bleak. You do get the feeling that Welles doesn't much care about pleasing anybody but himself at this point. Harry Cohn wasn't happy about that.

Welles couldn't get hired for another two years and then it was for an extremely low budget version of *Macbeth* shot for a studio, Republic, known best for serials and grade C westerns. After that he didn't work in Hollywood for ten years, though he made *Othello* and *Mr. Arkadin* in Europe. In 1958 he made the deeply squalid masterpiece *Touch of Evil*, a truly great film that the studio chopped up but which retains incredible strength and which has recently been restored to a condition much closer to Welles's intentions. *The Trial* (1962) came next, has much that is fascinating, and was shot and financed in Europe as are all the rest, which are few. *Chimes at Midnight* (1966), his Falstaff compilation of the Shakespeare *Henry* plays, and then the hour-long French TV production of Isak Dineson's *Immortal Story* (1968), and finally the documentary/essay compilation *"F" for Fake* (1973). Nothing else was completed and he died in 1985.

Introduction for screening in a film series curated by Poty Oliveira at YWCA Cine-Club, NYC, 2003

PETER SCHUYFF'S SHINING STUFF

PETER IS A GREEDY little twit who uses words like "twit." He likes to play billiards and squash and is a pouty bad loser prone to tantrums, and an insufferably smug and gloating winner. He's impeccably groomed and wears understated clothes of the finest fabrics and cut. He's good at dinner parties and knows the jokes of the moment. He's imperious and condescending at the first safe opportunity. He respects wealth, sophistication, learning, and skill.

I get pleasure from looking at his paintings, their serenely unassailable detailing of simplicity revealed in masses of color and shades of form, but when I tried to tell him so he undermined my response to him with a brush off that made me feel like a fool for trying to be nice. It's less that he's complicated than that he has a highly developed ability to intellectually protect his capital as an artist, that being his appeal to the rich people who he wants to buy his paintings. It must needs to embarrass Peter to have his work treated as anything other than a means to the achievement of (material) success.

The work is obviously and most definitely not "self expression" nor has it any message whatsoever. Painting is not a life-and-death matter to Peter ("romantic" is one of his most scornful epithets)—it is merely, or simply, one of his interests. Still it made him squirm and resist when

I pointed out that his claim to hate all his time spent in the studio, his satisfaction with Walter Robinson's characterization of his oeuvre as no more or less than "shiny things" (magpie appealing), and his insistence that he's comfortably chosen to work within a vocabulary arrived at

by his immediate predecessors, without aspiring to extend or enlarge upon it, all led me to conclude that as an artist he is a small manufacturer working in his own sweat-shop. Like most anybody, and artists certainly, he doesn't want to be nailed, especially not with his own hardware. That's legitimate: we're all bigger than anyone can ever know. One of the main jobs of an artist is to evade capture. The moment anyone—including oneself—fully "gets" you you've got to have moved on or it's all over. What is making art but trying to approximate how interesting things are and how they're interesting? On that scale, in that realm, the only thing you can fully get is dead, and that's the only thing good art can't be.

As I said, however difficult Peter makes it with his annoying eva-sions, I like looking at these paintings. They *are* shiny things, but of what nature? They are small but pure and final-seeming. They're not like music exactly, but maybe you could say that a given one is like a single note, wrapped in silence, nothing particularly special, but still, isolated like that, overtones and reverberations lapsing back into nothing, in-teresting and satisfying. (Their symmetry, entirely abstract nature, and their complexity-in-simplicity inevitably feels spiritual, but that's prob-ably best left incidental.) To me, they are even more pleasing seen in series, together.

Whatever else you might say about Peter, he is not pretentious, so I have not been pretentious for him. He told me he paints "for the eye and from the hand," and I appreciate that. When I asked him what response he'd like to elicit from a viewer of his work, he said "satisfaction," and he succeeds with me.

From Peter Schuyff *exhibition catalogue (Milan: Associazione Culturale Contemporanea Milano, 1996)*

CBGB AS A PHYSICAL SPACE

FIRST OF ALL, CBGB'S is located on the Bowery,* a street the very name of which has signified drunkenness, dereliction, and failure for as long as anyone can remember. Such is the mental space of its physical place. At present, though, that particular urban strip has become prime real estate. The most famous rock and roll club of all time, which has unquestionably done more than any other establishment to modernize the reputation of its area, has been priced out by bidders eager to install designer boutiques, upscale restaurants, and luxury apartments. When the dump opened its doors in December of 1973, it was typical of the rows of flophouses, low-rent restaurant supply corps, a sprinkling of struggling avant-garde theater venues, and, most abundantly and notoriously, countless ultra-cheap alky dives that, like civic backwater tidal washup, littered the Bowery, keeping it disreputable, dirty, dangerous, poor, and interesting, back then. Now the club is unique. Very soon it will no longer exist, except perhaps in whatever unlikely form can be transported to Las Vegas, where, as of this writing, it's been announced as reopening in 2007.

---

* I am writing in the late summer of 2006. By the time this book is published, CBGB's will no longer exist in the form and location it's held since it opened. It's still there now, though, so I'm going to use the present tense to describe it.

I remember the joint at the beginning. I was in the first band that brought the club attention and in two others that played there steadily in the place's earliest years as a rock and roll (cum "punk") club, 1974-1977. Pretty much every weekend in that period you could see one or more of the following groups on CBGB's stage (here listed in chronological order): Television, the Ramones, Patti Smith, Blondie,

The Heartbreakers, the Talking Heads, Suicide, Richard Hell and the Voidoids, and the Dead Boys. Its physical space, capacity about 350, has stayed amazingly unchanged. The front two-thirds—entranceway and bar area—of the single long room of the club proper, along with the toilet areas downstairs at the rear, are the same as they always have been. In the venue's first year or two there were a few minor rearrangements made in back, enlarging the stage and dressing-rooms, and installing a first class sound system; but the basic layout and construction, as well as the furniture, lighting and overall atmosphere, have not changed at all since 1974, except that the graffiti has gotten thicker.

The graffiti has gotten thicker, but that happened quickly too. It only took three or four years for the place to acquire the garish veneer within that's become its distinguishing mark: not the place's death-less overall wino-dive griminess, not the long procession of compact neon beer signs dangling like corrupt flags or coats of nauseous arms above the narrow public walkway behind the bar stools, not the blunt, ribbed, white tunnel-roof of canvas overhead outside with its innoc-uously ugly "CBGB and OMFUG" logo, all of which stylelessly sty-listic elements are virtually unchanged since Hilly Kristal re-named as CBGB what had once been the Palace Bar (adjunct booze hole to the Palace Hotel flophouse next door) . . . No, it would be a separate consequence of Hilly's stunning and consequential inertia that would ultimately proclaim his physical domain most powerfully—namely, his lack of interest in removing any defacement of the club's interior.

The result of that ultra-passivity regarding décor is the fantastic, ghostly, jewel-smear-for-walls of a palace-for-fun-seeking-children portrayed in this book. Analytically, all those spectra of marker scrawls, blurred spray-paint swaths, and day-glo stickers comprising the interior planes of a shimmering temple of impulse-to-assert, can't truly be seen as "self-assertion." It's more like mob behavior, like what goes on in a mosh pit, or like blank genetic reflexes, than anything to do with any-one's "self." It's just about leaving a mark, any mark. The specific words scrawled on the walls are irrelevant. Granted, a viewer almost can't help going in for close-ups and deciphering statements here and there, but the literal messages are unworthy of the overall effect, and interfere with it, like hearing Lindsay Lohan's words on a talk show. (The great '70s street graffiti kids, incidentally, who were of course in a different class altogether, would seem to have concluded the same, quickly evolving tags that were pure style, almost impossible to read.)

Above all, though, the effect of the surfaces of CBGB's dark, crazed insides is eerie, it's haunting. It's like a dead-quiet, chillingly colorful cemetery. Or autopsy: all of compacted history sliced open. It's not so much that the graffiti evokes the endless procession of individual kids who've attended the club, but that it evokes their absence, their faceless selves buried under the next pretty layer of pointless proclamation. The walls are an onslaught of death and futility as much as they are of life and vitality. The kids believed themselves to be unique individuals; the walls they covered with that claim are the proof that it's a delusion. Or is this what we knew all along, and the walls are sites of reveling in it, reveling in undifferentiation? Because it does seem sweet and innocent and loveable too.

Naturally, the graffiti in CBGB also has a lot in common with the style of music that made the club famous. It's not about an intellectual argument, it's not about opinions, it's about a condition, about being young and hungry; about energy, anger, and sex; pure formless assertion. Or not: It's about boredom and frustration. But boredom iterated and re-iterated, become drunk, passed out unconscious, and then beginning again. Funnily. It's horrible, but beautifully horrible, like modern ghostly Japanese horror movies with their derelict, peeling, void-riddled spaces; or like the abandoned west side docks of '70s New York where illicit, if somewhat defiantly public, sex was taking place everywhere among the filth and scribbled-on rotting wood. It's about abandon and abandon-ment made visible, and become the environment for where it's made audible as well. It's about ennui and inertia and their perfect realization in violence and sex. It's so pretty it hurts.

From CBGB: Decades of Graffiti *(New York: Mark Batty Publisher, 2006)*

LOVE

MARILYN MINTER

UP ALONG THE HEART of the galaxy slides a tongue. *I want the light on my tongue, always coming, coming from—everything. . . . the desire to orally know a photon.* The heart is ice cream. The floor is linoleum and has a puddle on it.

Everybody understands Marilyn Minter's work. She is a filthy sensualist, just like God. We were created to love Marilyn Minter.

Food and sex are life (which, to be inclusive, it should be noted is simply a livelier form of death) and the tongue figures heavily in both. Energy is conserved, and "inertia" means everything is inclined to continue. Let's fuck.

And the night-sky falls into your heart. Which is some kind of ice cream. The heart in flames of dark ice cream. Licked by death. I don't really see death anywhere in Minter's work (except as conceived as indistinguishable from life)—but for possibly in her photos of her mother, which to Minter herself weren't ominous or haunted at all, apparently. It's just that I'm so excited by my affinity with Minter I had to quote myself.

It's rare to see art works that, as Minter's do, purely fill you with life and happiness. Who else does that? Maybe an odd Koons, if you can adjust. Some Joe Brainard, though the Brainard will also probably be a bit poignant, a bit nostalgic. Who? Scattered early Claes Oldenburg things (drippy plaster food, for instance)? Matisse? Kurt Schwitters maybe? Walt Disney?

Minter's work staggers, weaving, in heavily chartreuse-enameled grimy toenails, around in mud-puddly time—the new work being the foundation for the early work, and, watching, one discovers how vistas of glistening orange caviar drooling from an extended tongue share aspects with a crumply sheet of aluminum foil across generic streak-patterned linoleum squares. Some of her earliest paintings—like the women's Pop-simplified fashion model faces intersected by grey similarly abstracted car bodies (from 1968, when Minter was twenty), or the crisp detritus (paper shavings, or aluminum foil, or a two-by-four, or a thin brown puddle) hyper-realistically isolated on that linoleum (from the mid-'70s), or the ben-day dots and paint-drips of food and pornography details in the subsequent fifteen years or so—all look consistent with trends in paint investigation of their times, but in retrospect they're not only terrific examples of their periods, and a genre unto themselves (Minter), but cosmic; the expanding universe, pure beauty from galactic glitter through jewels of spit to luminous electron smears. In the most recent decade of Minter's pictures nodes of gritty creased flesh isolated in extreme close-up can't immediately be told to be bare heel or thumb or nipple. The universe is infantile, glamorous, and dirty.

I intended to stay away from talking of Minter in ways not founded in the senses, but I can't deny that when I do the thought experiment—following her own lead—of imagining her overtly erotic imagery as being executed by a man rather than a woman, it changes my response to it. But, wait, on reconsideration, having just looked through catalogues of those sex-based works again, I believe they'd have the same effect on me if I knew they were painted by a man. I take that back. They're more fun done by a woman. The matter is murky, and it's ultimately uninteresting except politically or sociologically—ways that don't have much to do with art as art.

There's anecdotal interest in the way that Minter first started making explicitly "porn" pictures when she found herself stunned by

the brilliance of an early Mike Kelley show that "was basically mining
the contents of a thirteen year old girl's bedroom," and it occurred to
her that if a woman had shown those works, they would be dismissed
as banal and obvious. She wondered what imagery or subject would

be the reverse—predictably obvious for a male but out of bounds for a female. Hence her paintings based on commercial porn of women happily sucking cock and reveling in spurting hard-ons. Ultimately the subject or pretext or "content" of paintings itself is anecdotal and ephemeral, more or less ("Content is a glimpse of something, an encounter like a flash. It's very tiny—very tiny, content."—De Kooning as quoted by Sontag for "Against Interpretation"). But even if it fades over time, we're lucky to have it now, and in fact it's unlikely that cock sucking will fade. Not in our universe.

eat the light

From Marilyn Minter Pretty/Dirty *retrospective catalogue, ed. Elissa Auther (Gregory R. Miller & Co. in cooperation with the Museum of Contemporary Arts Houston and the Museum of Contemporary Art Denver, 2015)*

WRITING SEX

IT'S HARD TO WRITE ABOUT SEX. It's like writing about your mother. I mean your mother, not mine, and me saying things about her. Sex is charged. Some artists who treat sex behave as if people should respond to the sex in their work neutrally, as if it were any subject at all, but that's disingenuous or naïve.

One place the Bible makes sense is in Genesis where the loss of paradise is signified by the first humans' sudden shame at their nakedness (nakedness being genitals, being sex, of course). There's no going back. What removes us from the unselfconscious Eden of the other animals is that we have these oversized brains that aren't innocent. The god damned "human condition" is that we're physical creatures ceaselessly batted around by biological needs and impulses inherited from our instinct-driven ancestors while at the same time we've evolved these super-complex brains capable of imagining and desiring (and demanding) other, ideal, behaviors. It's embarrassing and infuriating, this discrepancy between what in some moods and states seems self-evidently desirable, even necessary, while in others seems depraved—or impossibly idealistic. (The very same activity can seem problematic because it's evil and because it's impossibly good, like, say, mate swapping, or having sex with your mother—that's *your* mother . . .)

But beyond a doubt: people have a visceral, involuntary response to the presentation of sex. So how can one write it well when people react to it irrationally? I don't know, but I think a way to judge one's success at it is by whether the writing makes enough readers interested in having sex with the writer. Really. Ultimately, art for most artists is an elaborate sexual display, and, so, specifically sexual literature would have to stand or fall according to its seductive powers. Of course there are many readers who are turned off by explicit sex writing, and the way to reach them lies elsewhere. But what an artist is doing is showing what he or she is made of so that the right people will be attracted. I do not think this is ignoble and I'm not trying to be a wise guy cutting down the pretensions of artists. I'm as pretentious as the next guy and I care more about books and writing and beauty than just about anything, but no more than I do about people wanting to have sex with me. Yes, art is also about making sense of the world (or excitingly reflecting its non-sense), and heightening the attender's own sense of being (inspiring him or her), and creating sensual and intellectual pleasure (beauty), etc., etc., but what are these but definitions of the seductive?

(In parallel, the act of writing itself is a kind of sex. That's not news either. Corny writers are always calling their books their children. But the need to write can also be a desire for immortality similar to what sex provides: reproduction. Sex is so pleasurable because our strongest drive is the preservation into further generations of our genetic material: a kind of physical immortality. Writing can be the means of doing this for a mind, a consciousness. A book survives because its author's consciousness as embodied in the writing is that interesting and affecting to readers. "Good" writing survives because readers like the company of the writer. Which brings us back to sexual display. . . . So suppose I'm writing about sex; then I'm having sex about sex in order to solicit sex! It's all sex!)

Probably the main objection to sexual writing is that it is vulgar, it violates refined discretion. Again, it's the reason we're not supposed to fart in public or to eat with our mouths open: embarrassment at our instinctual, involuntary, non-intellectual nature. I respect that—I try my best not to fart in public myself (though I enjoy it in private), while I regret losing the readers who can't abide sex-writing because it offends them. I don't claim that writing sex is right or good or necessary, and I'm not putting down readers who reject it. I just insist that it's legitimate. There is no subject that is beyond the bounds of good writing, just as there is no unworthy or indecent form or medium. I myself have a hard time reading very *long* works. So no matter how much I like Nabokov and Joyce, I've never read *Ada* or *Ulysses* all the way through. Though I read all the time, I haven't read *In Search of Lost Time* or *Don Quixote*.* I have never finished reading an epic poem. This is a handicap of mine, an unfortunate disadvantage. It doesn't mean that epics are inferior. By the same token I resent being sneered at or dismissed for writing sex. I believe it's the reader's loss to be unable to enjoy sex in art, however understandable his or her reflexive reaction may be.

In a way I think that writing sex is especially interesting because of its difficulty. The gender and sexual preference of the writer immediately render some kinds of writing more or less problematic. (Not to mention cultural background—writing about sex in France is different from writing about it in America, or Iran.) Say for instance I'm speaking of male heterosexual writing, then the writer must contend with: male readers tending not to like other men's sexual display, and women possibly being made to feel objectified and not liking that . . . The general difficulties have to do with penetrating (ahem) the readers' skepticism and resistance by winning their confidence with one's candor and depth of insight and (as above) one's personality, one's character, one's being itself as represented by the writing. (And again, finally, what other real standard for writing is there but that you like the company of the writer? You trust him or her, you like the shape of his or her mind and view of things, you appreciate the values inherent in the work . . .) It's hard! I myself have had writers I liked suddenly and fatally tainted because of what they revealed about themselves in

---

* I have to boast that since the publication of this essay I've read both *Ada* and *In Search of Lost Time*. The latter was one of the great experiences of my life.

their writing about sex. Just as readers do, writers of course have awful blind spots and handicaps in their psychology where sex is concerned, because it's such a complicated subject in which people have so much of themselves invested.

I think maybe gay men have the best chance of writing sex well. In fact when I think of good sex writing, the first names that come to my mind are Dennis Cooper and Allen Ginsberg and William Burroughs—Verlaine and Rimbaud were good too—not, say, Henry Miller and D. H. Lawrence and—who?—Philip Roth?—Erica Jong?—Kathy Acker? There's Nabokov, but he's really discreet. Apollinaire did some good pornography, but it was more purely pornography than these more "ambitious" kinds of writings I'm thinking of. (I believe pornography—writing done with the overriding purpose of arousing—is necessary and good, but that's a slightly different subject. The distinction is vague though; there's a lot of overlap. I've masturbated to Donatello and dug the formal beauty of photos in *Sister Spank* magazine.) There're Bataille and de Sade, but they feel too much like missionaries to me. The reason gay men writers have a better chance I expect is that gay male sex is more accepted as being largely about arousal and the path to its consummation (pure lust, in other words, rather than, however indirectly, the path to creating a family), so there's less room for confusion and ambivalence and fewer grounds for outrage and resentment in the reader. (Incidentally illustrating the difficulties I'm describing, I have to disqualify myself regarding lesbian sex writing because it makes me too jealous to assess it fairly. When I read it, if I like the writer, I want to be the person she's desiring. I haven't found a way into heterosexual women's sex-writing either. There isn't a whole lot of it by interesting writers. Lee Ann Brown is cool.) Allen Ginsberg's writing hasn't meant that much to me, but I think his sex writing is good for its unusual matter-of-factness, which I think largely follows from his queerness. Dennis Cooper and William Burroughs are two of the best American writers of the past fifty years and they both do a lot of sex and it's very good, conspicuously better than those heterosexuals, and I think this is made possible in part by this same advantage.

For some reason, I am interested in and compelled to try to know and describe dirty secrets of the sort that are obvious even though they're "secrets." Supreme examples being the biologically decreed pre-eminence of sex in our lives (and the sexes' separate interests there), and the inevitability of flat, final, death (and the implications of that). (Of course these are interestingly intertwined, being as sex provides the most effective way or two of detouring death.) But the list of such hypocrisies, illusions, and self-deceptions is endless (and the writers who've dwelt on them many—for instance, Voltaire, Swift, Flaubert, Nathanael West, Burroughs, Lenny Bruce—or maybe it's the only story there is—as Jim Thompson said, there's just one plot: things are not as they seem . . .). When I get uncomfortable with my own sex writing as I sometimes do (most often when I'm faced with reading it aloud in public, or when I think of relatives or "wholesome" people I admire reading it), or I'm subject to rejection or disapproval because of it, my justification for myself is always that I'm only being true to life. Maybe it is a poverty of material, but god knows it is half the material of our existence. (Or maybe I'm embarrassed because one doesn't like to be overheard shamelessly flirting. I think of writing as directed at one person, the reader. It's weird to have one's private offering, one's personal letter, heard by a crowd or discovered by one's family.) Then again, it's also embarrassing to have described my own sex writing as a solicitation of your favors, but if you encounter any of that writing and you're whom I care for you to be, the small embarrassment is worth the reward.

Introduction to Aroused: A Collection of Erotic Writing, *ed. Karen Finley (New York: Thunder's Mouth, 2001)*

CUNNILINGUS

I'VE SPENT MORE TIME at it than any other sex act, but despite my tendency to write about sex I can't think of any times I have written about that particular act ... Wait, now I remember there's once where I said how the

> [. . .] vagina would taste like warm folds of liquefying bubblegum and then like lobstermeat drenched in lemon butter sauce. The alternating flavors shifted like shafts of light reflected from the facets of a giant pink diamond.

How could I forget that, when it's one of the things I've written I've thought about most often? Maybe because it was about a sexually mutated deer (white doe with antlers), not a human woman. But it was a very womanly antlered doe.

And, no, yes, there's a scene in my novel *Go Now* too, come to think of it (though it also goes by quickly) where the book's narrator and central character describes having sex with his mother's sister:

> As I lick and jam my lips and tongue up into her cunt I press my hard cock against her hairless calf. Even her crotch which maybe in my whole life I have glimpsed once for a second as a child seems

so close, so known, while also lathered with all that sexiness of the control she is ceding me. It is soft and tender and the hair is silky and it smells so sweet. I hold her still-firm butt in both hands and push apart the crack and lick her asshole too.

Ho hum. But why do I have to make it bestiality and incest to use it? As I say I've spent more time engaged in it than any other sex act and, not only do I love it, I love it for the way women like it and what that does for me, but I think it's not something I like talking about too much. There's something about talking about it, about suggesting the image of oneself engaged in it, that seems obsequious, embarrassing ... How strange to realize that. When I thought I was happy to admit everything ... I guess it's one of those things that the men don't know but the little girls understand.

From Ecstatic Peace *"cunnilingus issue," ed. Thurston Moore, 2001*

MY NOTEBOOKS

I STARTED KEEPING NOTEBOOKS and journals in 1967, at the age of seventeen, after I left home and came to New York to be a poet. Those pages turned out to be useful, though for a long time I doubted that because, on the rare occasions when I'd look back at them, they seemed mostly full of boring angst and navel-gazing, along with fleeting enthusiasms for this or that, and ideas that were also forgotten as soon as they were recorded. I was still too close to that person to feel much but shame and frustration at his wild fluctuations. I kept at it, though, because I didn't know what else to do with my mind.

The pages held a roughly equal mix of personal experience (journals) and bases for works (notebooks). Actually, even though I advise my daughter now, when she mentions her journals, not to talk about feelings but to report experience, I've come to think about it a little differently. I'm glad I have the full record of what it was like to be that tormentedly young.

Eventually the literary fragments and ephemeral work-ideas came to have value too, even though I hardly ever carried them through directly ("movie: I want to play Roderick Usher"—summer 1974, or "Book: purely commercial collection of photos of disasters"—September 15, 1975). The spectra of scribblings eventually felt evocative enough that I published long stretches of them cold, in their full earnest inspiration

January 20/71

yesterday's identity switch comment
I find my "ability" to identify incredible—even with the vaguest literal
knowledge of some's work like Rimbaud Lawrence & Blake (like in today's
first actual work intimation of it from Blake) & Whitman—I have read somewhat
more of Millers work—or even Celine, Breton and others with slightly
less confidence,—I can be them amazingly & purely—like I am just a mass of
energy plasm on demand (with some right circumstances) in which these ones
can resurrect. A liquidy cloud like Genesis in which these forms appear
pushed up materializing like fish pushing up from the water still moist
and spraying with trickles down their side all as much a part of the fish—
more, his very life—this not usually noticed—the water an inseparable
part of the fish, more than his scales, or exactly equal—an outline drawing
of a fish looking like this—

fish rising from the see   fish rising from the sea
Rimbaud rising from me   Rimbaud rising from me
fucking there   fucking the air

They can arise from me into the air that way, still dripping and sheened
or obscured with "me" but that is inevitable and right bcause in ennabling
them to survive is indistinguishable from the life itself.
In fact occasionally I think just that energy and only manifest myself in
works through these animals inside appearing—though xkxx there are other
stimulus factors—objects, inserted emotions...play on me

Be a Great Metaphysical Pun, Final Paradigman in every channel, HI!

Paradigman

soap opera
so a pop era

(*Artifact*, notebooks 1974-1980, and then *Hot and Cold* which included 1988-1998).

Notebooks, it seems to me sometimes, are the ultimate art form. It's a bit like Borges's idea that, rather than create a book (such as a "collection of photos of disasters"), why not just posit that it exists? The published notebooks can also be seen as a sort of mirror image of that concept, namely that they themselves are fictional: they're like props for a movie or a play about a certain character ("me"), or they are novels themselves (which isn't to say that they aren't honest—on the contrary, they are honest to a fault). But regardless, I love the form of notebooks. Godard's movies are like notebooks, so are Dylan's songs, and Picasso's paintings.

The illustrations here are roughly chronological. Over the years I would cop and save images, too, that caught my eye, and lay them into the notebooks. That enigmatic Blimpie sub wrapper is an example. The marked-up and X-Acto-sliced transparent plastic sheet that comes

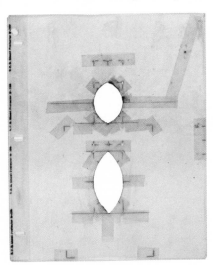

next was a template for use in the creation of a book I did publish, in 1971, called *uh* (subtitled "flip-movie dance alphabet peepshow toy enigma boring book"). It was an alphabet, one large letter per recto (like

(1)

1987 undated miscellany

first a list of (song) titles probably compiled from notes @ time of '85 band

Doomsday
Kiss Yourself Goodbye
I don't Know What to Feel About It
Bye Bye Boredom
Kids With a Con
Stealing for Fun
Cemetary Talk
Self Infliction [pain, "self"]
Who Do You Belong To?
X's for Eyes (Don't Get Y's)
Meet Your Maker
Science
Sleep
Not Stupid Enough
Don't Talk
True to Life
Slumber in the City
Slumber by Number
Forgive Me My Apologies
Glad to Be in Your Past
Take Me There
Get Outta My Dreams
Uncertainty [principle]
Sleepless Nights on Sheets of Paper
Red Noise
Rain Driver
Driving the Rain
Face Eraser
Puberty
Future Cliche
Monoral
Let's Pretend
Clinical Love
True Life Love
The End (Enter) of the World
Adolescent Girl
Mama You Lie
Pills Galore
Phony Grownups
Selling Myself
Don't Fit In
Like Your Sex Expensive?
I Am Worth a Fortune
The Truth Is in the Youth
Nothing is Enough
Nothing is More Than Enough
Saturated City (rain)
Song in a Different "I"
Don't Bug Me
Doin It on Purpose
Look at the Jill
So Good to Say Goodbye
Good Mouth Beats Gun

a flip-movie), reduced to so fundamental a set of curves that it was difficult to distinguish one letter from another. I attributed the book to "Ernie Stomach," which is consistent with the first two illustrations in this piece, written at age nineteen [not shown] and twenty-one, being that they are meditations and manifestoes rejecting the concept of a single identity, but instead affirming one's multiplicity and continuum of selves and that the

whole range of such selves should be cultivated for works (as opposed to the old-fashioned idea of narrowing down to "find your voice").

By late1974 I was focusing my energy more on music than poetry. I would be a professional musician for about ten years. That's illustrated by a page here listing prospective song titles. Then comes a big work intended for the magazine, *Slum Journal,* I was planning in 1978. It was going to be a tabloid, each page of which would work both as a graphic (like a poster) and as intellectual information (words). The face there is Jean-Luc Godard. By the early '80s I did as much drawing in my notepads as writing. That creature with the horizon behind its eyes is an example. Then a few pages of journals, including drawings, from 1986, after I'd retired from music. I started giving occasional poetry readings that year.

Now the selection skips to the late '90s [not shown]. By then the journals were pretty much limited to travel notebooks and graphics

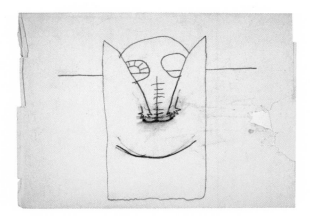

works, because otherwise my daily writing had become channeled into my novels and professional writing assignments.

The present, or recent, era in art is often characterized as the age of collage. Maybe it's seen clearest in painting, from which not only did the original "collage" designation originate, but where the old concept of the "masterpiece" has been superseded by the artist's streams of works

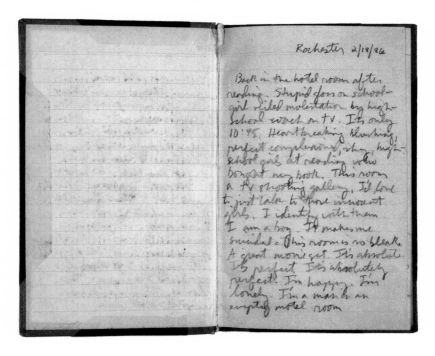

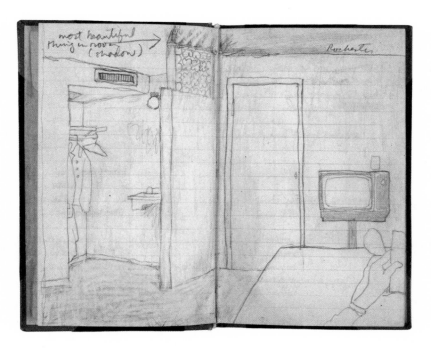

investigating or embodying every passing idea or insight, often gathered in "periods" or in concurrent discrete modes of style. The medium of the notebook inherently represents that mode of artmaking too. Notebooks might be as good as art gets in our time.

From Art Work: Seeing Inside the Creative Process, *ed. Ivan Vartanian (San Francisco: Chronicle Books, 2011)*

JOE BRAINARD: THE WORLD AS NANCY

JOE BRAINARD HAS BECOME legendary, though he's not included in standard narratives of 20th-century art history. Some of the reasons he's not in the conventional canon would be that: he didn't reconceive notions of painting or art the way that, um, say Picasso, Duchamp, Surrealists, Pollock, Warhol, for instance, are considered to have done; he was modest and unassuming and he worked small, more often drawing or making collages or small assemblages than painting in oil; and many of his works are collaborations with poets. The reason he's legendary is that he was an altruistic, reality-enthralled, self-inquisitor of artmaking whose ultimate achievement was himself. You could almost call him a conceptual artist, in the lineage of Duchamp and Smithson, in that his works, as interesting and good-looking as they are in themselves, are in a way merely the byproduct of his real project. For Duchamp and Smithson the real project was thought and ideas, for Brainard the real project was himself (his spiritual development, to call it something way more pretentious than he ever would have), and the happiness of his friends.

Nevertheless, all aspects of Brainard's legend are subordinate to the swoon-inducing, insouciant grace of his pictures. He was almost incapable of making a work not intensely pleasing to look at, and, furthermore, when he wanted, which was often, the works are not only as

cheerful, but as funny as they are lovely. These were ways he could con-
tribute to the happiness of his friends, or anyone who loved how things
look. He probably gave away as many works as he sold, and he tended to
price the rest low so that those who wanted them could have them. This
phenomenon of art made primarily as gift isn't entirely unprecedented
among sophisticated artists—Lewis Carroll, maybe?—but, needless to
say, it's rare (in the West anyway—it's perhaps more common in Bud-
dhist Asia). For Brainard, the commitment to art made in this spirit
contributed to his decision, in 1977, when he was thirty-five, to with-
draw from the art marketplace and cease to show new work. He lived
for seventeen more years, to the age of fifty-two (he was diagnosed with
HIV when he was forty-eight), and continued to make art, but at a reduced pace, and only to give to friends.

(There's another reason that he "retired," one that his closest friends
acknowledge while being uncertain of its importance: that Brainard had
become convinced that he was incapable of painting at the level of those,
such as de Kooning, whom he most admired. This doesn't have to be as
dramatic as it may sound at first: many people decide that they don't actually have the aptitude for carrying out their original vocational dreams.
But the reasons for such a withdrawal in the middle of a successful
career must be complicated or at least subtly mixed, and an equally convincing possibility—that's also a positive way of putting much the same
idea—is beautifully detailed in poet Ron Padgett's *Joe* memoir. It's that
quitting art followed from Brainard's values, his devotion to honesty,
clarity, simplicity and humility. Joe didn't have any big statements to
make and he didn't like the confining, confusing "public image" world of
the art market, so he just shook it all off and dropped out.)

The *If Nancy Was* works, nearly all of which were made in 1972, are
Brainard at his funniest. One sees in them his felicity as a draftsman,
his color sense and impeccable design sense, but mostly they're hilarious. (Incidentally, the twenty pictures exist as a group because
they were originally given by the artist to Fischbach Gallery's Beverly Zagor for not more than $20 each when, in the early 1970s, she
expressed her admiration for the lot but wouldn't accept them as a

SANTO NIÑO DE PRAGA

IF NANCY WAS THE SANTO NINO DE PRAGA.

present.) Joe was gay and these pictures are camp in their wit and care-free mockery, but Joe's version, unlike much camp, is malice free, as he himself was. Joe had admired Ernie Bushmiller's "Nancy" comic strip for its breezy clean style, forever, and had incorporated Nancy into works since 1963. One would guess that he had to have been aware of the "Nancy-boy" (queer) extrapolation to be made from this series (though there appears to be no record of his ever having referred to it, as there is none for that possible extra dimension to his fondness for painting pansies).

The pictures speak for themselves. The one thing I'd add is that it's fun to read them as Joe's world—Nancy being his stand-in or persona and the list of her incarnations being a representative sample of, a list that adequately evokes, the whole world. So, with the inclusion of the seven other known *If Nancy Was* works, that would make Joe's description of the world read like this:

> Art Nouveau, ashtrays, acting in porn movies, baby André Breton, Bright's Disease, underground comic book characters frenziedly masturbating, interior decorators, de Kooning paintings, having knowledge of the meaning of wearing green and yellow on Thursdays, old Kleenexes, Larry Rivers drawings, New York City buildings, being rich, heads on Mt. Rushmore, sailors' baskets, the Santo Niño de Praga, sexy blondes, national heroes' faces on stamps, balls, boys, drawings by Leonardo da Vinci, opening one's mouth so wide one falls in, acid freaks, terrible diseases, afro hairdos, and poets.

Or, to put it another way: Nancy is the constant, the immortal essence—everything else is costume. All the world is Nancy in drag.

From Art at Colby: Celebrating the Fiftieth Anniversary of the Colby College Museum of Art *exhibition catalogue (Waterville: Colby College Museum of Art, 2009)*

ARAM SAROYAN'S *COMPLETE MINIMAL POEMS*

THIS BOOK COLLECTS nearly all the poems Aram Saroyan wrote in the 1960s, when he was in his early twenties and, as he put it, "the only person available at a typewriter who didn't have some predetermined use in mind for it." The resulting pages, tapped in Aram Saroyan by his typewriter, were succinct. Saroyan was the master of the one-word poem. But his works were as musical and meaningful as more conventional poetry, too, and a lot more amusing. The minimal poems were eye openers, ear openers and mind openers, and no one else was doing anything much like them at the time, and no one has since.

Granted—as Saroyan has—he was smoking a lot of grass at the time. But every second person in the United States was, and is, on something or other often enough. The weed factor is interesting because: 1) it's typical of the era, always an interesting dimension of art; 2) one realizes it couldn't be an unfair advantage, since no one else wrote like he did; and 3) the reader's knowledge of it confers a nice extra little psychedelic ting to the pages.

Saroyan and his poetic cohort mostly lived in New York, and it was an exhilarating time for poetry—one of those extended moments, like the advent of Cubism in Paris or rockabilly in Memphis, where the artists who got it could do no wrong. Even the least writers of this

Second-Generation New York School, as it's sometimes called, were gorgeous and exciting for a while there, in the general vicinity of the St. Mark's Church Poetry Project circa 1966-71. Most of this material appeared in mimeographed pamphlets, but for a short time some of the wildest books were brought out by uptown commercial publishers too. Holt, Rinehart & Winston published Ron Padgett's starry, blue *Great Balls of Fire* (1969), and Ted Berrigan's *Sonnets* (1964) went into a second printing at Grove. Clark Coolidge's *Space* (1970)—he treated words somewhat similarly to the way Saroyan did, but more abstractly— was published by Harper & Row. Saroyan's 1968 volume *Aram Saroyan* was published by Random House. Its format was a nearly full-size representation of its contents as they would have been in typescript (or mimeograph), in the classic Courier typeface, looking unevenly inked, printed on one leaf-side each, for a total sheaf of only thirty poems. The book could be read in two minutes or so (as it was, aloud, by Edwin Newman on the "NBC Evening News" in New York), but one could look for a long time at its pages as well, repeatedly, and with great interest and pleasure.

Some of Saroyan's poems could only be looked at; they couldn't be pronounced:

lighght

(Jesse Helms would use "lighght" to mock the National Endowment for the Arts after Saroyan won a cash award for it.)

Some of Saroyan's other poems were about real-life phenomena made of words, so to speak, like the Joycean

whistling in the street a car turning in the room ticking

Others were more about the effects of the sounds of the words, as well as their appearance (similar sounding words tending also to look alike), tangled up with their denotations:

My arms are warm
Aram Saroyan

You could feel him in a room at his typewriter, like a monkey or a cat with a little extra brainpower.

Saroyan was known as a "concrete poet"—that is, he was writing poems meant to be looked at as much as read. Concrete poems aimed to be things as well as words, and they used all the resources of the alphanumeric page (or slab of stone, as Ian Hamilton Finlay did, or poster or other medium) rather than being merely linguistic expression of preexisting ideas or perceptions. All interesting poems do this to a degree, poetry being a recognition that consciousness is made of language, but concrete poems are an extreme example, which accounts for a substantial part of their poetic pedigree (and high-class license).

The back cover of Saroyan's second Random House book, *Pages* (1969) carried this author's note: "I write on a typewriter, almost never in hand (I can hardly handwrite, I tend to draw words), and my machine—an obsolete red-top Royal Portable—is the biggest influence on my work. This red hood holds the mood, keeps my eye happy. The typeface is a standard pica; if it were another style I'd write (subtly) different poems. And when a ribbon gets dull my poems I'm sure change."

Saroyan is more literary, though, than the label "concrete poet" might suggest. His ear is as sensitive and pleasure-hungry as his eye, as can be heard in that "This red hood holds the mood, keeps my eye happy," which is practically pornographic. His sensuality isn't obscene, though. It's clean and open and cheerful. His literary forebears were the rugged, unpretentious and openhearted Black Mountain poets and the Beats of the '50s, specifically Robert Creeley and Jack Kerouac. And as Saroyan has often described, he was a child of the '60s, with those values of community and peace and love. He's written, in fact, that the disillusionments of 1968—Vietnam, the murders of Martin Luther King and

Robert Kennedy—had a lot to do with why he stopped writing for the subsequent five years, and why he permanently dropped his minimal mode, which he associated with the innocent spirit of pre-'68. (He's also written that he'd simply exhausted that aesthetic for himself). The minimal poems are not just whimsical '60s trippiness. They're much more than novelties. This beautifully designed collection contains a poetry that shivers with itself, like something just born. Anyone interested in art made from words should have it.

From the New York Times, *2008*

THE HAPPY NIGHTMARE OF THE VISUAL

CHRISTOPHER WOOL'S PAINTINGS make me a little nervous. They seem impassive, they seem self-sufficient, they seem aloof, or at least indifferent to one's approaches, like a tree, or a corpse, maybe (cold and grey too). What's more alive than a corpse, though, from the point of view of a connoisseur? Nothing. There's nothing like a beautiful corpse, *nature morte*, to fascinate a person and stimulate meditation. I know Christopher insists on the strictly "visual" nature of his paintings—in particular the paintings in this show. But they provoke thought nevertheless. He also uses "alive" as the height of praise for the paintings of others he loves most. So maybe I shouldn't say "corpse," even just for dramatic effect, or to be a wiseguy. Obviously the word has negative connotations, but all is vanity, and furthermore nothing is truly dead except to the dead themselves. If we want to refer to how Christopher has said "no" to so many possibilities of painting (color, the sensual and homey hand-made-ness of the brush, representational reference . . .) maybe instead we could compare his paintings to movie stars, those drastically drained but beautiful and thought-provoking simulacra of soul, whom we know, but don't. Goddamn it, I'm sure I'm making Christopher mad now, but I will get to how purely and unequivocally tremendous his paintings are, before this is done, too. I'm a writer though, this is writing; all I can do is write! The main thing that separates Christopher's paintings from gorgeous corpses is that the paintings don't decay—on the contrary, they flourish. They grow and mutate and behave musically, as fully as one could hope from technically inert material, in the viewer's mind. (Then again, any "decay" is the flourishing of something else: energy is conserved . . .)

Christopher's pictures feel like paintings of paintings. They feel obstinately, aggressively a remove away, the way Andy Warhol or Richard Prince have been known to seem, while at the same time they feel hard won—strict chunks of physical interest wrested at pains from the scant areas available, as things have seemed for such as Jackson Pollock or Richard Serra. In a real way, all nonrepresentational painting is painting about painting (though of course Pollock—Wool's first master—in choosing not to paint from nature, intended to paint *as* nature). It could be said that Wool takes that a level further—paintings of paintings— while still making paintings *as* paintings. Wool's way with this can feel angry and mocking, defiant, almost resentful of the viewer's expectations. This, like the works' willful reduction of means, is something they have in common with punk music. But the mockery has another side too, arising from the pictures' flaunted remove, their apparent casualness: could they be exploiting our insecurity and vanity and goodwill? That of course is the argument that negatively has defined avante-garde art from Impressionism through yesterday: "A child could have done it." Sophisticated art critics of Wool typically base their skepticism regarding him on a slightly more complex twist to that same objection: they suspect that his success stems from underlying art-collector insecurity and philistinism that is comforted by the way his paintings might be read as providing great "great new painting" rather than great new painting.

Christopher's paintings do take place in a different area of the brain than other people's paintings, in a few different ways, which contributes to what makes them so good. At the same time that they provide foremost that "retinal" or sensual pleasure, they give the above-referenced appearance of proposing themselves self-consciously in a way that punkishly, maybe a little petulantly, endearingly boyishly, chip on shoulder, defies the viewer to doubt their legitimacy. Who knows how that apparent stance of theirs will shift in the future? Maybe the Wool paintings' "this is a good

painting whatever the fuck you think" attitude will eventually be lost or come to read as something else. But now it's still strong and appealing, and, because of the famous way an artwork wins any possibility of remaining interesting by the depth of its fidelity to its own original moment and place, chances are these pictures will keep their power to annoy and infuriate (like Matisse!) along with their elegance and intelligence.

It's interesting how paintings not only change over time, but are revealed and enriched by their position in the context of their author's body of work. The decisively "visual" mode of the paintings in this show coaxes from their surfaces that feature in Wool's earlier ones, such as, say, the word paintings or the patterned-roller paintings, that might have read more "conceptually" before. In this show's works, Wool is reveling in the thoughtless eye's dimension. "You could almost say I'm picturing something in a nightmare, or a dream . . . You know how nightmares can be so unbelievably powerful without really being about anything? Sometimes I have these terrible nightmares and I wake up and Charline asks, 'Well what were you dreaming?' And I was sitting in the park and there was something—it was the scariest thing that ever could have happened. But nothing happened." Rather than pulling the wool over our eyes, he is taking it aside and doing things to it, and doing other things to it, and then stamping that up against the wall for the eye's ecstatic enjoyment (transcendent Wool gathering).

Everyone knows how the human eye searches for its home, the human face (and figure), in everything it sees. Nonrepresentational painting has to be really abstract to foil that tendency. But even devoid of all hint of the figurative, a painting has a personality—it has a personal style and a character just as faces do, but more truly, since a painting is purely surface (even if it's a roiled, convoluted, surface providing some illusion of depth) and so by definition is faithful to its perceived "personality." Christopher's paintings have movie star faces, once removed: faces like stills of movie stars. Faces effect much subliminally by their expressions in pure repose, even the most classically beautiful—which one might expect to be uniform or bland—as perfectly exemplified by movie star stills: Joan Crawford is always angry, Renee Zellweger concerned and innocent, Meryl Streep exalted. These paintings are stills of a star (who resembles cloudscapes and stained driveways and smeared sheets of anonymously asserted existence) in whom we recognize serenity, delicacy, wit, spontaneity, and an all-encompassing power that is lighter than air. They're positively funny in places, a little whimsical, and always chic, like Audrey Hepburn (frowning perhaps) (or what if she agreed

to do *The Paris Hilton Story*?). They are stars who maintain their dignity without sacrificing naturalness. We recognize that they refuse to give us much except for their beauty and the behavior they depict when called on to exhibit it for their audience. We respect that.

I more than respect that, I am exhilarated by it, if a little ashamed to have strayed so far from the paintings' true ground: the two-dimensional field wherein Christopher has disposed and disported some proposi-tions as being worthy of one's eye's capacity. Everyone knows the Redon drawing of the Eye-Balloon (or its etched version *The Eye Like a Strange Balloon Mounts Toward Infinity*), wherein a giant eye, floating as a light-er-than-air balloon, iris pointed skyward, carries in its suspended basket a disembodied head. Maybe Christopher has painted here what that balloon eye, rolled upward, sees. Oops, I've done it again. Frightmare. Please enjoy the pictures is what I want to say. They are so great looking.

From Christopher Wool show catalogue (Los Angeles: Gagosian Gallery, 2006)

WHAT I WOULD SAY IF I WERE
Christopher Wool

I DON'T WANT MY WORK to feel all sweat-soaked and tortured. I'd like to be like a crooner, effortless seeming, smooth. That doesn't mean it actually is easy. And it doesn't mean you don't have backbone, or even aggression. Like Frank Sinatra. Or Miles Davis, maybe. It's like magic. I want my things to just appear. Not be painted. Just appear. And that is scary, too. It's not magic like Tinker Bell. It's more like the writing on the wall.

Why do I sometimes leave empty space at the bottom of the word paintings I make? It's a question. It's like the huge margins in old illuminated manuscripts, or early printing. That's where the commentary goes, the reader's reactions. Or like the silence in the room after something unexpectedly emphatic has been said. It's the pause for the laugh. But really, you answered your own question. It's the Q & A after the lecture. It's the gutter for the runoff. I'm starting to feel like Cole Porter—it's a Bendel bonnet, a Shakespeare sonnet, it's Mickey Mouse. It's a kind of respect for the viewers. You want to give them a moment to compose themselves. To absorb what just happened. Between you and me, it's more technical. I like things "off-register." I like to disrespect the boundaries, the edges of the surface, and let things trespass or ignore them. So the picture, and the markings, are not hemmed in, not so defined.

One thing that can work is to take one idea, one quirk, or technique, you've noticed in someone else's work, and make a series of paintings exploiting that, using it as a starting point and exaggerating it, or exploring it. Sometimes I see the starting point in the world, or sometimes in my own work. Why not? No one ever knows about any of it unless you tell them. Or maybe they do, but it's legitimate. Like what the Cubists did with Cézanne. Sometimes it's all a kind of exciting fashion game. That offends some people. They think it's disgusting. But everything you do in life is a kind of game. Nobody really understands anything. The only reason to go on is because you're interested in the course of the game. You want to see what's going to happen next, and possibly try to influence it. Or at least play your cards.

In addition to all that, or despite it, there is so much of interest in the world. You almost have to filter a lot of it out. You do have to filter it out. Or anyway be attuned to the things of interest that are currently being neglected. In a way art is nothing but that: the drawing of attention to interesting things in the world that no one seems to be noticing at that moment. That's your "style," your "character," your individuality as an artist: what things you can see as interesting that are being overlooked, that you can bring to attention. And if you're lucky enough to succeed, you not only make some good paintings, but you've literally enlarged the world a little bit, or slightly altered it. Andy Warhol, for instance, made grainy newspaper photographs—the kind we were surrounded by all the time—beautiful, so that suddenly everybody in the country was newly surrounded with beauty every day. Because they were surrounded by smudgy newspapers.

Then again, even though I don't think about it as such, I can't deny that I am aware that the paintings are about how "beauty" might be completely abstracted, separated from all the world, and completely empty of everything, even prettiness, or you could say, even beauty. For painters like me, the visual is a condition of its own, separate from thought at all, which is kind of frightening, too, like ghosts, like hallucinations. But "beauty is the beginning of terror," they say. I actually don't like the word "beauty" at all. "Beauty" is something that should be seen and not heard.

From Whitewall *magazine, 2007*

FILM COLUMN:
Eternal Sunshine of the Spotless Mind

director: Michel Gondry; script: Charlie Kaufman; cinematography: Ellen Kuras; cast: Jim Carrey, Kate Winslet, Kirsten Dunst, Tom Wilkinson, Elijah Wood, Mark Ruffalo, David Cross

THE HYPE ABOUT CHARLIE KAUFMAN'S mind-blowing scripts has kind of put me off. There've been four filmed in the five years prior to this one: *Being John Malkovich, Human Nature, Confessions of a Dangerous Mind*, and *Adaptation*. His high-concept mind-mixed-with-"reality" stories are not as shockingly original as they're sometimes made out to be. I know he himself would acknowledge this because he's copped to a weakness for 20th century writers who've explored a lot of that territory— Stanislaw Lem (author of *Solaris*) and Kafka (whose most famous work of course is about a man who wakes up as an insect) and Philip K. Dick (source of *Blade Runner* and *Total Recall* and *Paycheck*, etc.), for instance. Kaufman's self-consciousness, carried to neurotic extremes of self-reference in *Adaptation*, is also common in literature (and in adventurous film-making like Fellini's *8 ½*, and nearly all of Godard).

But as I say, Kaufman shouldn't be held responsible for the inflated claims of his wildest enthusiasts. And the last couple of his movies have made me a believer. The guy has really got balls for one thing, as full of self-doubt as he keeps reminding us he is. Courage is often what sets the first-rate apart. You've got to be willing to trust your instincts and go past the frontiers of convention, not faltering, even when the convention becomes "going beyond convention" and you find yourself feeling morally obliged to go beyond the convention of "going beyond convention," and then beyond even that and in fact do falter and then push through that and maybe make a complete fool of yourself. Another thing that separates Kaufman from the rest is that most of the other recent mind/reality-meld movies use their premises (What if you were to find out you were not human but a machine? What if "reality" was actually a creation manipulated by unknown outsiders?) in the service of typical mystery/suspense/thriller shoot-em-ups, while Kaufman's scripts are about confused and complicated real people getting exposed in the course of the conceptual switchbacks. And of course he's funny too and I'll get to that in a minute. Granted, the movies have dull spots, and irritating ones, and logic-holes, but that's almost inevitable when you're working on the edge. It's worth it, and the possibility also remains that at some future viewing one of the dull spots could turn out to be brilliant.

Eternal Sunshine is Michel Gondry's second film. The first was the excruciating *Human Nature*. He was a music video whiz (as was Spike Jonze, whose first two movies were also written by Kaufman). Gondry made the amazing White Stripes Lego clip ("Fell in Love With a Girl") and their "Hardest Button to Button" (where each beat creates another identical drumkit/amp/mic across the landscape) as well as lots of famous Bjork extravaganzas. Music videos are basically ads and they tend to be decoratively flashy and slick, even when straining to be "dark" like the obscene David Fincher, but Gondry is well suited to direct *The Eternal Sunshine of the Spotless Mind*. His videos are full of loops and multiplications and people sleeping and vehicles, all of which figure strongly in this flick. In fact the Kaufmanesque original idea for the film was actually Gondry's. It concerns a guy, Joel Barish (Jim Carrey), whose relationship with his girlfriend, Clementine Kruczynski (Kate Winslet), has been disintegrating when he discovers that it's worse than he realized: she has undergone a procedure to have him him erased from her mind. This pains Joel so much that he resolves to do the same, but during the process he realizes that despite everything he doesn't want to forget her. Most of the movie is spent in his mind as we trace back his memories of her and he starts trying to hang on to her by hiding her in unlikely recollections where the professional memory-removers won't know to look.

I'm way into Jim Carrey. I've liked him since *Ace Ventura*, *Dumb and Dumber*, and *The Mask*—his amazing triple-stage 1994 star-birth—up through the transcendent *Cable Guy* (thank you, Ben Stiller). He's made a few dubious flicks since but he's genius for sure. In this movie he does his insecure "little guy" schtick, a whole lot of which is terrible posture, and it works OK. It's not what you most hope for from him, and it can seem unreal because so much of him says "over-the-top comic star," but you're still happy to watch him.

Kate Winslet is ravishing. I boycotted *Titanic* and have somehow, possibly defensively—she's so attractive it hurts—stayed out of her way otherwise. What a girl. That smile kills me, the way it looks almost like a grimace at first and then apologetic and then vulnerable, and then heart-breaking, stretched there *au naturel* across her super-pale but orgasmi-cally flushed face. Again, the only problem is that she's a bit too appealing for the role. Here I blame the filmmakers: there's not enough story info to make her supposedly tawdry, self-hating, personality believable. It's like she's an angelically radiant, smart, spontaneous Kate Winslet going around with a placard hanging from her neck that reads "alcoholic slut."

As I was saying, Kaufman scripts are funny too and a lot of the humor comes from how imaginative and perceptive he is in how he plays out his trippy premises. Gondry is good at executing this stuff. Music videos are ideal training grounds for ways of expressing in imagery states of consciousness and emotions. For instance probably my favorite passages of *Sunshine* are the bizarre, ecstatic scenes of Joel sneaking Clemen-tine into his childhood. There's this one where he's an eighteen-inch tall infant (Carrey and big furniture) playing beneath the table in the bright idyllic '60s kitchen where his young mother is puttering around and then there's Kate Winslet too, the same age as his mother is, and full size, but she has her punkette day-glo streaked hair, and she's so thrilled to find herself there and she's so desireable and she lifts up the front of her skirt for little Jim! That scene is practically worth the price of ad-mission. The film works. It's good. It moved me and I didn't expect that.

BlackBook *film column #1, Spring 2004*

FILM COLUMN:
Tarnation

director: Jonathan Caouette; script: Jonathan Caouette; cinematography: Jonathan Caouette; cast: Jonathan Caouette, Renee LeBlanc, David Sanin Paz, Rosemary Davis, Adolph Davis

WHAT DO GAYNESS, YOUTH, WIDE-OPEN SEX, poverty, mental problems, despair, cruelty, silly drama, and cheesy pop culture have in common? Besides inherent fascination . . . No maybe it *is* simply inherent fascination: the allure that creates the market for exploitation tabloids. Because there is definitely a kind of tabloid, sensationalist, element in the pleasure to be found in the small quasi-genre of films from the last fifteen or twenty years I'm thinking of, the content of which more or less corresponds to the above list. But these films I'm thinking of are also among the most interesting films being made these days, whatever their sensational subject matter may or may not have to do with it. Other qualities they share are that they're usually played by non-actors and are made extremely cheaply. Harmony Korine's *Gummo* (1997) is the archetypal masterpiece of the trend, but that's a dumb thing to say. These movies don't derive from *Gummo*—they just have certain things in common with it, and *Gummo* is the most bountiful of them so far. Some films that qualify preceded *Gummo* too, for instance Todd Haynes's amazing *Superstar: the Karen Carpenter Story* (1987) in which the non-actor performers are actually Ken and Barbie dolls. The original examples would probably be Andy Warhol's movies and maybe Jack Smith's—even Robert Bresson, at a certain remove (John Waters is too much satire though his heart's in the right place).

The film that set off these thoughts is *Tarnation*, a movie cooked up by thirty-year-old Jonathan Caouette from his collection of mostly home-produced media, reaching back to the first videos he shot at the age of nine in Houston, where he grew up, and earlier than that for snapshots and imagery copped from mass culture, and extending, through answering-machine tapes and pop music clips, up to digital video, including some "reenactments" of moments in his life, shot recently in the Queens apartment where he now lives. The movie was constructed by feeding that raw data into his boyfriend's Macintosh computer and manipulating it with the Apple iMovie editing and special-effects software that comes free on most Macs. The press release lists the budget for the film at $218. (This figure doesn't include the multi-thousand dollar cost of getting the computer's Mac-burnt DVD version converted into projectable 35 mm film, or the expensive rights to songs he uses on the soundtrack, or the expenses across decades of accumulating the personal archive, but it's a valid way of describing the cost of making the film.) The movie is billed as a documentary, but it reads more like a diary or self-portrait or memoir, though the director refers to himself in the third person in his voiceover. It's the revery of his own life by a person who grew up unsupervised, a small-child witness to his mother's rape, abandoned to foster care, reclaimed, abused, and gay in Texas, never knowing his father, and whose glamorous heartbreaking mom was deranged, largely as a result of the countless shock treatments she received as a child with the approval of *her* parents . . . The kid/filmmaker himself ends up with what he describes as "depersonalization disorder, which is defined as a feeling of disconnection from the body and a constant state of unreality," though I'll be so presumptuous as to say that he doesn't seem crazier to me than half the people I've known. And the film is not merely squalid or melodramatic— it's smart and pretty and fast. One thing for sure is that Caouette is a born filmmaker, as well as a born actor.

Those clips he uses aren't ordinary home movies of course. Then again maybe they are, in the same sense that part of what's so interesting and satisfying about the films I'm talking about is, wait . . . I'm tired of saying "the films I'm talking about"—can I come up with a name? . . . I'll call

them . . . Candy Acid . . . Candy Asséd . . . *Candy Assid* movies. Part of
what's so interesting about the Candy Assid movies is that they depict
what is actually the real present, the real America, the America of junk-
strewn tract houses and cheap motels and PCP and crank and psyche-
delicly unhinged sex and nonstop television and franchise businesses and
sudden violence and bad health. And they give us that as an environment,
not a "subject." They are exciting, colorful, and often funny. Sublime, as
well as boring sometimes, but that's because they're about real life. I'd
count Bruno Dumont's *Twenty-Nine Palms* as Candy Assid too, and it's
neither gay nor especially coming from trash culture, but is boring in the
most compelling way. The leads don't "act," and hardly anything happens,
though the mundane settings look glorious. There are gas stations and
motels. The movie is unmitigated life. People are not especially attractive
and they don't understand each other but still they want to fuck as much
as possible, and then suddenly it's over in the most definitive fashion.
Twenty-Nine Palms is the movie of these most clearly descended from
Bresson, who was the original genius of the non-actor in poor everyday
situations shown sublime.

Gus Van Sant's *Elephant* is another Candy Assid high achievement,
and in fact Van Sant came onto the production team of *Tarnation* once
it was made, as "executive producer" to help get it attention and distri-
bution. There are real-life scenes in the movie unique in film history.
For instance a sequence Caouette shot when he was eleven years old,
with a stationary video camera alone in his room, of himself uncannily embodying a distraught female hillbilly testifying, as she nervously
tugs at a forelock, that, to start off, "Jimmy says when I wear too much
makeup it makes me look like a whore . . ." I asked the director about
this, and he told me he was imitating his mother whose second husband had been beating her up. The sequence ends with eleven-year-old
Jonathan-as-Renee lisping stone-coldly, "I blew his ass away." Caouette
tells me he'd also been watching earlier that day (twenty years ago) an
episode of *Bionic Woman* that featured Lindsay Wagner imprisoned and
that Lindsay Wagner had always reminded him of his mother, and that
that contributed to the scene, and that furthermore later the same night

he'd seen a PBS broadcast of *For Colored Girls Who Have Considered Suicide/When the Rainbow Is Enuf* with Alfre Woodard and he probably stole some ideas from that. So we have an eleven-year-old boy in drag filming himself acting his hysterical mother using inspiration from "Bionic Woman" and Ntozake Shange. The whole movie is as trippy and chilling and endearing as that. And his pre-adolescent acting is the equal of Brando. But the main thing is that the movie feels like everybody's real life. In this time and place, as in most other times and places, people's actual lives are as screwy as these movies. It's only the really perverse people in the ad agencies and political campaigns and bible groups who try to pretend otherwise. And this is just five minutes of the movie I'm talking about. Just as significant are the moody, gorgeous montages cut to snatches of evocative pop music that alternate with what Caouette calls the "verité." The film is a knockout. If it plays anywhere near you, you should go see it. (Then make one yourself.)

BlackBook *film column #3, Fall 2004*

ARIANA REINES'S *COEUR DE LION*
and *Mercury*

ARIANA REINES, NOW THIRTY, has a curriculum vitae that could make her look like a star of academia. She graduated summa cum laude from Barnard and then studied with the most rarefied, radical philosophers and literary theorists at Columbia and at the European Graduate School in Switzerland. She has translated two books from the French for *Semiotext(e)*, as well as Baudelaire's *My Heart Laid Bare* for her own tiny Mal-O-Mar press. In 2009 she was the youngest ever Roberta C. Holloway Lecturer in Poetry at UC Berkeley. Her first book of poems was *The Cow* (2006), followed by the two reviewed here, and she's the author of a play, *Telephone*, inspired by Avital Ronell's extravagantly intellectual prose and graphics treatise extrapolating schizophrenia and modern culture from telephone technology, *The Telephone Book*, which Reines play awed reviewers and won two Obies in 2009. She is interested in and has studied performance, and is an irresistible, waifish, wisecracking public impresario of her poems. She's discussed endlessly on the Web. Whatever all that might suggest, her heart truly is in the gutter with the filthy and distraught and impossible and she's one notch above a bag lady herself, literally. She is about nothing but poetry—poetry and decency, probably in that order.

Coeur de Lion, originally published in 2007, is a long poem-series written in a confessional mode, intentionally blog-like, in which the author kisses off a boyfriend whose love letters to another girl Reines has found by hacking into his e-mail account.

> This morning you wrote
> Back to me. You said that
> What really fucking pissed
> You off was that I seemed
> To have made a "whole project"
> Out of reading your emails
> And that I ran through the whole
> Devastating thing with "relish."
> It's true, I did make a project
> Out of it. Right now
> I'm listening to Stevie Wonder
> Sing "Ma Cherie Amour." I fucking
> Love Stevie Wonder. I could fall
> In love with him a hundred times.
> I know what he means when he says
> La La La La La La.

Reines, riffing on themes of *Coeur*, expanded, "There's also the kind of creaturely smegma of living in your imagination and feeling that nothing human is foreign to you, that you can veer into all kinds of creepy territory." "What is smegma exactly?" this reviewer, uncertain, inquired. She replied, "I have no idea. . . . Is it an ooze, like pus?" According to dictionary.com, smegma is "a thick, cheeselike, sebaceous secretion that collects beneath the foreskin or around the clitoris." Which Reines would love because cheeses (not to mention genitalia) play an important role in *Coeur de Lion*, for one because the title signifies a brand of cheap Camembert—along with, of course, King Richard Lionheart, whom she annexes in the book for his mixture of aspirations to the literary and his Jew-killing (Reines is Jewish and her mother's parents survived the Holocaust in Poland)—but also because it's Swiss cheese that, in the book, her literarily aspiring, borderline anti-Semitic boyfriend says her pussy smells like (in a good way).

The book's material is daily life treated without restraint, like the gossip and chatter of self-dramatizing students, or a brainy seducer free-associating into your ear at a party—but it keeps digging down and veering off and adding up until it's profound. It's practically novel-istic in the fullness of its portrait of this nerdy but sexually uninhibited couple in their smegma of other recent lovers, classes with Alain Badiou and A. Ronell, vacations in Venice financed by parents or student loans, fucking in the woods, references to Stefan Zweig, Rimbaud, Nabokov, Leonard Cohen, Arthur Russell, etc., insecurity and fear, pussy licking and cock sucking, ego and bravado, evocations of true horror and suf-fering, as for instance of the poet's mother, who has pretty much lost her mind and wanders the streets penniless . . . And it is all real, it's the truth, and you're touched and inspired by Ariana Reines, and it goes the ultimate dimension and is poetry.

The new book, *Mercury*, is longer, more complex, and in ways more ambitious than the two previous, though consistent with them. Reines likes to let a metaphor emerge as an organizing principle to charac-terize and partially generate each book, and make that literal by using it as the book's title. *The Cow* could be seen as interior, personal. Reines is a once and future vegetarian (as cows are ruminative grazers, and in being slaughterhouse victims a whole other pertinent symbol), and she's obsessed with the identity of her biological, cultural gender ("cow" also being specifically female, etc.). The book is also "interior" for con-taining some of her most beautifully musical/abstract poetry: "A gelid streak of apple goo a purl of it I peel away from me and eat. // I know that really beautiful women are never alone. // Their intelligence curls up like a fist in them and sweetens the shutter on their clits." *Coeur de Lion*, with that title's associations, is about personal relationships. Mercury refers to the metal, of course—quicksilver—obviously potent metaphorically; and to alchemy, which in a way is rooted in metaphor, being an attempt to link material substances with spiritual ones; and the planet and the god. *Mercury* is about everything interlinked, the universe. It's still gritty and first-person, but it's the "Aria" in "Ariana," it's 239 pages into infinity, on winged heels and a prayer. "Aria" is the book's first poem (Wednesday, as well, is Mercury's day—Mercredi—in French):

> It is Wednesday
> I don't know who I am.
> How did I get here? I don't know.
> That's a lie.
> Not totally.
> It keeps me empty
> Just empty enough
> for you to enter me

On both the page and at the podium, the art of Ariana Reines is, in a way, charisma. It's perfection, but not flawlessness—rather grace and shamelessness. The works are riveting at baseline, but they also ray and reverberate with each lovely, funny recovery from, each redeeming transformation of, an endless series of errors. It's alchemy achieved, and so vital as to exemplify poetry today in its guttural full glory.

From Bookforum, *2012*

ROBERT CREELEY'S *IF I WERE WRITING THIS*

WHAT STRIKES ONE FIRST about *If I were writing this* is that it's a death-conscious view from advanced years; the poet is seventy-seven. But more importantly, the poems feel material, as if they were born of physics and acts of chance rather than a person's thought processes. They seem to be as much written by language itself as by a person, while still making interesting and useful sense. It's a strange phenomenon, as if the rain caught in a door screen formed legible glyphs, or like some kind of stage magic that no one can explain. Creeley's sleeves are rolled up, he uses nothing but his hands making simple motions in a closed empty room. Where did that *pic vert* (or *pic noir*) come from?

> Have we told you all you'd thought to know?
> Is it really so quickly now the time to go?
> Has anything happened you will not forget?
> Is where you are enough for all to share?
>
> Is wisdom just an empty word?
> Is age a time one might finally well have missed?
> Must humanness be its own reward?
> Is happiness this?

How could those unremarkable, almost banal, lines add up to something so moving and heartening? It reminds me of when I saw Iggy Pop, who's as old for rock and roll—fifty-seven or so—as Creeley is for poetry, last year doing his incomparable one- and two-chord Stooges songs, shirtless, all defined veiny muscles, dancing furiously the whole set, and shouting between numbers, "You make me so happy! *I am you*! I am you." In fact Creeley has a poem in this book called "For You" which goes in its entirety, "At the edge, fledgling, / hypocrite reader, *mon frere*, / *mon semblable*, there / you are me?" The "hypocrite reader" and the French are taken right from Baudelaire's "To the Reader." Everyone is everyone!

Or at least the artist and a receptive audience are one. Baudelaire is taunting us with this complicity of author and reader, while Creeley, like a fledgling of the abyss, is more tentatively positing unity. With Iggy it's the music that's merging us. But in fact it's music that's at work in Creeley too. That's what puts the "fledgling" at the "edge." There'd be no "fledgling" if there were no "edge." That's the magic he's working: surrender to music. Try to count all the rhymes and half-rhymes and rhythm-turns and recurring consonants winding like an unpaved road through a virgin landscape in the stanzas above. He's good enough to let the landscape do the driving.

Creeley started off as a poet angry and aggressive and ambitious, back at the very end of the '40s. His compadre Charles Olson asserted their credo in Olson's famous manifesto "Projective Verse" (1950) that included Creeley's high-decibel pronouncement, "FORM IS NEVER MORE THAN AN EXTENSION OF CONTENT," and together the two of them disseminated their ideas at Black Mountain College, where in the early '50s Olson was rector and Creeley edited the influential *Black Mountain Review* as well as taught. Creeley doesn't need to shout any more. In fact he said in his 1988 *Autobiography*, "Now I might say equally, 'Content is never more than an extension of form.'" And Projectivism's aims now seem less exceptional than typical of the era, sharing values with the Beats and New York Poets as well as action painting and bebop jazz. The polemic and campaigning fall away, and what's left is a few poets and some poems. (Which isn't to say that the Projectivist pair's efforts weren't fruitful. The recent publication of the smart, comprehensive *Black Mountain College: Experiment in Art* is sumptuous evidence of their inspirational force.)

Creeley has always used words to make spaces between them to look through, and has made poems that are charged objects as much as messages. This focus on words at their most material level, where they're like irregular masses inspected in the light, to be arranged in sculptural constructions, was a big influence on the "concrete" poets of the '60s and '70s. An example of this kind of poem from Creeley is, say, "Here" (ca. 1974), which goes: "Here is / where there / is." (Forgive me for remarking how such enigmatically oracular poems always seem stoned to me too.) He still writes poems that feel like certainties struck from the entirely uncertain, that teeter on the edge of sense while being indisputable, but now they're more complex and explicit:

If it's there, it's something—
And when you see it,
Not just your eyes know it.
It's yourself, like they say, you bring.

These words, these seemingly rounded
Forms—looks like a pear? Is yellow?
Where's that to be found—
In some abounding meadow?

The Creeley who promoted his literary values so hard for so long when he was young has come to attribute nearly everything he's achieved to chance, and even his very possession of a life—that has any more palpable existence than "echoes," "a sense of shadow," and the "comforting poignancy of old affections"—to (charmingly, strangely) having written it. "It is the pleasure and authority of writing that it invents a life to live in the first place."

Creeley's poetry is now at a tremendous peak.

From Bookforum, *2004*

JIM CARROLL MEMORIAL REMARKS

I FIRST KNEW OF JIM when I was eighteen, which was when he was eighteen, since he's two months older than me. He already had out a great little pamphlet called *Organic Trains*.

To me Jim was a poet above all, one of the rare ones who was just jacked in to the underneath and always had been. It was one of those ordinary miracles of New York (though at the time it pissed me off too).

The first personal memory I have of him comes from a year or so later. I told this story to the few people who were at his wake so forgive me if you've heard it before. But back then, at nineteen, Jim and I were both hanging out a lot with or were the boyfriends of a couple of great art world women who were about fifteen years older than us, and these two women were each other's best friends: Patty Oldenburg, whom I was living with and who had recently separated from Claes Oldenburg, and Clarice Rivers, who'd been married to Larry Rivers. One night Patty was talking on the phone with Clarice and laughing and having a good time and when she hung up she told me that Clarice had Jim there in her bedroom and had him dressed up as a girl and was putting makeup on him. This was 1969. Sure there was Holly Woodlawn and Jackie Curtis, but Jamie Carroll? At nineteen, I thought that was about as glamorous a poet story as I'd ever heard.

A few years ago, when the incident came up between us, he said to me, "I have no shame about this stiletto-heeled foray into the anima. I made a really fine looking chick when I was eighteen or nineteen."

"Stiletto heeled foray into the anima." All right. The man had a way with words.

We gave a few readings together over the years. One of the very first, if not the first, was here in the church. It was a great reading and very memorable to me. For one, because I closed my reading with a short poem that ended with the words, "I want to fuck you in the ass / so much," and afterwards a tall blonde girl came up to me and told me how much she liked that particular poem and we then saw each other for about a year.

But it was memorable also because Jim read this amazing little segment of prose that he said came from the novel he was working on. In it, the young protagonist, named Billy, is riding on a long-distance bus in the rain. The guy next to him introduces himself as being a writer. Billy, after a moment of detaching himself by staring out the window into the rain, turns to the guy and asks, "How many people have you disappointed?" The kid starts raggedly counting on his fingers and finally comes out with something like "seven, maybe eight." Billy replies, "I have disappointed thousands. Literally thousands."

If I understand correctly, he was still working on that novel when he died.

In the last ten years, out of the blue, he sent me series of emails a few times. He was kind of excited when he got his own email address and he would mess around online. We didn't really hang out and were even a little rivalrous when we were young—back then he would sometimes talk in interviews about knowing me when I was Richie Meyers and I was fat. I wasn't really fat and no one but my mother and Jim ever called me Richie.

When he was fooling around online and writing me, he found this page on my website where I answered a few questions that site visitors asked. One of them was "What is your deepest shortcoming?" I said, "I'm self-absorbed. And I don't care. That's two." Jim wrote me, "The character in my book is self-absorbed too. But I think I'm even more self-absorbed than you. There. Back to work. I'll see you at some bullshit function we were both suckered into." And here I am!

I have to insert, just because it's so typically great, the email lines he wrote me about Christo's Central Park artwork, *The Gates*, "I saw the Christo thing. Pretty fucking big. I read that they have many Cop surveillance cameras monitoring the thing, but with an industrial box cutter, how long could it take to slash a couple of those saffron things & toss them into the back of a pick-up? They are made of some pretty tough polymer fabric, however. I have studied them for tensile strength. I need some new window shades."

In that same flurry of emails, in 2005, he began one of his messages with this little versified shred:

> It is good to have made contact with Hell
> If I establish intermittent
> Correspondence with Hell
>
> Perhaps, I will build
> Some homeopathic immunity
> By the time I get there.

That is pretty funny, and I was secretly really flattered to be in even such a toss-off and ambivalent work of his.

I want to read a short poem in tribute to him that's actually by Rimbaud. It's an early poem by Rimbaud written when he was sixteen or seventeen. The odd translation is by me, but it's a lovely poem and it's a sonnet and it rhymes.

EVENING PRAYER

> I, an angel at toilette, sit
> forever with beer, and smoking tobacco

and drinking my beers my head full of shit
(*dreams*) and I'm wacko

my head full of dreams that burn like phosphorous
heart like a hunk of raw torn wood
my head unwilling to act as the boss for us:
sad heart crying its gold sap blood

and once I've carefully swallowed the dreams
I turn from the beer and leave the room
to meadows outside where the burning deems

me Lord and I sweetly piss in the womb
of the dark skies high in glorious streams
that bless and gratify every bloom

Delivered at Jim Carroll's memorial, St. Mark's Church, NYC, 2010

MOUTH OF HELL COLUMN:
The Gates

CHRISTO'S AND JEANNE-CLAUDE'S *GATES* in Central Park have just come down. I went through a couple of phases regarding them before I ever saw them first-hand. At first I was looking forward to them. They looked pretty in the preliminary drawings and I'd always wanted to see a large-scale Christo. The wrapped-up Reichstag (1995) looked eerie and hilarious in photos. Then the week *The Gates* opened I saw one of the Maysles' documentaries on the artists (the Maysles have been filmically documenting the wrappings, etc., for decades). The movie was about the big umbrellas that C and J-C put up in California and Japan, which seemed like the thing they'd done that was most similar to *The Gates*. The umbrellas looked garish and intrusive, though the impression they made wasn't helped by the way that everyone in the film was so effusive about them. (Tears would come into their eyes as they spoke! One bystanding woman could think of nothing to compare the beauty of them to except the experience of giving birth to her daughter!) The big umbrellas, blue in Japan, and yellow in CA, poking into the landscape, looked like litter to me, like defacement. So all of a sudden I was pessimistic about a trip to the park.

But, in fact, it did turn out to be kind of thrilling. As obnoxious, or obvious, as this may sound: you had to be there. Photographs don't convey it. It's not just the three-dimensionality but that the installation was on the scale of the environment. Seeing a photo (or drawing), even news-footage on TV, can't tell you about the experience any more than, say, looking at a still can tell you about a movie.

When I first walked into the park, with the gates trailing orange across my field of vision, I was still skeptical. Then, as I got in deeper, the first surprise was their scale. They didn't feel big. You could reach up and touch the bottom hem of a flap. That kind of endeared them to you a little right off. The next thing that hit you was the fluidity of the experience. With every step you took, with every shift in your viewpoint, the way they looked changed, around you as well as winding off in the distances. They might look aggressive and inappropriate for a moment, but then you'd swivel and they'd look sweet and funny and pretty. Then the strongest reaction took over: how wacky it was. How pointless. And, all else being said, that was the best part of it. They just existed to make you wonder about them. They didn't make any sense. They felt like an "adult" version of the focused handiwork of a slovenly kid, like in "Drunken Boat," where, "If I desire the waters of Europe, it's the puddle / Black and cold, where, towards fragrant twilight / A squatting child full of sadnesses, releases / A boat as frail as a butterfly." Not to get too literarily overblown or sentimentally nostalgic, but the whole endeavor, with its two-week lifespan, reminded me of a kid alone scratching out a project of twigs in a dirt pile in his back yard and then going and getting a friend to show it to and three days later it's as if it never happened. Basically, Christo did that for the whole city and it was cool.

Monthly column for Noel Black's Colorado Springs, CO news tabloid, Toilet Paper, *published 2004-2006*

FILM COLUMN:
Jesus Is Magic

director: Liam Lynch; script: Sarah Silverman; cast: Sarah Silverman, Bob Odenkirk, Brian Posehn, Laura Silverman

IT'S OCCURRED TO ME more than once that I wish I could frame my whole life as a comedy routine. What does this have to do with movies? Well, if you knew that I intended my whole life as a joke, that question would answer itself. Maybe everybody really has two lives: what they experience as it happens, and then how they experience it in retrospect. The first time is tragedy, the second farce, as Karl Marx put it. Or, as Charlie Chaplin said, life is a tragedy when seen in close-up, but a comedy in long shot. Where am I going with this? To Sarah Silverman, and her beautifully coiffed and lilting anus (you have to see the movie). Sarah is so quick that she makes the tragic comic while it's still happening.

But really I do think that to be a standup comic is the highest calling on earth. I'd give anything to be a good comic. I may still try. It's the hardest job in entertainment (slash "art"), and the most satisfying (that feeling you get when you get a laugh). And the good thing is it's really ephemeral, which is admirable, a kind of higher truth in itself, because nothing really lasts. Standup comedy does not survive. Lenny Bruce himself is a trial to sit and listen to at this date. I wonder how much longer Andy Kaufman will stay funny. Maybe he'll be an exception. But for the most part standup is either topical or gets a lot of juice from attacking the boundaries of propriety, both of which things date fast.

Though there are immortal, archetypal jokes. That's what *The Aristo-crats* is about. The jokes are eternal and the comedians are their humble media. (Speaking of *The Aristocrats*, I thought it was weird that no one commented on the political content of the central joke. The comics who analyzed it got it backwards. The fact that the joke's punch line reveals that a pornographic vaudeville family act of spectacularly bloody and scatological grossness calls itself "The Aristocrats" is funny not because of its stupid inappropriateness, but for the exact opposite reason: its surprising insight. Take Prince Charles—please. Not to mention Paris Hilton.)

But what a beautiful vocation: to show how ridiculous everything is all the time. To make that your whole life and reason for being. And the success criterion is so clean. It's even more clear-cut than athletics. If you get laughs, you win, if you don't, you lose (though here's another place where Andy Kaufman may have finessed the law). I like the mutual-support aspect of it too. Maybe I'm naive, but comics seem like natural, inevitable, support groups for each other, like war veterans or recovering drug addicts. They share an extreme experience which creates a compassion and appreciation for each other that shows in practice (as in *The Aristocrats*, or the recent Seinfeld standup documentary *Comedian*, or *Broadway Danny Rose*). Because, of course, standup does have its dark side. What performance trade is more stressful? It's said that surveys show that the single most anxiety-provoking experience Americans can think of is public speaking, and standup is public speaking to the nth, which is part of the reason it's as aggressive as it is, aiming to "kill" the audience. There's the standard explanation for this that the comic is getting back at all the people who've tormented her over the years. But it's also a weird syndrome of the performer resenting the paying audience for taking this position of ruthless judgment, no matter that the crowd's been most fervently and obsequiously solicited by the comic . . . Anyway, there's a lot of tension and hostility involved.

But back to Sarah Silverman. Normally I wouldn't write about a concert movie, because there isn't much movie to it: you point your cameras at the stage and there it is. But results are what count, and this show is a great time. Anyway, films have always been as much about their stars as anything, there's no getting around it. A concert film is a kind of ultimate star vehicle, and Sarah Silverman deserves it. She's been real good for a long time, although she's only thirty-five and looks ten years younger. She actually wrote for and appeared regularly on *Saturday Night Live* all the way back in their 1993-1994 season. She's had troubles with censors the whole time too. Her first bit on *SNL* was as a commentator on the "Weekend Update" discussing the twenty-four-hour waiting period for abortions required by certain states: "Quite frankly, I think it's a good law. I was going to get an abortion the other day. I totally wanted an abortion. . . . And it turns out I was just thirsty." And she is still embarrassing NBC in the new century. Four years ago the network decided to apologize to Asians when there was protest over Silverman's account to Conan O'Brien on *Late Night* of how she'd wanted to avoid jury duty: "My friend said, 'Why don't you write something inappropriate on the form, like "I hate chinks"?' But I didn't want people to think I was racist. So I just filled out the form and I wrote 'I love chinks.'" This is all mild compared to what she does in her stage act, which is what *Jesus Is Magic* is, though many will know more or less the style to expect from seeing her on the Comedy Central Pamela Anderson Roast in August. She doesn't hold back.

You can't talk about Sarah Silverman without mentioning her appearance. Not only is she wildly lovely, but she has the charismatic immediacy, the physical expressiveness, of a star actress. These things add a nice piquancy to her frequent references to her own asshole. Richard Pryor had similar luck with the way he always looked like a cute nine year old while he was talking about drug-whores and beatings and starvation. Silverman relies a lot on adopting the persona of a ditzy JAP type who does things like authenticate her compassion for 9/11 victims by comparing their plight to the tragedy of her discovery that her daily soy latte actually contained NINE HUNDRED CALORIES. The show goes pretty far out, but Silverman pulls it off, with a bright smile, whether because her ways of mocking attitudes towards 9/11 and AIDS and race-hate work as real insights, or just because she's good enough to say "fuck you" to everybody because she's a bad-ass comedian and fuck you. She overreaches with the four or five musical numbers though. Movie critics want to be comics and comics want to be pop singers. But she is great and the movie is funny.

BlackBook *film column #9, Fall 2005*

FILM COLUMN:
Wassup Rockers

director: Larry Clark; script: Larry Clark, story by Clark and Matthew Frost; cinematography: Steve Gainer; cast: Jonathan Velasquez, Francisco Pedrasa, Milton Velasquez, Yunior Usualdo Panameno, Eddie Velasquez, Luis Rojas-Salgado, Carlos Velasco, Iris Zelaya, Ashley Maldonado, Laura Cellner, Jessica Steinbaum

I HATED LARRY CLARK'S FIRST MOVIE, *Kids* (1995). It was a long voyeuristic leer pretending to be a socially concerned AIDS exposé. It was fucked up to see a teenage girl's HIV used as the excuse to show endless soft-core kiddie porn. The director was fifty when he did that.

Clark had made his reputation as a still photographer decades before, with the books *Tulsa* (1971) and *Teenage Lust* (1983). *Tulsa* showed his gun-playing, drug-shooting, teenage boyhood crowd in Oklahoma; *Teenage Lust*, fifteen-year-old runaways/prostitutes and their hi-jinks in New York. Both books were packed with youthful hardons, bedraggled pussy, blood-wet drug needles, and other unsupervised poor-peoples' scenarios of pleasure and destruction, all in battered black and white. Most of the kids looked like they were having a fairly good time. The books exposed a typical American way of life that had never been presented to the public so fully and explicitly before. They were great pictures.

There are a lot of missing years in Clark's artistic bio between *Tulsa* and *Kids*. He spent some of them in penitentiary and most of them on drugs. Up until he turned fifty, his output amounted to one thin collection of photos every ten years. But those first two books were brilliant. In contrast, his films have been frequent—five made before this new one in only ten years—but seriously defective. The actors in *Kids* were unknown New York skateboarders and club kids, and at least it had the virtue of realistic characters, even if most of them were creepy. Its follow up, *Another Day in Paradise*, used a weaselly James Woods and a grotesquely faked-youthful Melanie Griffith, both out of their depths and misdirected in roles we had already seen played a thousand times anyway: the semi-charismatic outlaw drug-head losers of Scorcese, Tarantino, Gus Van Sant, etc. The young actors (Vincent Kartheiser and Natasha Gregson) who played the protégés of Woods and Griffiths were just as painfully unreal as their elders.

In around nine months stretched across 2000-2001, Clark made three more films: *Bully, Teenage Caveman*, and *Ken Park*. Each was awful and featured many more skinny teenagers doing sex and crime offensively if unconvincingly.

To give the director his due, the movies have had one consistent strong point, their photography. They're made quasi-documentary style, with a lot of hand-held camera, and are full of spontaneous-seeming cool ideas of what to shoot in a scene and how to frame it. The location settings—motel rooms and suburbs and highway strips—are good looking and atmospheric too. (The music has been more than decent as well—choice pop and "underground" records mostly.)

But, surprise, all that is a prelude to glory.

The new movie, *Wassup Rockers*, is a gem. It's about a set of young Latin skateboard punks in L.A. The immediate thing that sets it apart from Clark's earlier films is that for the first time the kids are likeable. They're irresistible, and not just for their charisma, their star-quality youth, but for their charm and openness. At the same time they are not any softer or safer, or less preoccupied with sex, than everybody in the earlier movies. These kids have actually lived most of what was filmed, in the deep ghetto of South Central L.A. But, despite the pressures of those surroundings, they seem to have kept not just a basic good will but a kind of pacifism. The word they use for their opposition numbers in the world is "haters." You can see why they wear tight pants and tight t-shirts and relate to the Ramones. They're like the young Ramones: street hardened but not looking to fight, and funny in a way that depends on a kind of amazingly preserved innocence (though it's an innocence that's almost knowing, cultivated, if that can be), and happy in each other's company. *Wassup Rockers* is a perfect title, too: these kids are a personification of rock and roll: sexy, tough, open, young, funny, sharp, and real.

Clark didn't just stumble on the movie. Not only does it proceed from his usual preoccupations, but he spent a year hanging out with the cast to gain their confidence and learn about their lives. Maybe this film is so much better than his others because its methods are more in line with what made his early books so good. The people here are ones the director lived among, and most of the movie comes from experiences of theirs, much of the dialogue improvised. He doesn't have to direct them how to behave, but rather to know how to use their natural behavior.

The film begins with a documentary clip of the main character, Jonathan Velasquez, telling anecdotes about his friends directly into the camera. Then the fictional story kicks in, the narrative line coming from two ideas of Clark's. One was his imagining of what it might be like if two rich Beverly Hills airhead sex-dogs, Paris Hilton and Nicole Ritchie types, were to encounter the skaters; the other suggested by the old youth-gang movie *The Warriors*, a favorite of Clark's, in which a New York gang is forced to travel across the turf-borders of rival gangs on their way home. In *Wassup Rockers*, the kids have to find their way back to South Central after a Beverly Hills cop-encounter and a skirmish with the rich girls' boyfriends.

The movie is full of new touches for a Clark movie, too. For one thing it will actually make you laugh. Not just because the kids are naturally great, but because the director wrote some types into the Beverly Hills scenes that are as flamboyantly entertaining as the best John Waters characters. For instance, a falling down drunk, if buff, matron in formal gown, gesticulating and smiling and slurring to Kiko, "With a face like that you're gonna get plenty of ass . . . With an ass like that, you're gonna get face. I mean with a face like that you're gonna get a lotta girls . . ." "When?" he suggests. There's some weird slapstick that actually works too, and a couple of strange inspirations, such as when, as the boys are hightailing it off the grounds of mansion #1, one of them scoots back into frame to plant a kiss on a piece of sexy statuary.

The movie is kind of a contemporary combination of *Rebel Without a Cause* and *The Wild One*. It made me realize that maybe the most kind, or even fair, way to look at Larry Clark films is as sensationalist youthsploitation in the vein of movies like those from the '50s. They are like modern drive-in flicks (*I Was a Teenage Caveman*). In that light, they're not so obnoxious, and this new one is positively transcendent.

BlackBook *film column #12, May 2006*

FILM COLUMN:
A Scanner Darkly

director: Richard Linklater; script: Richard Linklater, from a novel by Philip K. Dick; cine-matography: Shane F. Kelly; cast: Keanu Reeves, Robert Downey, Jr., Woody Harrelson, Rory Cochrane, Winona Ryder

RICHARD LINKLATER IS ONE of a set of directors—mostly in their mid-'40s—who have in common that they first got national attention fifteen or so years ago with low budget independent features, went on to make standard Hollywood commercial films, but still continue to make other more personal and "experimental" films. I'm thinking of Gus Van Sant (*Drugstore Cowboy* but also *Finding Forrester*), Steven Soderbergh (*Sex, Lies, and Videotape* but also *Ocean's Eleven*), Kevin Smith (*Clerks* but also *Jersey Girl*), and Linklater (*Slacker* but also *Bad News Bears*). Gus Van Sant, who's a little older than the others, is an interesting guy. His shot-for-shot remake of *Psycho* was ballsy and worthwhile, and so was *Elephant*, his avante-garde description of the few minutes in the lives of some high school students just preceding a Columbine-type slaughter. Linklater is interesting too, and appealing as a director. *Slacker* was a really good movie. (Criterion, by the way, has released a fantastic two-disc DVD set around it, with a lot of director commentary, hours of Linklater's pre-*Slacker* movie-making, and lots of other bonuses.)

Linklater is a wholesome, unpretentious guy who still, after years in cut-throat big-time kiss-ass filmmaking, maintains his loyalty to a philosophy of individuality, of non-conformity. He likes bohemians and mavericks, people who are thoughtful and questioning and obser-vant, who don't care about conventional worldly success. Those are the kinds of people he makes his movies about. His three best films, *Slacker*, *Waking Life*, and this new one, *A Scanner Darkly*, all flatter with attention the kind of late-night rap-session philosophy and mental riffing most people outgrow by the time they start working for a living. *Waking Life* was basically about how there's no distinguishing between waking and dreaming. How much slacker can you get than that? It was a lovely movie. (Unfortunately, it seems Linklater has also remained about fifteen where boy-girl romance is concerned. His whole conception of ideal masculinity as evidenced by his use of Ethan Hawke in *Before Sunrise / Before Sunset* and Matthew McConnaughey in *The Newton Boys* pretty much ruined those three films . . .)

A Scanner Darkly was made using the same rotoscoping technique as in *Waking Life*. The script is played by actors for the camera, but their film images are then reworked by animators using specialized software that turns the actors into moving paintings. The resulting images are still basically faithful to the subtleties of what the actors did when playing the scenes. It ends up like an animated graphic novel.

The movie is based on Philip K. Dick science fiction (as were *Blade Runner, Total Recall, Minority Report*, and *Paycheck*), which means that it's about the impossibility of separating reality from imagination/delusion/hoax. In this instance, though, the story is, more than anything else, a requiem for Dick's friends—and he, himself—who were killed or permanently damaged by drug use. He was a heavy drug user who wrote his first eighteen books on speed. *A Scanner Darkly*, published in 1975 and written about seven years before he died of heart failure at age fifty-three, was, according to Dick, the first novel he wrote without amphetamines. But the story is basically about amphetamines and the accompanying paranoia, Dick's massive fear that nothing is as it seems, nothing can be trusted (including oneself). The movie, which is very closely based on the book, feels not just profoundly sad, but profound, which isn't something you'd expect from either animation or pulp science fiction. (Or paranoid speed freaks for that matter.)

The main actors in it are Keanu Reeves, Robert Downey, Jr., Woody Harrelson, Winona Ryder, and Rory Cochrane. Downy and Harrelson are inspired as crazed speed-freak types. Their paranoid, deluded, meg-alomaniacal improvisations-become-script are major contributions to the film. Cochrane does a destroyed nervous-system pretty well too. All the casting seems almost laughably "type," but these actors carry their weight. Even Keanu Reeves's inevitable quasi-Eastwood, but weary, monotonous mutter, works. In fact, the only problem with the flick is that the performances are so good that one misses seeing them directly filmed rather than processed for animation. I understand though that the rotoscoping made it possible to do the movie for $6- to $8-million, rather than the $20- to $25-million it would have cost to build the sets and do the special effects. So the trade-off is understandable; and the animation has its own attractions too.

The story, which is set "seven years from now" (in the book it's 1994), is about the group of grungy brain-damaged drug heads infiltrated by a grungy brain-damaged undercover cop. The sympathies of the story are clearly with the addicts, but at the same time it's impossible to tell the addicts from the narcs. In fact, the main character, Arctor (Reeves), is an addict who is also a policeman who reports to his boss on his own activities as well as those of his friends. He informs on himself not only to protect his "identity" from the police—since he and his fellow cops all wear special electronic "scramble suits" that make them unidentifiable multi-person "blurs" when they're not in the company of their drug-user targets—but because he can't really tell who he is anymore. Ev-eryone is equally innocent and guilty, and it's impossible to know with certainty who is who and what they're doing to whom and why. One thing is known beyond a doubt: the drug rules. It's an irresistible powder ("You're either on it or you haven't tried it") that slowly destroys people's brains. It's made from a little blue flower, and is known as "Substance D," or just "death." Life (the drug) is death: the writer nailed it. Probably the only unequivocally repudiated people in the story are "straights," the ordinary working citizens with small predictable lives. Arctor had once been a straight suburban family man himself, but in a sudden revelation realized he hated his life and was ready to leave it for "this dark world where he now dwelt [in which] ugly and surprising things and once in a long while a tiny wondrous thing spilled out at him constantly."

This attitude, of course—rejection of the straight world—is typical of Linklater's movies. I couldn't help recalling his Criterion bonus voiceover commentary to *Slacker*, which repeatedly names certain (mostly young, and seemingly carefree) cast members as having died in the fifteen years since the movie was made. The *Scanner* book and the movie made from it end with a dedication to a long list of Dick's friends who've been killed or badly impaired in their pursuit of a life devoted to "playing." "They remain in my mind and the enemy will never be forgiven. The 'enemy' was their mistake in playing. Let them all play again, in some other way, and let them all be happy."

It's a kind of "punk" movie really. It's about people who can't accept limits and want life to be more—even if it kills them. They're not really admirable. The Downey character informs on one friend and casually allows another to die, but somehow there's still something innocent and sympathetic about him. It's all sad and interesting and confusing and beautiful.

BlackBook *film column #13, July 2006*

SEX ON DRUGS

MY BUILDING HAS BEEN HOME to many poets, and still is. When I moved in in 1975, Allen Ginsberg had already lived here for a few years. He moved out in the mid-'90s when he made a lot of money from selling his archives, less than two years before he died. Rene Ricard, the notorious poet and aesthete lived here in the '80s, drug- and clothes-rich via art gifts from the painters he'd helped to make glamorous, like Jean-Michel Basquiat and Julian Schnabel and Francesco Clemente, and subsequent hopefuls and admirers. He was smoking a lot of chemicals at the time and had to leave the building after he nearly burned it down twice. Jim Brodey lived here. Larry Fagin lives here and so do Simon Pettet and John Godfrey. (Look them up.)

John Godfrey is a real good writer, sort of a poet's poet, and he lives in the apartment directly above mine. After I gave him a copy of my first full scale book of poetry back in 1991, he said he could tell what drug I was on when I wrote each poem. This kind of hurt my feelings but I had to laugh because the truth was I usually was on something or other when I wrote the things in that book (because I was usually on something or other at all times). I could also laugh because by then I felt pretty secure that the drugs hadn't done the writing any damage, except for in my case reducing its quantity, which, I guess, on second thought, is a serious type of damage . . . But I do think there have been a lot of good poems written on drugs, and even more good sex enabled. It's too bad the drugs are so wearing on both one's body and judgement.

I think every drug that has any recreational appeal improves sex, if for no other reason than that they all reduce inhibitions. Even the ones that make you nervous, like speed, also make you aggressive and seductively eloquent and increase your consciousness of your nerve endings, the greatest number of which per square millimeter of course are concentrated in the classic erogenous zones (as opposed to the romantic erogenous zones, like ankles and necks). Furthermore, the very act of two people using drugs together is a kind of demonstration of willingness to surrender to and even transgress in favor of the sensual.

Probably the most eccentric acts of sex I had under drugs took place on cocaine. I had a couple of serious cocaine periods when the drug was widespread in the late '70s and early '80s. I was a tired heroin addict at the time and the coke livened things up and since my band was pretty popular locally I could get together income as needed. I had the committed street junkie's snobbery and preferred to shoot every drug. I would have injected marijuana if I could—in fact I did shoot up THC a couple of times. In the cocaine era I'd sometimes go for days shooting up every twenty minutes or half hour. The scab on my forearm was like a long brown zipper. I used to cut the toe out of a sock and pull it up to the elbow of my left arm whenever I needed to wear short sleeves in public. (I remember I once went to visit my mother at her house near the coast in Virginia back then. We'd go to the beach and I had to wear the sock. My sweet mother didn't like to know about bad news and weirdness, but finally towards the end of the week she had to ask. I was ready. "Everybody in New York wears them," I scoffed.)

But yeah, back to sex on cocaine. My fondest memory is about a technique I developed in the darkest days of that era when I'd often find myself crazed in my apartment at 2:00 or 3:00 AM after many hours of solitary cocaine use, having arrived at a state where I was unable to think of anything but sex. Actually there were two techniques; this is the first one. I didn't just want sex, I wanted it precise and detailed and extended.

Cocaine abuse brought out the megalomaniacal scientific erotomane. I wanted sex that was both as dirty and as everlasting as possible. I hit on the idea of calling up a likely girl and asking her to come over and let me draw her naked between-legs. That seemed like a good point of departure. It was effective. She'd come over and take off her pants and underpants in the dead silent 3:00 AM apartment and lie on the bed with her knees up and parted and I'd stretch out on my stomach between them with a drawing pad and pencil until we both came. (The other technique was what I used when the paranoia level got too high to make phone calls: substitute a full length mirror for the girl.)

I haven't done LSD or any other heavy psychedelic since I was in my twenties, except for psilocybin once or twice when a girl I liked turned out to have a mushroom bent (we ended up standing in makeshift scant costumes against opposite walls of the room staring at each other and jerking off). (To revert to the poem/drug subject for a moment: the only deliberately drug poem I remember having a hand in was a collaboration done on mushrooms alternating turns at a typewriter trying to spell "psilocybin." I still have that sheet of paper somewhere and it makes me feel a little stoned whenever I come across it.) I always craved sex when I was high on acid, but I think it was too exhausting. You don't want to be profoundly uncertain about what just happened and feel yourself disperse and clump and merge with an alien cohort and see your pulsing components glow and splotch, and be pierced by the significance of some new commonplace again and again, etc., etc., etc., multiple times with no respite or end in sight all that often. Things are complicated and demanding and confusing enough already. And anyway I mean "psychedelic orgasm" is kind of redundant.

I was never much into tranquilizers either. I had sex on quaaludes a few times. All I remember is pillows, that and breasts. Brain feathers, big rubbery nipples . . .

Contrary to conventional wisdom sex is really best on heroin. First of all heroin doesn't make you crazy like cocaine does. You don't end up down on your hands and knees picking at white specks in the carpeting, in a state of feeling continuously startled, like a horror movie.

No. Heroin is cozy. Heroin is voluptuous. It also seems to stretch time, most certainly does in the case of a user's erection. I remember laughing to read in *Bird*, the Charlie Parker oral history, amazed anecdotes about his sexual stamina (there were also awed accounts of his uncanny ability to nap on the bandstand and then rouse himself just in time for a solo). Dope works wonders. True, if a user is inclined to try to maintain the most extreme near-comatose level of opiate intoxication sexual potency might suffer, and doubtless there are those so single minded that any distraction from their desired nod is considered obnoxious, but as a general rule, a good high holds a plump sweet spot of eight to ten hours the entire length of which it's simple to elongate a single amazing fuck. The ideal way to spend a rainy day.

For what it's worth, I haven't done drugs in a long time. I don't even drink or smoke any more. It doesn't feel like a loss. Frankly, whenever I hear anyone refer to drugs casually, presuming a naughty shared affection, it annoys me, gives me the creeps. I'm not a member of that brotherhood in smirks. On the other hand I'm not ashamed of my history, obviously. Drugs are now so pervasive that there's no real stigma attached to using most of them anyway, with all the psychoactive "therapeutic" ones available, even the many which are physically habit forming, like Xanax and Ativan and Klonipan. My feeling is that the influence of a drug, if it's a drug powerful enough to noticeably affect the experience of sex, in a real way subsumes the experience into itself. When you have sex on drugs, you're having sex with the drugs, not sex with a human. That's cool too, I'm not denigrating it. Everything is chemical after all, most emphatically including people. One could make a case that sex itself is a drug: it sure does flood the nervous system with pleasing molecules. Or, on the other hand, that love is the drug that does the most to make sex good. That's another subject though and one too corny or at least too complex for me to try to treat here.

From Nerve, *nerve.com, 2003*

MUSCLE CAR BLISS

LIVING IN NEW YORK, where a car is usually more trouble than it's worth, I'd never owned one and knew nothing about them when I got a yen a few years ago. I consulted my trusted car-guy buddy—Bill from Detroit and the Lakeside Lounge—and he said the main thing was to go for an American car circa 1968-1971, the last cars made before environmental fears started restricting motors, a *muscle car*. They were not only fast and sharp, but big, with humongous trunks, seats like couches, and huge engine compartments where all the working parts were accessible. Plus, there're still enough of them around that they aren't hard to find.

I decided to go to California to shop for mine because the climate there is kind to cars and the highway culture means they're well kept. Inside of two weeks I'd found a gorgeous canary yellow '68 Plymouth Satellite* in San Jose, $1,900. I haven't been the same since. I swear that for the first few weeks I had that car I would lie in bed at night thinking of it and then have to get up and get dressed and go out to look at it just to admire it and make sure it was OK ... The closest I've ever come to suicide happened when I put a long slashing dent in the passenger side rear quarter the week

---

*"Only" a 318, but just newly rebuilt/bored, with 340 heads, a four-barrel intake with Holley Pro-Jection fuel injection, dual exhaust ...

I got it back to New York. ("*Nothing* lasts. What's the use? I should jump out the window.")

What makes a muscle car? Well, historically, they're the machine embodiment of the peak moment of innocent (or deluded) American joy, independence, and power. They coincide with the baby boom's teenage years, the final years of that collective confidence in endless resources and "manifest destiny" (the first and last muscle cars were built during the Vietnam War). In the '50s, when gas was cheap and the economy booming and highway construction rampant, cars got more and more powerful and large, but also ornate. Fifties autos were garish spacewagons for the prosperous suburban modern-age families founded after the Second World War. The cars of the '60s were built for the children of those families, who preferred no-frills speed and candy-colored muscular fun to chromey fins and pseudo-luxury.

This was when cars were named for wild animals and untamed forces of nature: Mustang, Galaxie, Comet, Cobra, Cyclone, Cougar (Ford); Charger, Challenger, Barracuda, Demon, Super Bee (Mopar—the gearhead term for Chrysler/Plymouth/Dodge, from the name of their parts division); Firebird, Wildcat, Impala, Nova, Tempest (GM) . . . Compare "Lexus," "Accord," "Camry" . . . My favorite though, and the one that best represents what I love about them all, was named after a wiseguy cartoon: the immortal 1968-69 Road Runner. This car was the result of Plymouth's inspired determination to build a machine that could break 100 m.p.h. in the quarter mile but cost less than $3,000. It's more or less the Clint Eastwood of cars: long, wide, lean, slit-eyed, roomy, not showy, but with lots of teeth, and very bad when threatened. Its standard engine was the Mopar 383 c.i.d. V-8 four-barrel, but with heads, intake/exhaust manifolds, and other parts from the high performance 440 V-8, a 4-speed manual shifter, and of course dual exhaust. Not to mention the Warner Brothers bird logo bolted to the sheet metal, and a horn that went "Meep-Meep" instead of "honk" (really). The car was a high-spirited blue-collar dream, and for '68-'69 130,000 of them were sold. Consequently, it's still not hard to find them; in fact if you shop a little you can still get a nice one for $3,000!

Driving back roads—setting out with no particular place to go except away from civilization, and no itinerary but to find out what there is to see (and eat and smell and listen to), and then to start watching for a nice funky mom-and-pop motel come around dusk—is what I most like to do now. This requires a car of the type I describe. Listen to me, life is sweet.

From GQ, *2000*

MY BLUES BAND: THE ROLLING STONES

"A swift, too-pretty grackle swarming over a plate of noodles."
—Brian Jones on the Stones*

WHEN I WAS A FIFTEEN, I had three music albums: *The Rolling Stones Now*, *Bringing It All Back Home* by Bob Dylan, and *Kinks-Size* ("featuring 'All Day and All of the Night' and 'Tired of Waiting'") by the Kinks. I really liked all three though I didn't think about it. (I remember I was suspended from school for a week in the ninth grade and my mother made me paint the house. I ran a cord to a little portable record player in the yard and had those records repeat while I painted. The Stones one started to melt and warp in the sun, so that night I put it between two frying pans in the oven and the next day it sounded even better.)

At that time I didn't know what the music classification "the blues" meant. I had the vague idea of it being the sad folk music of African-American slaves and their oppressed sharecropper descendants. But you'd hear jazz people and TV singers claim it too. Anyway, I thought of it as dated and corny, and the oppressed black people when I grew up weren't listening to it much either; they'd more likely be listening to Otis Redding or Mary Wells or Marvin Gaye.

I've done some research and I know what people mean by blues music now, and the Rolling Stones, back then, in the mid-'60s, were a blues

* In a dream I had.

band who also did some R & B, and they were good. They were my blues
band and I will defend them.

Muddy Waters himself admitted to Robert Palmer in the '70s, "They
got all these white kids now. Some of them can play *good* blues. They play
so much, run a ring around you playin' guitar . . ." He added, "but they
cannot vocal like the black man," and I grant there's not much denying
that, but I'd propose Dylan as an exception*, and also, with some ca-
veats, Mick Jagger. Of course the teenage Rolling Stones, unlike '30s
Delta farmhands, learned most of what they played from records, but
that was often true of black blues musicians too by the mid-'50s, and
it was the music of the R & B and Chicago blues players of that time
that the Stones grew up loving and imitating when it was current:
Muddy Waters, Chuck Berry ("rock and roll" but who was brought to
Chess Records by Waters), Howlin' Wolf, Bo Diddley, Jimmy Reed,
Arthur Alexander. Keith Richards is always saying there's only one
song. That's a stretch, but in a few real ways there is only one blues
song—almost anything that can be called a blues follows a I-IV-V
chord progression, and there are thirty or forty lines of lyrics that show
up in half the songs that count as blues. The original country blues
players shuffled those lines continuously, depending on circumstances,
not only among songs but within a given song. Players would habit-
ually take credit for composing songs they recorded that were only a
few words separated from their pre-existing sources. The composition
was really in the delivery.

The Rolling Stones were scrupulous about crediting their models, but
they did carry on in this spirit of the blues recombinant dreamlike history. For instance Muddy Waters's first commercial recording, for Chess
in Chicago, 1948, was "I Can't be Satisfied" and it was a huge regional hit;
the Stones covered this song on their second album *The Rolling Stones No.*

---

* Exhibit "A" being the famous 1966 "Royal Albert Hall" live date, where, incidentally, of fourteen original compositions Dylan performs, three happen to be pure
blues constructions: "She Belongs to Me," "Just Like Tom Thumb's Blues," and
"Leopard-Skin Pill Box Hat."

2 (British Decca, 1964); and then a year or two later their original international smash was "I Can't Get No Satisfaction." "Satisfaction" is a rock and roll song and it's only related nominally and in spirit to that earlier blues but it's consistent with the history, and is an extension of the tradition. Of course the Stones took their very band name from a Waters tune.

It's a progression and all one thing going from the earliest turn-of-the-twentieth-century first person country blues prototypes that were never recorded—with their repetitions, calls and responses, and African rhythms and African musical value of roughness (Palmer cites for instance early New Orleans jazz horn players pressing their necks between frying pans)—to the "ramblin'" showmen, buskers, and Saturday-night dance entertainers like Charley Patton and Son House and Robert Johnson whose music we have some direct record of and whose recordings were popular only among blacks and primarily in the south during their lives; to the Delta-drawn Chicago electric bands of Waters and Wolf and Reed, boogie of John Lee Hooker and Texas-rooted style of Lightin' Hopkins, who made nationwide hit records that were still half-hidden from white listeners as "race" records; to the Rolling Stones who had worldwide mega-hits (their 1964 British number one hit version of Howlin' Wolf's "Little Red Rooster" was the first and only authentic blues song to ever top the pop charts there or here). The progression took place over a span of only about sixty years, and though at each stage the music became a little less local and eccentric, it's all blues, until it disperses into a kind of loamy "pop" that the blues (and other folk music) made possible, like the Stones and Dylan, and Jack White.*

I was amazed when I heard the original versions of those records of '50s electric blues that I'd first heard in the Stones' renditions. The thing that amazed me then was how ludicrously blatant the ripoff was; how the

---

* Palmer didn't really say that thing about horn players pressing their necks between frying pans. He did say they'd use handfuls of kazoos as mutes. And then, further, regarding blues recording history, there's a lot to the point made by Robert Gordon in *It Came from Memphis*, paraphrasing his friend Jim Dickinson, "The best songs don't get recorded, the best recordings don't get released, and the best releases don't get played."

Stones would imitate the originals not only in arrangement and guitar tone for instance, but also how the vocals imitated the accents of those southern black men and the twists of the styles of their singing, line by line. By comparison Elvis Presley's cover songs of early R&B were awesomely creative. At the same time you could make a case that the Stones' versions of Muddy Waters were to him as he was to, say, Son House. It's true that the homogenization of the sound at the Stones' level is mostly in the singing. What Robert Johnson and Howlin' Wolf and Muddy Waters did with their voices has not been touched by a white rock and roll singer (except, I'd maintain, for Dylan). The way those great blues singers cut loose, playing their voices like something they're beating on with sticks, while also whistling through like horns, and somehow at the same time talking in words like possessed confessors, interspersed with yelps and moans in seeming spontaneity of excitement or anger or pain is only barely hinted at by Jagger. Jagger is good though and in other ways than by mimicry. That adolescently fresh-voiced snotty-kid defiance of his, mixed up with of all things a lisping femininity—his outrageous girlish threatening contempt—is completely "rock and roll," completely weird blues. It works, and ultimately it's probably the biggest actual contribution to the "canon" the Stones make as a blues band.

But the Stones aren't legitimate as a blues band only because of their musical ability anyway. There are qualities of blues—as well as its extension rock and roll—that get expressed by other means than musically, or of which the music is just one of the ways they are put across, and a major set of these is that weirdness, that insolence and snottiness, as well as miscegenation—sacred profanity, say, heartfelt entertainment, loving cruelty, say, black whiteness, happy sadness, say (rhythmic blues)—a swaggering freak, mutant thing of self-involved promiscuity and slick showoff duds, and the Rolling Stones were there by their ordinary nature. They were these ugly skinny all-jawed girly-haired British working class kids dressing like romantic dandies singing the folk music of another race of another country in obscene sibilant taunts and come-ons. Like Tommy Johnson and Robert Johnson they sold their souls to play the way they did. You can only play that music if you don't give a fuck. What could selling your soul mean but never worrying about restraining your evil impulses anymore? And any way you look at it, they're corrupt. It cuts in the most mundane and pathetic ways too—the Stones immediately dropped their old friend and original band member, pianist Ian Stewart, from the group because their first manager thought his looks didn't fit in with what could be popular at the time. Chuck Berry was maybe the most corrupt of all. All his songs were written specifically to appeal to white high school kids. Charley Patton himself was looked down upon by many in his time and place for being too much a showman, pandering to the crowd. Nothing is pure in this world.

"Nothing is pure in this world." There are those who revel in that perception and take it as a license. I am not among them. But I did get a lot from the Rolling Stones when they were new and I think what I got was pretty much the same as what Saturday-night dancers to Robert Johnson got on the plantations and in the roadhouses in the '30s: some raw emotion, strong pride, sharp attitude, ideas about what clothes would attract sexy women, and a kind of dance music that physically felt good and made you want to jump around and take off. The Rolling Stones had that effect on me because they were a real good blues band.

From Martin Scorsese Presents the Blues, *eds. Peter Guralnick, Robert Santelli, Holly George-Warren, Christopher John Farley (New York: Amistad, 2003)*

SONIC YOUTH'S *GOO*

"Here it comes again out of the rain
seems to have a new kind of same"
—Thurston Moore, "Disappearer"

SONIC YOUTH SAY, "GOO." Thurston, puppet of evol, shears the wires leading to his head and knees and collapses to the floor, breaking his fall with his guitar. "Ow," his guitar says, mildly. Thurston tells it to go to the corner and stand facing the amp. Piercing wails. Meanwhile, Kim (is that your own hair or did you scalp an angel?) is projecting into the microphone, a fifteen- year-old's perfect but unattainable older woman. When you hear a girl arguing with a boy out in the park, and they're too far away for you to make out the words, the man's voice sounds like a monotonous hum that the girl's is making a song around. Kim is both of them, with the kind of voice that can get you to bark like a dog when she says so. And that dance that looks so solitary that you want to be invited in. Why are this blond husband and wife behaving this way? In passion for Lee Renaldo. Lee leaps aboard Steve Shelley, his cute android thoroughbred, and plunges, loping, towards the storm of noise like it's a stampede he's pushing ahead . . . Then everybody exchanges places.

Sonic Youth were my favorite new band for years before I ever heard them, just for their name. When I heard them their name just improved, gaining further suavity, brains, and sex appeal . . . These are four white kids whose emotions are interesting and who know how to make a noise similar to real life of this moment intensified and stroked and given a beat in such a way that you also get a little beautiful relief from it, or at least support. Their music is also a lot like weather catastrophes (the sun comes up, etc.) at their most thrilling.

The group is well known now. In so many ways New York doesn't seem like part of America, but Madonna had NYC credentials too. If you think about it Sonic Youth has all the qualifications for popularity that a U2 does while being also funny and unpretentious. Though I think ZZ Top is more the class of band whose shoes they'd like to fill, whose tracks they'd like to cover, nationwide and bad, winding their way up the charts . . .

But then there's even room in their hearts for Karen Carpenter. In one of the two or three best songs on *Goo*, "Tunic," Kim sings in the persona of Karen arriving in heaven, "Hello Janis . . . Hello Elvis . . . Dreaming dreaming of how it's supposed to be . . ." They've always incorporated into their songs whatever survived their attention spans that day. They don't try to play pop stars (while they do play at playing pop stars), but remain with us stranded here in the electron torrents.

Daydream Nation was the album I played most last year. A friend, hearing it at my house one day, surprised me by wanting me to turn it off because it was "sad." I suppose I know what he meant, but that sadness is also funny and isn't something that makes me feel bad or unhappy; it makes me feel good. It sounds the way the world is. As a matter of fact, all the three or four other great double albums—*Blonde on Blonde, Exile on Main Street*, the Velvets live in Texas (*1969*), maybe *London Calling*—have that same quality that *Daydream* does of an edge of weariness: strong emotions recollected in noise, only pointless blizzards of which seem able to approximate the way feelings feel these days, or at least it takes hurricanes of it—storms so overwhelming that they become almost tranquil, serene, detached, "sad"—to muster the power necessary for a feeling to arise from the strew and babble of our normal lives.

Speaking of Hullabaloo, the sound of *Goo* most resembles late '60s crazed psychedelia. "Journey to the Center of your Mind." Spirit, Iron Butterfly . . .

I like Sonic Youth songs more without knowing the lyrics. The message is carried by snatches of phrases and misheard words. Music is emotion and energy, not thought or ideas. A lot of people in the underground-network music world that this band comes from make the mistake of trying to think, snobbery worse for being misplaced. Bands like Sonic Youth, or, say the Replacements, get put down for becoming more polished or writing more conventional songs five or six records into their career (the same thing happened with the Velvets' *Loaded*), especially if they sign with a powerful label. It's true that Sonic Youth has become more formularized, but I like their formula and you can hear its origins, its amorphous first state, in early records. You can see how it grew from there, and I think it's endearing the way they've come to psychedelic music from the other direction (relentless, obnoxious, kitschy, crude, New York racket, rather than "rock 'n' roll"). It's not selling out; it's just where their development took them. Doubtless, it will take them elsewhere soon.

Goo is not that much of a departure from the group's most recent records, while not being quite as great as *Daydream Nation*. But that standard is high and there are songs on this album you don't want to miss. Sonic Youth are really great and this record is no exception.

From Spin *magazine, 1992*

IN MEMORIAM HILLY KRISTAL

IT'S FUNNY, I REALIZE that when I think of CBGB's I think of bikers and winos and hillbillies, not kids blasting guitars and yelling their heads off. That's how strong first impressions are—and how far back I go. But really it feels like the crazed music is temporary. That Hilly has just been hospitable and so the bands that dropped in have never left. Then again I've always thought of the music the place is famous for as White Urban Folk Music, and that is the equivalent for its time and place of "Country/Blue Grass/Blues."

Hilly seems to me as if I knew him when I was a little kid, like in Kentucky. He was there when we were growing up, and he was watching and helping. I'm glad it was Hilly who was there with that club. Nobody was as decent and also as professional as he was. CBGB's always had the best sound system.

I'll always be grateful to him. Thanks Hilly.

Delivered at Hilly Kristal Memorial tribute event, Bowery Ballroom, NYC, 2007

FILM COLUMN:
Brokeback Mountain

director: Ang Lee; script: Larry McMurtry, Diana Ossana, from a story by Annie Proulx; cinematography: Rodrigo Prieto; cast: Heath Ledger, Jake Gyllenhaal, Randy Quaid, Anne Hathaway, Michelle Williams

ANG LEE MAKES ME THINK of the old-time Hollywood studios and the tradition of the "quality picture." He's like MGM, as MGM was in the 1930s and '40s, making skillful, classy, affecting films in all genres, set in many periods. In those days, individual directors were that versatile, too. William Wyler is a good example. (Interestingly, he was also, like Lee, an immigrant, from a fairly comfortable family background, arriving in the US in his late teens: Wyler a German Jew from Alsace, Lee a Chinese Taoist from Taiwan.) Wyler won three best director Academy Awards—exceeded only by John Ford's four—and made everything from westerns to family dramas to musicals. He was a great director of actors, too, helping boost to stardom many Hollywood legends—Humphrey Bogart and "the Dead End kids" in *Dead End* (1937); Henry Fonda in *Jezebel* (1938); Laurence Olivier in *Wuthering Heights* (1939); Montgomery Clift in *The Heiress* (1949); Audrey Hepburn in *Roman Holiday* (1953); and Barbra Streisand in *Funny Girl* (1968)—all in good movies that betrayed no identifiable director's personality or "touch."

So, as unusual as it is in these days of specialization and auteur consciousness, there's plenty of precedent for global, near-anonymous directorial skill. Personally, I wouldn't seek out Wyler's movies, though, whereas I wouldn't want to miss an Ang Lee. I've always liked his movies a lot: *The Wedding Banquet* (1993, a comedy about gay Chinese-American immigrants), *Sense and Sensibility* (1995, late 19th century Britain—Jane Austen—more or less introducing Kate Winslet), *Ice Storm* (1997, perceptive, intimate description of weird cold upper-middle-class 1970s American suburbia, introducing Tobey McGuire), *Ride With the Devil* (1999, Midwestern Civil War pic), and *Crouching Tiger, Hidden Dragon* (2000, period Chinese martial arts flick, introducing Ziyi Zhang). *The Hulk* was the exception that proved the rule of his ultra-competence. Now, people are talking Academy Awards for Lee's new film, *Brokeback Mountain* (*Crouching Tiger* won four, including best foreign language film). It's already won the Golden Lion, the top award at the Venice Film Festival.

Brokeback is about the love affair between a couple of cowboys in Wyoming between 1963 and 1983. On one level, it's a classic (or "ordinary") story of an affair between two people who can't let their relationship be known, whether because it's adulterous or because it defies cultural taboos—racial, political, or whatever. On the other hand, any kind of depiction of gay love that's not essentially comedic is a pretty new thing in a mainstream American movie.

It seems to me that the first thing to be noted about how these two cowboys are portrayed is that neither of them is ever shown to be effeminate at all. In a way, I suppose, that's progressive, but there are other things about the lead characters that make me wonder whether their "romantic" love is actually "gay" in essence. Maybe that's the point: that the dividing line between "gay" and "straight" is elusive or even nonexistent. Both men get married and have children, too. But you get the feeling that these men's backgrounds are so emotionally impoverished that they're both stuck at a barely adolescent stage, or at least a place where they're more at ease with men than women—the way a lot of boys and men are in fact. Often that's actually thought of as a "macho" trait. It's funny. The film is like a buddy movie that goes that one extra step. Nothing we're shown about them suggests that their relationship differs much from that of any two guys who like to go hunting and fishing and drinking together—except that these two just happen not to mind actively assisting in each others ejaculations. Of course, the problem is that, where they live, such behavior can get a person bludgeoned to death by the more sexually insecure he-men in the area. (As per Academy Award-winning *Boys Don't Cry*.)

The film is as satisfying in its presentation of a cultural milieu as Lee's various other movies have been. The details of the leftover-cowboy purlieus of backwater Wyoming and Texas—omnipresent huge sky, broke-down trailer offices, small-town rodeo queens, half-dead ranch operations, swaggering farm-machinery salesman as patriarchal success story, etc., and the dominating interludes of sheep-herding and camping in the wild mountains—are all seductively handsome and realistic.

The script was written by Texan Larry McMurtry, author of such novels as *Lonesome Dove* and *The Last Picture Show*, and his writing partner, Diana Ossana. They were faithful to the convincing West of Annie Proulx's original short story, which has been much admired and talked about since it appeared in *The New Yorker* in 1997. Nearly all the dialogue published in Proulx's story was kept in the movie, for obvious reasons ("Tell you what, you got a get up a dozen times in the night there over them coyotes. Happy to switch but give you warnin I can't cook worth a shit. Pretty good with a can opener.").

The acting and casting are superb. I won't be surprised if Heath Ledger receives an Academy Award for his Gary Cooper-to-the-point-of-autism version of a close-mouthed but lustful fucker of Jake Gyllenhaal's lonesome butt. It's the kind of thing the Academy does award. These actors were pretty brave. The recurring image that remains for me is a brief shot in a tent of Jake's frightened and amazed but grateful face as on his hands and knees he first takes it from Heath up behind him. This is what people will be paying to see. Not really. People would go to this movie if Jake was a girl, too. The picture has those classic good-movie qualities that have made the other Lee flicks worthwhile (great art direction not least among them). Though I have to say that, while his soundtrack music has always been pretty conventional, it was positively irritating in this, being mostly spare, pretty, wistful-sounding acoustic guitar picking signaling romantic sadness and nostalgia.

But, to repeat, I've always liked Ang Lee. I respect his intelligence and professionalism and skill and have even appreciated the near-invisibility of personality in his filmmaking—I think there's explicitly something of the values of the Tao (pre-Zen Chinese philosophy) in it, which is an intriguing twist to the Goldwyn-Mayer-Thalberg principal of high-class entertainment, as opposed to "self expression." And this movie has all those virtues, plus the intrigue and novelty-value (or what have you) of watching two manly movie-star cowboys making out. So that's a pretty good deal.

BlackBook *film column #10, Winter 2005/2006*

FILM COLUMN:
Palindromes

director: Todd Solondz; script: Todd Solondz; cinematography: Tom Richmond; cast: Emani Sledge, Valerie Shusterov, Hannah Freiman, Rachel Corr, Will Denton, Sharon Wilkins, Shayna Levine, Jennifer Jason Leigh, Ellen Barkin, Stephen Adly Guirgis, Matthew Faber, Debra Monk, Richard Masur

TODD SOLONDZ FILMS ARE GUILTY pleasures by definition: their pleasure comes from close attention to everybody's continuous excruciating meannesses to each other, and that "everybody" includes you. Granted, they're meant to make you laugh and they succeed at that, but now even the comedy seems to be getting removed little by little. *Welcome to the Dollhouse* (1995) was his funniest, most consistent, integrated, film, while the ones that followed, *Happiness* (1998), *Storytelling* (2001), and now *Palindromes*, have each gotten a little more purely acidic, with more and more places in them where the acid burns through, leaving strange-smelling, fuming holes.

The overall bitterness of his movies would seem to indicate that the director was traumatized in youth to discover he wasn't regarded as a magnetic personality. And it's true of him as an artist too: no matter how smart and insightful, Todd Solondz is not a director you love. In every movie he makes there come a few points where you lose your patience, where his focus on hypocrisy, cruelty, and selfishness seems too narrow to carry a film and starts getting tedious. But he always recovers. This new film is the most arduous, with more dicey stretches and the longest wait for a redeeming payoff, but it does end up succeeding, and it's more ambitious than the others in many ways.

Solondz has said all his films are love stories, and there's truth in that—he's mostly written about people hoping for involvement with other people. It sure has taken him to some funny places, though, such as when thirteen-year-old wallflower Dawn Weiner in *Dollhouse* is invited out on a first date by her tight-lipped classmate hero, Brendan, with, "You get raped. Be there." Or in *Happiness*, when the mild, slightly stunned-looking, psychologist played by Dylan Baker gets exposed as a pedophile, and his pubescent son, with whom he has a caring, honest relationship, asks him tearfully, "Would you ever fuck me," and the father assures him, "No. I'd jerk off instead." Or, in *Storytelling*, when the small boy of an upper-middle class family finds their housekeeper weeping and, once he draws from her that it's because her grandchild has just been executed for rape, asks, "Consuelo, what is rape exactly?" and she replies, "It's when you love someone and they don't love you and you do something about it."

Lines like these are comic, more or less, but they're not mocking or exploitive the way they might seem in different circumstances. In the movies, they're considerate. Solondz doesn't condemn his characters— each tends to be mean and innocent equally. That's what keeps the stories interesting. People can't help what they're like. If we could, we'd all be beautiful and popular.

This new movie is Solondz's strangest yet, with very little in it that's laugh-out-loud funny, but more than ever that's taboo. His just-previous, *Storytelling*, opened with Selma Blair's contorted face and naked upper body writhing and bouncing in erotic abandon atop a sexual partner who, when the camera panned down, turned out to be a guy with his clawlike left forearm pinned to his torso and his mouth pulled sideways by cerebral palsy. *Palindromes*, for much of its length, seems to be made exclusively of that kind of material (which isn't comedy), while, unlike the cruel "fiction workshop" *Storytelling* segment (which got pretty brilliant pretty fast), this new film's provocations don't, at first, seem to add up to much.

Palindromes follows the quest of a barely pubescent girl to get pregnant so that she can "have lots and lots of babies, as many as possible, because, um, because that way I always have someone to love." Those words are spoken by a little black girl, Aviva, the lead character, who looks about six, to her mother (Ellen Barkin). In the next scene the same little girl, now white, and a slouching, overweight, expressionless thirteen or so, is on her way with her parents for a friendly visit with another family, the dull young son of which Aviva will promptly induce to impregnate her. (It turns out that the Aviva role, a thirteen-year-old girl, is played by eight different actors: two grown women, four girls thirteen-fourteen years old, one twelve-year-old boy, and the one six-year-old girl.)

Now that Aviva has become pregnant, she's forced by her parents to get an abortion. In the wake of that medical procedure, the hurt and horrified girl runs away from home. Hitchhiking, she tries to obtain a new pregnancy from a truckdriver whom she follows into his motel room, but disappointingly is provided only anal consummation. The next morning the trucker abandons her. Following this, the exhausted child (in the form, now, of an obese black woman who looks about twenty-five) is taken in by a fundamentalist Christian couple devoted to adopting variously afflicted and congenitally disabled children—heirs to Down's syndrome, leukemia, missing limbs, epilepsy, cystic fibrosis, etc.—whom they pamper with love as well as teach to perform fancily choreographed gospel songs for presentation at religious gatherings.

This takes us about halfway through the movie. There's been hardly any comedy and the acting is rudimentary (most of the Avivas are non-actors). The pacing is slow and the story grim to no apparent end. It occurred to me at this point that maybe Solondz's reason for the multi-actor role-fill was to complicate things in hopes it might keep our attention. The viewer, drifting and flailing for some kind of grip, also starts to pick up on indications that maybe the film is about our current socio-political situation: Aviva makes up a story about her parents having died in the September 11 attacks, and there's all the screen time for "Born Again" Christians, and constant treatment of abortion matters. So, giving the filmmaker the benefit of the doubt, one wonders if that's why things feel difficult—that maybe it's supposed to be appropriate to the subject of our ugly times. And perhaps the multi-Avivas as strictly a thought-stimulant . . .

But, then, what's the "palindrome" angle? There's a character in the film who seems to be its "Greek chorus" commentator, or Solondz-surrogate: Mark Weiner (Matthew Faber), the brother of Dawn Weiner, heroine of *Welcome to the Dollhouse. Palindromes'* opening credit sequence features Mark's funeral eulogy for Dawn, who, it turns out, has committed suicide after becoming pregnant as a result of date rape. Aviva is Dawn's cousin. It's Mark who will introduce the title-subject, asking Aviva as she's leaving home, "Did you know your name is a palindrome . . . It's a word you spell it backwards and forwards it stays the same, never changes." Mark reappears at the end of the film and elaborates on this theme, of nothing ever changing, etc., in a little philosophical monologue that puts the movie in a fresh light, and for me saves it, making its difficulties seem worth while. That was an unusual experience, to find an "art" movie that seemed mostly failed suddenly get, in its final minutes, its parts clicked into place by one character's brief remarks, but that's how this film operated for me. As problematic as the movie is, it's equally thought-provoking.

BlackBook *film column #7, Spring 2005*

DAWN IN NEW YORK

IN ANCIENT GREECE, "rosy fingered" Eos, the personification of dawn, had an insatiable desire for young men. In New York City, Dawn is the name of a topless dancer. Nothing changes. (Though one also recalls Dawn Weiner, of *Welcome to the Dollhouse*. That Dawn, it turned out a movie or two later, committed suicide after becoming pregnant by date-rape. Not really a very dawn-like thing to do. Except perhaps in these apocalyptic times. But then her name was no doubt meant ironically.) I love dawn in all her rosy New York parts. But dawn is really for the young. It's all beginning.

Nearly every New York dawn I've seen has been the previous day extended. The first specific one that I remember happened in the spring of 1974. It's just one image. I'd spent the night inside the Club 82, a dark little transvestite club on East Fourth Street that had been appropriated that once for rock and roll by the New York Dolls, who were at their peak at the time. Johnny Thunders was nineteen or twenty years old. The group, in a curtsy to tradition, had just put on the only show they ever actually performed in drag (only macho Italian Johnny refused—which ain't to say his skintight pants, platform high heels, and gigantic ratted hairdo wouldn't have raised eyebrows on Mott Street). David Johansen wore a strapless dress. The club was wired happiness, faces wall to wall like flowers floating in front of the roaring music. I think it might have been the first time I spent all night in a rock and roll club. It was literally underground; when I finally climbed up and pushed open the door to the street I was surprised by the pale light. Everything was so quiet, the air was fresh, and there a few yards in front of me was Johnny ducking into a taxi alone. It's hard to convey how thrilling and inspiring that was. As much for the taxi as anything. I could never take a taxi because they cost too much.

Until this week, the most recent association I have with seeing the city that early is about ten years ago when I spent some sunrises walking along the East River all love sick and self-doubtful about the woman to whom I'm now married. The thought of downtown dawn still carries a suggestion of unbalance from then. But dawn really makes everything into itself. Even New York is subordinate to it. I went out the other morning and double-checked. There are local details—the all night coffee shop diners; the noisiness of the birds in the vacant-lot parks; yellow taxis whishing in the rising light with their headlights still on. A person out at that hour feels especially, fantastically, alone; the presence of any others, like de Chirico solitaries in the landscape, inculcating both intimacy and fear. But truly, at dawn, the city is not "New York," but a chance for the glow and colors to make everything. Though I guess there is something pretty "New York" too about the feeling it gives you that the future is possible to create.

From the Brooklyn Rail, *2008*

A FAVORITE BOB DYLAN SONG

TALKING ABOUT DYLAN is too complicated for just a few words. You can see why everybody writes books about him. It seems that anyone who likes him at all has a relationship with him, whether they admit it or not, that's just about as personal as any they have with people they actually know. He's been that useful, meaningful, and exasperating all your life long. No wonder he resents his fans. And the song I picked to write about, "You're A Big Girl Now," is the one for me that's the most revealing of his bewildering powers because it's the one that has the greatest distance between its emotional impact and its actual words. How does he make those silly words so affecting? It would take a book to sort out. "Time is a jet plane, it moves too fast." Where is the poetry in that? It's banal. The metaphor is obvious and the observation commonplace. But in the song it breaks your heart. I think maybe it's something about both his openness and the way his mind skips around in his condition, somehow thereby indicating the shape of everything and I mean everything. In other words, in a song like this one, it's how the lines turn into each other. For instance, the whole beginning of that stanza goes, "Time is a jet plane, it moves too fast / Oh, but what a shame if all we've shared can't last. / I can change, I swear." No one line is much more than banal, but it's how they're presented as following from each other that makes that "I can change I swear" choke me up every time. Or is it his delivery?

Or the melody? (It's partly the way the phrases are bound together by the flowing sound of the words themselves: plane, shame, change; fast shared, last swear . . .) Or is it the weird way saying "You're a big girl now" is inherently sarcastic, a sneer, when obviously what's going on is he wants her more than anything in the world? It's all the currents, nothing left out, in something apparently so simple and ordinary. There's no explaining it.

From Mojo *magazine favorite song survey for Dylan issue, 2005*

MOUTH OF HELL COLUMN:
Winter Holiday Issue

MY DAD WAS A JEW, but he had no religion. He was a communist organizer as a very young man, which I suppose is actually a Jewish thing to do, but it's also atheist ("Religion is the opium of the masses.") (Which insight might actually be topped by its counterpart, "Opium is the religion of the masses."*). But when I was a kid we did full-scale Christmas without ever giving a thought to Jesus. You know, we chose a tree, decorated it, put presents under it, hung stockings, last-minute additional gifts provided by Santa—bingo, Xmas morning . . . It was great. I never knew my father any better than a seven year old could anyway because that's how old I was when he died. My ma, who came from poor southern Methodists, had no religion either (As a kid I asked her if there was a God, and she said maybe the sun.). She was good for Christmas too though. Other people have mixed feelings about Christmas, but I'm into it.

Now, when I see those street decorations coming out the week before Thanksgiving, I do resent it. But what the hell. You have to love capitalism. It's so eager to please. And it's created such great packaging. I mean, we know it's greed masquerading as cheer, but the cheer is so pretty. Look at Brillo boxes. (As Andy Warhol did.) (For some reason soap has the most beautiful, happy, deathless packaging. There's even a detergent that's named "Cheer.")

---

*As remarked by John Bevan.

My wife and I went to Macy's on Saturday afternoon two weeks before Christmas. We were dreading it, but thought we had to find what we needed. Macy's is eight or nine stories high and a full New York city block of buildings merged into one, making over a million square feet of floor space. The streets outside it were almost impassable with shoppers. Inside the building though, we adjusted. It was festive. There were so many various examples of everything, including people, and the light was cozy, and all the Christmas symbols and signs were glittering and glistening and harmonizing everywhere. (A lot of stuff was on sale too.) There was also a surprising amount of warm old wood in the structure— many of the escalators' steps and trimmings, for instance, were actually worn wood, looking not deluxe but homey. We passed a door opening onto smiling young hirelings in elf outfits beaming at a line of little kids being admitted to a hidden room for a puppet show. And while all the merchandise was organized and displayed to best sales advantage, that mostly meant "pleasing to the eye," and the place was ramshackle too, with floors rising and dropping as the original buildings required, and different sales departments contributing their separate styles.

When we left, it was dark. Outside, there was a crowd around the display window by the revolving doors. In the window was a giant book lying on its side. In a moment, hidden machinery opened the book and, panel by panel, a cartoon stage-set panorama unfolded of cutout wintertime holiday revelers, the colored lights on them shifting in syncopation, backed by music. Everybody was into it, though it appeared that a couple of the pieces failed to move into position. Then we saw someone pointing a digital camera upwards, and we looked. Looming directly way over us, huge but manageable, and lit at the top like fluorescent green and red icing on a birthday cake was the Empire (!) State Building, against the black sky, the moon right beside it—though half the moon was dark—magnificent and spooky. We went with the flow.

Monthly column for Noel Black's Colorado Springs, CO news tabloid, Toilet Paper, *published 2004-2006*

ART IS THE DRUG:
Top Five Junkie Literature

FIRST, I SHOULD SAY that *Trainspotting* would easily make the top three but I'm not supposed to use it because it already gets enough play here. I don't think I should use my own book either because I'd look like an asshole. So, rather than struggle and equivocate to make a ten-long list, I'm going for the crème de la crème and keeping it to five.

I was surprised it was so hard to make the original quota. There are a few lowlife/addiction writers whose names always come up, but to my mind, now that the novelty of the drug story has worn off, these writers don't have much left. I want to recommend really good writing, not just honest accounts of addiction. Nowadays you can get that at your local Narcotics Anonymous meeting.

If I were going to list more books than I have I would have gone to writers of longing and emptiness and compulsion and obsession whose books don't technically deal with dope, like Dennis Cooper, like Baudelaire and Huysmans and Poe, or *Dracula*. Then there is alcohol, speaking of Poe—a case could be made for Raymond Chandler's books as addiction literature, not to mention, say, *Under the Volcano*. Addiction is a condition that doesn't necessarily result in opiate abuse. I allowed myself this latitude just once, in number three below, because I didn't want to get too cute. I'm sure I missed some real good books but I looked pretty hard.

I found that in the context of this list there was an easy test for defining the class of "good books." The fine but second-rate addiction literature was depressing, and furthermore was contagious, capable of kicking up, at least in me, a sneaky little what's-the-use urge to get high. The really good books—the top three books for sure—were just as accurate and relentless in drug need depiction, but they weren't depressing. They were exhilarating and they didn't make me want to use drugs. Good art makes a person feel better. Art isn't the facts, it's the truth, and the truth will set you free! Art is the drug.

1. *Jesus' Son* by Denis Johnson (Farrar, Straus, Giroux, 1992) This is that rare kind of book that strikes you with awe line after line, paragraph after paragraph, page after page, so that you don't even know when to call up your friend to tell him or her about it, because your faculties are all flummoxed, and it's indescribable anyway. Johnson (like Dennis Cooper, like Mary Karr, and me, and Eileen Myles and Jim Carroll) wrote poetry first, though please disregard this if it puts you off. There's nothing precious or pretentious about this book. It's short but in no respect slight, and it's billed as "stories," though I read it as a novel and still can't help thinking of it that way. The writing takes place in this misty chemical haze through which the details of the sentences pierce with a lurid glaring clarity so precise and heartbroken, you want to laugh and moan at the same time. It's the same guy talking all the way through and what he does is tell you about how things look and seem from inside the final throes of his drug-life in the lost and loneliest corners of the American midwest. "Down the hall came the wife. She was glorious, burning. She didn't yet know that her husband was dead. We knew. That's what gave her such power over us. The doctor took her into a room with a desk at the end of the hall, and from under the closed door a slab of brilliance radiated as if, by some stupendous process, diamonds were being incinerated in there. What a pair of lungs! She shrieked as I imagined an eagle would shriek. It felt wonderful to be alive to hear it! I've gone looking for that feeling everywhere." I am not kidding when I say it's funny though. There's one story about the spaced-out garbage-head

orderlies in a hospital emergency room that had me laughing out loud more than I can ever remember laughing at a book before. Incidentally, after I read this book I got all of Johnson's previous novels (there are four) and, with possibly one exception, they are just as good, though they don't deal with drugs.

2. *Junky* by William Burroughs (Penguin, 1977, originally published 1953) Burroughs is beyond death. It's amazing that a book of this genre—cheap sensationalist confessional (packaged as educational cautionary) for repressed thrill-seekers, or pulp fact—could be as unqualifiedly good as it is. It really does seem as if his voice comes from beyond, like the detective sent back from death, with no illusions, no polluting vested interests, nothing to live up to, no regrets: a perfect resigned disinterest. And, once again, it's hilarious. His meticulously sawn and nailed deadpan prose, matchless ear, and complete lack of fear continuously create scenes and lines that are funny just for the unfamiliar shock of their truth-to-life. About a fellow inmate at rehab: "There was no stopping him. When people start talking about their bowel movements they are as inexorable as the processes of which they speak." The book is a first-person account of the life of a seedy dope addict and small time criminal of the time, set mostly in New York. I can't help wondering what it must have been like to be a precocious teenager in the '50s, a connoisseur of the culture's secrets, and to come across this book in a rack at a bus station. Talk about happy face.

3. *Dr. Jekyll and Mr. Hyde* by Robert Louis Stevenson (Bantam Classic, 1981, originally published 1886) Like *Frankenstein* and *Dracula* (both of which have mythological/folk-tale precedents, however, and neither of which is as well written as *Jekyll and Hyde*), *Dr. Jekyll and Mr. Hyde* is one of those lucky stories that though written by a specific mortal seems like it must have existed forever. (Why are they all "horror"?) It's an allegory of cocaine addiction. I don't know if Stevenson consciously intended it so—probably not, or it wouldn't be as good as it is—but he is known to have used cocaine, and the book works near-perfectly as such.

Here is Jekyll's description of the transformation his chemical formula works on him: ". . . I came to myself as if out of a great sickness. There was something strange in my sensations, something indescribably new and, from its very novelty, incredibly sweet. I felt younger, lighter, happier in body; within I was conscious of a heady recklessness, a current of disordered sensual images running like a millrace in my fancy, a solution of the bonds of obligation, an unknown but not an innocent freedom of the soul." The essence of Hyde is that he is dissolved of all restraints (and feels really good). In the context of Victorian England, and in this book, that is evil, but it is also irresistibly thrilling and very much like coke. It's a great book. Incidentally, Stevenson died at forty-four of a cerebral hemorrhage, and his last words were, "What is this strangeness? Has my face changed?"

4. *Straight Life: The Story of Art Pepper*, by Art Pepper and Laurie Pepper. (Da Capo Press, 1994, originally published 1979) There are a number of memoirs and thinly fictionalized street-writing accounts of lives spent on drugs. This book is to my mind the best of them. Pepper was a jazz musician (he died in 1982, at the age of fifty-six) most of whose life was spent stoned, primarily on heroin and liquor, and who also logged a lot of time in jail and other institutions. One wouldn't call the book well written but then it wasn't actually written at all—he spoke it into a tape recorder—but it's completely vivid and relentlessly (500 pages plus) revealing. Talking about his childhood: "I was afraid of everything. Clouds scared me: it was as if they were living things that were going to harm me. Lightning and thunder frightened me beyond words. But when it was beautiful and sunny out my feelings were even more horrible because there was nothing in it for me. At least when it was thundering or when there were black clouds I had something I could put my fear and loneliness to and think that I was afraid because of the clouds." Passages (sex and crime, etc.) will blow your mind. I can't deny that it's depressing; but if you want to know what it's like, typically, to be a hopeless junkie, there's no better book to read than this. If you do, I recommend picking up a few of Pepper's CDs for a break from the

story now and then. His playing, mostly alto sax, is beautiful and relieves the claustrophobia.

5. *The Basketball Diaries* by Jim Carroll (Penguin, 1987, originally published 1978) and *Confessions of an English Opium Eater* by Thomas de Quincy (Carroll & Graf, 1985, originally published 1822) Couldn't decide between them so I'm using them both. I've got to say *Basketball Diaries* doesn't do for me what it did when I was younger. I remember reading it in mimeo magazines in the '60s and being very impressed and jealous. I prefer J.C. as a poet. The stuff I like in the *Diaries* is the more poetic stuff. Lines like, "Bob Dylan, he's in the radio. He glows in the dark and my fingers are just light feathers falling and fading down . . ." Maybe the movie ruined it for me—those kids just seemed so obnoxious, ugly mean-spirited, not just tough and wild. I wanted somebody to shut them up. That wise-ass stuff doesn't do it for me now. Still it's got a lot of funny anecdotes, and it's cool when he lets down the front. As for *Confessions of an English Opium Eater*, it has its points but is kind of irritating too. De Quincy is so in love with the sound of his own voice—a typical junkie failing. Still he's got a pretty good voice, even if those elaborate sentences can get on your nerves: "Here was a panacea [...] for all human woes; here was the secret of happiness about which philosophers had disputed for so many ages, at once discovered; happiness might now be bought for a penny and carried in the waistcoat pocket; portable ecstasies might be had corked up in a pint bottle; and peace of mind could be sent down in gallons by the mail coach." A lot of his surmises regarding the character of the drug and addiction itself are quaint and dated now, but the book is interesting historically, plus the guy is as honest as he can be, very smart, and, as I say, capable of a good line: ". . . [I]f you eat a good deal of it, most probably you must do what is particularly disagreeable to any man of regular habits, namely—die."

From Esquire *(UK), 1997*

FILM COLUMN:
Notre Musique

director: Jean-Luc Godard; script: Jean-Luc Godard; cinematography: Julien Hirsch; cast: Sarah Adler, Nade Dieu, Rony Kramer, Simon Eine; as themselves: Jean-Luc Godard, Mahmoud Darwich

I'M A LITTLE EMBARRASSED to be writing about Godard since I promote him incidentally all the time already. I should use the little space I have here to talk up directors more in need of attention. Godard is probably the most written-about director alive. People used to call the Rolling Stones the greatest rock and roll band in the world and, though the loudest of those people were probably hired by the band, still, it probably was true for a couple of years. Well, Godard has actually been the greatest filmmaker in the world since about 1959. (Though Bresson and Hitchcock, thirty years his elders, and Welles, fifteen years older, overlapped him a little.) I know it's wrong to call any one artist the best, but Godard is in a class with Picasso or Bob Dylan for childishly too-much talent and vision exercised through phase after phase into great old age. And, what can I say, his new movie is the best one I've seen this season.

Godard is seventy-three and has made more than thirty features, but his late films are the work of an old man in only the best senses: he's been around the block; is death-conscious, tending in mood to the contemplative bleak; impatient with vanity, inanity, and deception; and crazy with insight. He's also often clownish. Most importantly, he knows how to get cinematic elements to do about anything he could ever want them to, and his recent movies are as stoked with ideas and spirit as his earliest ones were. Maybe his endless inspiration comes partly from his approach to artmaking, one he also shares with Picasso and Dylan and for that matter Frank O'Hara, and that's that he makes works like superior notebooks. He goes on nerve. Since he's obsessed with cinema, his creations are as full of filmmaking ideas as they are about whatever else he's feeling or thinking or fantasizing, but he knocks out his movies the way other people talk on the phone or write email or keep journals. This means he's prolific, but it doesn't mean the works are thin: he's prolific vertically as well as horizontally. There are almost always four or five interesting threads and levels happening at once in a Godard movie, so even his weakest moments have something worthwhile going on if you're willing to shift. Sometimes he'll do something just to see what happens if he tries it, and/or to keep conscious that it's "only a movie." This brings to mind probably the most famous instance of Godard's inspired nonchalance: the jump cuts in *Breathless*. That innovation—the removal of frames from the middle of shots, resulting in the stuttering jump of an action from one moment to a few moments later—gave the movie a feeling of dangerous vitality and caused a lot of comment. Godard dubiously explained the technique as his way of shortening a film which ran too long. The point is it did give a new kind of kick to the film, as well as make one think again about what cinema itself is. Nobody else makes serious movies that do things like that (unless you count Jerry Lewis . . . there's Scorsese, but he would do it only with a distinct narrative purpose). It also demonstrates how with Godard, the most intellectual of directors, film is physical.

I was a little dissatisfied with *Eloge de L'Amour* (*In Praise of Love*), his film prior to this one. As always with Godard, it had much beauty and provocation, but it felt relatively flimsy and haphazard. *Notre Musique* ("our music"), on the other hand, is the first movie I've seen in as long as I can remember that I didn't want to end. This may have something to do with the way its final ten minutes are set in heaven and that the movie is fairly brief—seventy-nine minutes—but still, I didn't want it to stop.

The film features Godard himself traveling to Sarajevo to participate in a literary conference, and is divided into three parts: Hell (ten minutes),

Purgatory (one hour), and Heaven (ten minutes). (Godard often structures his movies in advance into chapters that seem to help generate content. Apparently his titles serve this purpose too—the director says that since the '60s he's thought of his titles in advance of the movies.) The "Hell" sequence is a video montage of war and genocide, both "documentary" (war cine-records) and "fictional" (Westerns and War movies). It's horrifying and garish, but the graceful, fast-streaming imagery is also seductive and in a strange way consoling, even soothing. It feels good to consider from the vantage of a movie audience the moving, lyrical, continuous and boundless viciousness of people towards each other. Thus is introduced the main thrust of the movie, which is a consideration of the mutual dependence of certain dualities ("our music"): death/life, darkness/light, negative/positive, imaginary/real, criminal/victim, shot/reverse shot. Godard's whole career could be seen as a meditation on film's mixed identity as documentary and fiction, and this movie is an advanced example of it. The haunting centerpiece is a lecture on "The Text and the Image" that Godard gives a small group in a dark side-room of the half-destroyed city. On either side of that, the story of the movie follows the separate missions of two young Jewish women who've come to Sarajevo, one a French-Israeli journalist—who wants to bring things "to light"—and one a suicidal, guilt-ridden Russian-Israeli, moving into the darkness. Both the women, similar-looking in their seraphic freshness, have come to Sarajevo to learn more about the conditions they inherit as Jews. The journalist, Judith Lerner (Sarah Adler), visits a French diplomat (Simon Eine) who hid her grandparents from the Nazis, and interviews an eloquent Arab poet (Mahmoud Darwich as himself). Olga Brodsky (Nade Dieu—And what's with that last name? Is that a punk-rock name?), who seems both fragile and unshakably committed to her beliefs, talks to her uncle (Rony Kramer) about her determination to kill herself as the only solution possible to her pain and guilt about Israeli treatment of Palestinians.

The viewer welcomes the presentation of the torn-up old graceful city itself, too, with its ruins remaining from the siege bombardments, as well as its regions of ordinary ugly modernity. It's an underrated high virtue of films to present the true feel of a place in time. *Notre Musique* is a physically lovely movie about irreconcilable oppositions accepted, not complacently, but with compassion and from honest necessity (necessary honesty), as separate faces of the truth.

BlackBook *film column #5, December 2004/January 2005*

FILM COLUMN:
2046

director: Wong Kar Wai; script: Wong Kar Wai; cinematographers: Christopher Doyle, Lai Yiu Fai; production design: William Chang Suk Pin; art director: Alfred Yau Wai Ming; cast: Tony Leung Chiu Wai, Gong Li, Takuya Kimura, Faye Wong, Ziyi Zhang, Maggie Cheung

WONG KAR WAI MOVIES are lightweight, like smoke, like the sound of rain, like light itself, like this sentence! I really love his new movie, more than any of his others. Some of the earlier ones were more or less boring: *Happy Together*, *In the Mood for Love*; or annoying: *Fallen Angels*; or lovely and moving (if sometimes boring and annoying): *Days of Being Wild*, *Chungking Express*; but *2046* is elixir, it's magnificent, the essence of sad, fake-tough gorgeousness.

The principal quality of Wong's movies is their style, their visual and aural style, and the style is so stylish—meaning just at the frontiers of where "real life" (fast food joints, crummy apartments, industrial landscapes, sentimental pop music) meets the utmost aestheticization of things (extreme wide angle lens, slow-motion, hand-held camera, highly coordinated color schemes, garish over-exposure, opera, voice-overs)—and the stylishness is so intense that it overwhelms anything else. It becomes the content in a way that can ultimately feel frustrating because the style keeps saying "this is lovely and fascinating" no matter what's going on: cold slaughter, a lover's indifference, boredom, hopelessness, passionate emotion, locking your father in the bathroom, anything. Everything is so pretty and chic-looking. Is memory really the chic-ification of one's reality? It has almost seemed like that in Wong Kar Wai.

Because his movies are mostly about memory: about loss, transience, and, as a result, hopelessness.

Though I suppose this, this gorgeousness of things in Wong's memorial universe, makes sense. One might well resent being dominated by a traumatic past, but at the same time, why not live in memory—it's where a person can keep things from changing. It's the place where the consciousness of the romantic, sentimental schoolgirl (possibly living inside the whore) and the haunted lonely tough guy (her lover) intersect: the territory of Wong's movies.

As the director's films increase in number (*2046* is his seventh feature since the first, *As Tears Go By*, seventeen years ago), the sources of his preoccupations and themes become more apparent. Wong is an exile whose movies are suffused with loss. Born in Shanghai, in Communist China; his family emigrated to Hong Kong when he was five in 1963 (a date featured prominently in his movies), but because of political turmoil his brother and sister were forced to remain behind. In Hong Kong, where his family lived in poverty among other poor Shanghainese immigrants, Wong didn't learn the local language until he was thirteen. His father was a sailor and later a nightclub manager. Wong spent most of his time with his movie-loving mother. The director seems to have a strange nostalgia for this period in Hong Kong, as the definition both of beauty and of loss. The otherworldliness of his childhood seems to have fixed him in it. Only a kid or a professional killer or a drama queen could take seriously the conception of love his movies purvey, namely that "the only love is first love, before love has had a chance to change at all." But you don't have to take it seriously in order to appreciate him, any more than you have to take seriously the emotional preoccupations of Douglas Sirk or Jerry Lewis or Martin Scorsese to appreciate them.

Wong's best work is more like poetry or painting—collaged and abstract—than it is like stories, but poems that can hold their own with the most affecting pop songs, or the most satisfying crime novels, rather than the cross-eyed soft flowers, sunsets and wistful sweetness often called "poetic." (Though there's plenty of whimsy in Wong—it's one of the things that can get annoying, though he usually pulls it off.) They're poems in that they make patterns that have the logic of their maker's inner world rather than being cut to fit a pre-existing form, the way movies usually are. On the other hand, strikingly, *2046* is a genre film. Most of Wong's movies have the mood and sensibility of classic "film noir." They're about men who are cynical about romance because they were originally hurt so badly in love, they're about urban alienation, they're about cheap rental rooms, about casual extreme violence, they're full of rainy streets and darkness and shadows and loneliness and erotic cigarette smoking. *2046* is the apotheosis of this: it's noir distilled to its essence, without end or beginning.

Also, as in modern poetry or painting or jazz, Wong makes up his movies as he goes along, improvising, and fills them with overlapping quotes and signature references, variations on his themes. He shoots many more scenes than he uses and any story (usually rudimentary) is created in how he edits the results. Neither the actors nor the director know what will happen in the movie until the movie's release. During the making of *2046*, it was often described as a science fiction film. There's hardly any of that left. The remnants turn out to be scenes taken from a science fiction story that the film's protagonist, Chow (Tony Leung Chiu Wai), is writing. That story, which is about the year 2046, contains bits and pieces translated from Chow's "real" life (the narrative of the movie we are watching). This, in turn, parallels the way that *2046*, the movie, cannibalizes and refers to characters and incidents and data from Wong's previous movies, the same way the movies use Wong's own experience as their source. He does this fractal repetition of motifs and patterns very well—it doesn't feel contrived, but in fact true-to-life in a genuinely poetic way.

2046 is about the hard-bitten pimp-like pulp fiction writer, Chow, in the Singapore of 1963 and the Hong Kong of 1966-69, and his relationships with a series of women. The most prolonged relationship is with the resident of room 2046, Bai Ling (Ziyi Zhang). The charm of the actors can't be overstated. Ziyi Zhang is as unaffectedly, quiveringly sexual as Marilyn Monroe, while as elegant and self-possessed as Audrey Hepburn. Her ordinary speaking voice is sexier than most women's nudity. Tony Leung in his role has been compared by Wong to Clark Gable, but Humphrey Bogart would be just as apt. The look of the movie is breathtaking. There were actually two separate moments when I gasped and felt my eyes start to well, solely in reaction to a shot, an image, distinct from any narrative meaning. I wanted to be part of the culture that wanted from its movies what this movie provides its audience. But, I suppose, by loving the movie, I am part of that culture. And this, in turn, one could say, resembles how Wong in his movies, by longing for evanescent beauty renders it permanent.

BlackBook *film column #8, Spring/Summer 2005*

FOUR LESSER-KNOWN WRITERS
I've Loved and Learned From

TOM VEITCH

In the 1960s and early '70s there was a bunch of young poets in New York centered around the St. Mark's Church Poetry Project in the East Village who, though mostly pretty well educated, were "anti-academic." They were street poets, who, rather than trudge to respectability through college literary magazines and teaching jobs, did drugs and scrounged and traded partners and flung out crazed and beautiful mimeo pamphlets of each other. One of the greatest examples of the many great stapled, mimeo publications of that moment was the work of a guy named Tom Veitch [pron. *Veetch*]. Veitch has never been as well known, even in those poets' tiny frame of fame, as some of his friends, and furthermore he eventually dropped out of poetry altogether, and ended up scripting sci-fi comic books for a living. There were a few years, too, in the middle of his poetry period which he actually spent cloistered as a Benedictine monk in a Vermont monastery. The following three poems are taken from a collection mimeo'd at that time, in 1967, entitled *Toad Poems*. The book is attributed only to "Pseudonym"—Veitch's name isn't on it anywhere, and sometimes it still gets listed in dealers' catalogues without reference to him. His close friend the great poet Ron Padgett wrote a classy short intro to the pamphlet, in which Ron says that he (Padgett)

had "always dreamed of a poetry that would be, without any special connotations to the word, bad, as well as pleasurable" and that "before I'd
read TOAD POEMS several years ago, I'd never read anything so genuinely sub-intelligent and unconcerned, yet perfectly aware of itself."

Ladies and gentlemen, three toad poems by Tom Veitch . . .

CATS CLIMB TREES

Cats climb trees because they are
Afraid of Dogs.
My dog was not afraid of me,
So I never climbed any trees.
Twenty years ago this happened.
Since then my dog has died
and been buried under a tree
in our front yard.
Today I climbed that tree for
the first time, to chase down a
cat named Melvin who had got
caught up there after running
from my new dog whose name
shall not be mentioned
(We call him Ron)
My Sister wrote that.

SOMETHING TO EAT

I asked for something to eat,
Something outside my own body,
And in came a hunk of greasy cheese,
fresh from the mouse-trap.
Now a dagger appears between the
pages of your mind, and the
envelope seals itself

under your magic pencil.
What he means is that bitter cheese
is better than no cheese at all,
and Indian varmints on
painted horses are better than
no Indians at all.
Quite the contrary in fact,
No less true of course, no matter
how you look at it.

COWBOY SONG

Wait until the revelation
Of embarrassment encompasses
Your last compass-curved thought
And the contradiction of
Contradistinction has enveloped
Your last turd—
Then my little girl
I will pat your hair
And comb your werewolf
lips; love lost on a banshee
Always backwards
into nothing
Border fire
Burning down Fear Village
And last week's jokes.

DENTON WELCH

Denton Welch was an upper middle class English guy born in 1915 who
died at age thirty-three (1948). As a twenty-year-old art student, he'd
been bicycling in the country when he was struck by a car, fracturing

his spine and injuring him internally so badly that he finally died of the effects thirteen years later. Those thirteen years were largely spent bedridden, often in terrible pain, alternating with short periods when he could live almost normally. All his writing was produced after the accident, under those circumstances. His stories and books—three short novels and two small story collections—were presented as fiction but all were detailed description of experiences of his. They earned him praise from the most sophisticated stylists and poets of his time, such as W.H. Auden, Cyril Connolly, C. Day Lewis, E. M. Forster, Elizabeth Sitwell, Herbert Read, Vita Sackville-West, Edmund Wilson, and on and on. He's rarely remembered as among the great writers of his time though, probably because his material is so plain-spoken and unpretentious. After his death his primary, most distinguished, American appreciator would be William Burroughs, and the first passage here tonight is a lot like Burroughs in Burroughs's earliest, straightforward style, as in *Junky* and *Queer* and *Interzone*.

FROM *MAIDEN VOYAGE* (1943)

The next morning I began to draw. I sat in a corner of the deck and drew the coiled ropes, the lifeboats, the ventilators and any other strangely shaped thing. It made me happy and contented. I did not think about myself at all. When other passengers came up I held my board very close and frowned as if I were in deep thought. They usually muttered something like, "I won't disturb you, I see you're concentrating," and then moved on, but one woman would not leave me. She was between fifty and sixty and the ends of her silk scarves fluttered in the wind. Her head and neck were like the Roman symbol of an axe embedded in a bundle of sticks. The neck was all broken up into wrinkled skin and corded muscles, and the head jutted out at the top.

I could see from the color of the scarves that fluttered and slapped against her that she was "interested in Art." They were puce and peacock blue. She was persistent as a bird, swooping down to peck at my drawing every moment. At last I gave it up and leaned back against the side of the ship as she talked.

She was going to India to meet her husband. She had no children of her own but she had several nephews and nieces who were extremely clever. One of them was going to an Art School. She ended up by telling me her name. It was Mrs. Wright.

There was a moment's pause and I felt her eyes on me. I looked up suddenly and caught the glint of curiosity. She dowsed it instantly but I knew what was coming. She began with more skill than I gave her credit for, and I found myself answering her questions with only slight resentment. She soon knew that I had run away from school, that I was going to China and that I was not quite seventeen.

The reaction came after she had left me. I brooded on my dislike of her. I hated to think that I had satisfied her curiosity. She was like a greedy, sinewy spider.

In the evening I walked round the deck, passing constantly the portholes of Mrs. Wright's cabin. On one of my rounds I stopped close to them and leaned against the side to rest. My eye caught something gleaming gold and blue just inside the cabin. It was a still unopened box of chocolate. It lay on the sill of the open porthole.

"The greedy bitch," I said to myself. I thought of her sitting up in her bunk, wearing, perhaps, a boudoir cap with lace and blue ribbons; reaching for the chocolate without taking her eyes from the page of her novel.

I imagined her face when the groping hand told her that it was not there. I put my hand in, picked up the chocolate and walked on swiftly.

When I reached the stern I leant over and watched the wake disappearing into the collecting darkness. I tore the shiny paper off the chocolate and threw it down so that it was swallowed up in the churning of the propellers; then I began to eat.

It was like a communion feast. I was eating Mrs. Wright. Not for love but for hate, so that later she should be ejected from my body to go swimming down with the rest of the ship's sewage. I put large pieces in my mouth and savoured them deliciously until the whole pound was finished.

At dinner Paul asked me why I ate so little. He asked if I felt seasick.

FROM *A VOICE THROUGH A CLOUD* (1950)

It was horrible; they were going to abandon me, and my legs were bristling and burning and I could not move them, and my head was throwing out waves of black sickness which seemed about to drown me. I began to talk to the nurses wildly. I asked them questions; I told them things; I laughed and smiled. And all the time I knew they were watching me and judging me. They were not taking anything I said seriously.

Then the pain, like some huge grizzly bear, seemed to take me between its paws. I screamed from sheer shock at its sudden increased violence.

"Stop it," the nurses said together. "You'll wake the others." They seemed about to stifle me if I dared to make another sound.

I must have screamed again, for all I can remember is a shriek and a pain invading my whole body. The shriek seemed to be following the pain into every limb. I was nothing but a shriek and a pain. I was sweating. Everything was wet. I was crying. Saliva dribbled out of my mouth.

In the middle of the furnace inside me there was a clear thought like a text in cross-stitch. I wanted to warn the nurses, to tell them that nothing was real but torture. Nobody seemed to realize that this was the only thing on earth. People didn't know that it was waiting for them quietly, patiently.

I felt that if I bore the agony a moment longer it would split my skin. It was such a growing and powerful thing; it would burst out of the tightness of my body.

I heard footsteps hurrying away; then silence. One of the nurses was still holding me, trying to stop me from moving.

At last the other one came back and she had a dainty dish and a little gun or model road-drill with her. It struck me that these articles were so small and finical that they could only be drawing-room tea-toys, and I thought that they should have been made of silver and not chromium.

The nurse lifted up my arm, swabbed a little place with cotton wool. I realized that she was trying to help me. I knew what the gun was for now, but I did not believe in its power. It was still associated in my mind with sugar-tongs and tea strainers.

But the moment she pricked me so heartlessly, pushing the needle right in with vicious pleasure, I had faith; I knew that it was magic. It was like the Sleeping Beauty magic. Exactly the same, I thought, amazed at the similarity. Everything was there, the sudden prick, the venomous influence wishing me evil; then there would be the hundred years' sleep. I knew it in spite of the pain. The pain did not abate at all. It was still there, eating me up; but in the hundred years' sleep it would die. It couldn't live for a hundred years. And brambles would grow and turn everything marble-grey. The dust would be as thick and as exquisite to the touch as mole-skin; and there would be moonlight always.

FROM *THE JOURNALS* (1984), from entry for 12 MAY 1946

[. . .] then I went to Wrotham, where I found in the not very promising shop there a little emery needle-cushion beautifully made in the form of a tiny stool. It was so much a stool and so little a needle cushion that I wanted it at once for the dolls' house. It has minute needlework on top framed in kid leather; the legs of the stool are covered in morocco, with gold trimmings. Where the needles should go is faced in faded rose watered silk.

So much work and love just for a needle-cushion, and quite a usual one at that, I suppose. I like to think of the early-Victorian girls poking their needles in and out to make them glisten.

The little stool makes one think that civilization is fastidiousness.

People will call this missish slop, trivial, shallow; but it is they who are trivial with their blunted coarseness.

If people doted on their needle cushions more, a great tree of civilization would grow out of them instead of a wave of bad smells and famine.

BILL KNOTT

The American poet Bill Knott was born in 1940. His first substantial book, *The Naomi Poems: Corpse and Beans,* came out in 1968 but on it's cover the book was attributed to "St. Geraud" (named, it turns out, for the lead character in an obscure 18th century French pornographic novel) and the author's dates on the poetry book were given as "1940-1966." On the back cover, though, it was printed that "Of himself the author says: 'Bill Knott (1940-1966) is a virgin and a suicide.'" It turns out that Knott had, in 1966, sent out an announcement that he'd killed himself because nobody loved him. The 1968 book comprised mostly love poems and anti-Vietnam War poems. It was sensationally pow-erful: poems of love, despair, horror, outrage, and loneliness written from this surreal imagination that mixed self-disgust with adoration and awe (mostly for particular women) in a big disgust-bowl of adoration-struck awe self. Three years later he published the book *Nights of Naomi*, from which the four poems for tonight are drawn. The poems in that book are a relentless rush of his style of writing distilled to its essence, without any of the usual pace-changes or shifts of perspective or modulations or asides. It's just this prolonged spurting gush of pure Knott, from 1971. Incidentally, the poet is still at it now, forty years later. For some years he's been keeping up a blog where he vents his works and thoughts and anger nonstop, and offers for free PDF versions of nearly all his books. Now it looks like he's dropped the poetry blog in favor of selling his paintings on line. He also runs a poetry workshop at a small college in Boston.*

---

* He died in 2014.

FROM *NIGHTS OF NAOMI* (1971)

Fluent in all claws
Her lips flare like others' nostrils flare
Stabbed by quicksand she montages purple invisibilities
Where there are twins one is wearing a mask
Of her clear eyes and cloudy nipples
Dressed in a dairy of sheep's shrapnel
A ripped venom grovels at her brow
Gloating like the writhe-scent
Of her sweat's landing-instruments
Of coiffured ingots
Screeching like the cocoons on her whip
Which sheds the muteness
I lick
When I pick up a new poetry book
I always glance first at the biographical note
If the poet has children I don't read the book

———————————

Your clitoris is my boyfriend
Like a cameo on fire it has the best view in my dreams
I kiss your clitoris of syringe laughter
With all of DroolQueen's tattoo levitations
With my asshole on a snapping cushion held forth by double sperm
Like nights sheered
By vestigial moss of nipples
The howling rubble in your scrotum carves a loftiness
Upon the applause
Purple as a sink made of swans
Where the blindfold fish blow on their abacuses
To set us floating down the semen to the ocean
Which writes help on a donut and throws it out the window

To inlay ballerinas as stop-and-go lights in the floors
Of statues of spurting pinpricks
Often a maskflurry face slashes
Incisions in my flesh then pours in your eye-makeup
So I will see for the first time

Tanager moos of starfish
Marquee of stranglers
Diamond putty
Palette of birthmarks on fatal blackboards of needles
Skintight test-tubes of maze-breathing swoops
Coma of rusty-hinged wafts
Growing on decks of jelly pencils
Somersault-ore tress propped by yodeling pings
Key flooded by display-cases of mauve deathmarches through stereo
cilia whose
headmasters were warped off my tanager moos of sandstorm

Cueballs have invented insomnia in an attempt to forget eyelids.

GÉRARD DE NERVAL

Gérard de Nerval was a French poet born in 1808. He often had a hard time distinguishing between common reality and the unique worlds of consciousness triggered in him by ordinary events. He was well aware of this problem, though, unlike the classic conception of the deluded hallucinatory madman, and one of his most famous works, the prose confession "Aurélia," describes the phenomenon in heart-rending detail. He was perhaps the most eccentric and tortured of all the eccentric and tortured 19th century Romantic poets, but he was probably also the most loved. The classic anecdote of Nerval described him discovered walking the gardens of the Palais Royal with a lobster on a blue silk leash. He explained that the lobster does not bark and knows the secrets of the deep. Towards the end of his life he spent extended periods in a mental asylum. He was found dead at the age of forty-six, apparently by his own hand, hanging from a lamppost in a poor neighborhood of Paris.

OPENING PARAGRAPH OF *AURELIA* (1855)
trans. by Geoffrey Wagner

Our dreams are a second life. I have never been able to penetrate without a shudder those ivory or horned gates which separate us from the invisible world. The first moments of sleep are an image of death; a hazy torpor grips our thoughts and it becomes impossible for us to determine the exact instant when the "I," under another form, continues the task of existence. Little by little a vague underground cavern grows lighter and the pale gravely immobile shapes that live in limbo detach themselves from the shadows and the night. Then the picture takes form, a new brightness illumines these strange apparitions and gives them movement. The spirit world opens before us.

FROM *THE CHIMERAS* (1854)
trans. by Richard Hell

GOLDEN LINES
"And so! Everything is alive!"
 —Pythagoras

Man, free thinker! Do you believe you alone can think
In this world where life bursts forth in everything?
Your freedom disposes what it may
But the universe is beyond you.

In animals honor the mind acting:
Each flower is a soul disclosed by Nature;
A mystery of love lies concealed in metal;
"Everything is alive!" and has power over you.

Beware in the blind wall a gaze that watches you:
The heart of matter holds a word ...
Make it serve no impious use!

Often in the obscure being hides a God;
And like the eye born under the eyelid's veil,
Pure spirit grows beneath the skin of stones.

From "autobiographical" reading at Justine's Brasserie, Austin, TX, 2011

SADNESS NOTES

THE TRUEST ART IS SAD. A work of art is good, is "beautiful," to the extent to which it seems to correspond to "how things are," which is a kind of definition of "God." Unfortunately,* "how things are" is a phenomenon that's indifferent to us—while, on the other hand, we *are* how things are: we can only know what we're physically capable of perceiving; and we ourselves follow from, are literally born of and controlled by, "how things are." It's all mirrors and ouroboros and there's no exit. Art is boring (which is especially sad considering how much one loves it and needs it). The subject brings to mind that classic suicide note, "All this buttoning and unbuttoning."†

But what do I know about philosophy? I should leave that to Schopenhauer: "No little part of the torment of existence lies in this, that Time is continually pressing upon us, never letting us take breath, but always coming after us, like a taskmaster with a whip. If at any moment Time stays his hand, it is only when we are delivered over to the misery of boredom." Furthermore, "In early youth, as we

---

* If such a word can be applied to existence, which itself defines "fortune" of course.

† Thanks Mette Madsen for bringing this line to my attention. It's attributed to an "anonymous 18th-century suicide note" where it appears in *The Oxford Dictionary of Quotations*.

contemplate our coming life, we are like children in a theatre before the curtain is raised, sitting there in high spirits and eagerly waiting for the play to begin. It is a blessing that we do not know what is really going to happen. Could we foresee it, there are times when children might seem like innocent prisoners, condemned, not to death, but to life, and as yet all unconscious of what their sentence means. Nevertheless, every man desires to reach old age; in other words, a state of life of which it may be said: 'It is bad today, and it will be worse tomorrow; and so on till the worst of all.'"*

I admit those lines are pretty funny, but funniness is another quality of the best art. In fact, sadness is funny, because it's so useless. The funniness gets swamped and mutilated by the very pointlessness though (viz. Beckett).

The great poet of sadness is Paul Verlaine.

III†

It rains gently on the town.
—Arthur Rimbaud

It weeps in my heart
as it rains on the town.
What is it that indifferently
slices into my heart?

The rain sounds sweet
on the earth and the roofs

---

* Both quotations from "On the Sufferings of the World" (from *Parerga, 1851), as translated by* T. Bailey Saunders in *Complete Essays of Schopenhauer* (New York: Willey Book Co., 1942).

† From *Songs Without Words* (*Romances sans paroles*, 1874), section *Forgotten Songs* (*Ariettes oubliées*). Translated by Richard Hell.

to the soft bore-
dom in my heart.

There's no reason the sky
weeps in my disheartened heart.
No betrayal?
Grief without reason.

It's worse
for having no reason.
Without love or hatred
it rains in my heart.

[Which incidentally brings to mind these lines of the poem "Nine All Night" by our exhibition's Rene Ricard: "Now the lights are slowly going out in the Bronx . . . no / The lights go out one by one in Queens / Love is gone / And the lights are going out one by one in my heart."*]

Two sorts of experience are the most sad, though they are related complexly. The first is the sadness of innocence, which, of course, like everything in language and human existence (except poetry, "spiritual transport"), only exists in relation to its violation, its loss, absence, or opposing counterpart. The other is the sadness of betrayal—not of being betrayed, but rather the act of betraying another. These plights are built deeply into our self-conception, of course: paradise and its loss; and the human betrayal of "God"—which is another aspect of the (biblical) description of our being and its origins—though Judas is a purer example. I have two stories about the first type of sadness, both of which have to do with my daughter, and which are moments that felt gorgeously sad. The first one was funny too.

When Ruby was around three years old, one day I was alone with her in an elevator going down on our way to the playground in the park. I'm

---

* From the periodical *CUZ* #1 (New York: 1988, The Poetry Project, Ltd.).

tall, and, as I spoke to her, in order to see her face to face I squatted down on my haunches. She immediately did the same thing, defeating my purpose. She thought that if I did it, it must be the proper way to behave.

Another time when she was a small child and had done something wrong, misbehaved somehow, I had the sudden realization that, "There will come a time when she won't be forgiven."

Sad literary masterpieces of the 20th century . . .

In Search of Lost Time (*À la recherche du temps perdu*). The title speaks for itself. Though, to give pleasure its due, the book does inhabit a realm very close to happiness, which is sad.

Levi-Strauss's anthropological dissertation-memoir, *Tristes Tropiques*, one of the most beautiful and melancholy of books, could be regarded as a long meditation on the corruption of innocence. It's also partly about how the study of something—in this case Amazonian tribal peoples— tends to destroy the thing under examination (and corrupt the innocence of the student as well—there's always another area of innocence!). But, so: in studying sadness, we destroy it!

Beckett.

Sebald. Cioran. Cormac McCarthy.

In Borges, another indisputable literary master of the century, futility suffuses all. When asked during a late interview what he felt at the prospect of death, he replied, "Hope. All I feel is hope, knowing the certainty of escape from this miserable existence," and a moment later, "Free will is an illusion, but a necessary illusion. To quote Spinoza, we are like an apple that falls, but feels that it wants to fall."* (The greatest of filmmakers, Robert Bresson, also believed all existence to be chance and predetermination.)

Eve betrayed God and so did Judas. What could be more sad than their fates? And any God worth the name is in us already. Those acts of betrayal are also losses of innocence. There's no more (deliciously?) sad

---

* On April 8, 1980 in a public interview at M.I.T., Cambridge, MA.

thing than self-corruption: to profoundly know one is doing wrong, but persist. One also knows, all along, that the punishment, no matter how hidden, must be greater than the reward. Still, the fall is voluptuously inevitable. One takes one's own innocence, thereby demonstrating the fundamental grotesqueness of our position, halfway between mud and "angel"—as beings purely chemical, physical, mechanical, fore-ordained, but with brains so big and heavy that the brains are conscious of themselves and capable of imagining behavior other than the one that actually imprisons us. It's hopeless.

So what do we do? Make art, for one thing. As Borges also said, in a preface to one of his books, "The learned doctors of the Great Vehicle teach us that the essential characteristic of the universe is its emptiness. They are certainly correct with respect to the tiny part of the universe that is this book. [...] It is all just appearances, a surface of images—which is why readers may, perhaps, enjoy it. The man who made it was a pitiable sort of creature, but he found amusement in writing it; it is to be hoped that some echo of that pleasure may reach his readers."*

Art, like life, is a matter of killing time.

Finally, I'd like to quote the poet John Weiners: "I want to write a poem about an old person dying of loneliness. I want to write a poem about an old person, alone in a room, dying of hunger and loneliness. No one has ever written a poem about an old person dying in the cold, of hunger and loneliness. Except of course Ava Gardner, who is always our master."†

From Sad Songs *exhibition catalogue (Normal: University Galleries, 2005)*

---

* From 1954, *A Universal History of Iniquity*, in *Collected Fictions* (New York: Viking Penguin, 1998).

† In a 1984 interview with Raymond Foye, published in *Cultural Affairs in Boston* (Santa Rosa: Black Sparrow Press, 1988), p. 17.

CREDITS

Page 32: painting © Christopher Wool: Untitled, 1987, enamel and flashe on aluminum, 72" x 48". Used by permission of Christopher Wool.

Page 34: two page spread from Secession catalogue © Christopher Wool: *Chistopher Wool* (Vienna: Secession, 2001). Used by permission of Christopher Wool.

Pages 36, 37: photos © Christopher Wool: *East Broadway Breakdown* (Berlin: Holzwarth Publications, 2003) 8.5" x 11". Used by permission of Christopher Wool.

Page 39: painting © Christopher Wool: Untitled, 2000, enamel on aluminum, 108" x 72". Used by permission of Christopher Wool.

Page 70: drawing © Richard Meyers: Fountain, ca. 1975, pencil on lined notebook page, approx. 8" x 6". Used by permission of Richard Meyers, courtesy of Fales Library and Special Collections, New York University Libraries.

Page 77: painting © Richard Meyers: Untitled, 1997, oil on canvas panel, approx. 18" x 24". Used by permission of Richard Meyers.

Page 78: dust jacket design © Richard Meyers: preview edition of *Hot and Cold* (Ancram, NY: Vehicle Editions, 1998). Used by permission of Richard Meyers.

Page 152: painting © Peter Schuyff: Untitled, 1994, acrylic on canvas, 23.62" x 23.62". Used by permission of Peter Schuyff.

Page 155: two photographs © GODLIS: CBGB interiors, 2006. Used by permission of David Godlis.

Page 163: painting © Marilyn Minter: Orange Crush, 2009, enamel on metal. 108" x 180". Courtesy of the artist and Salon 94, New York.

Page 163: painting © Marilyn Minter: Spill, 1977, oil on canvas, 60"x 60". Courtesy of the artist and Salon 94, New York.

Page 164: one panel detail of four panel painting © Marilyn Minter: Porn Grid, 1989, enamel on metal, single panel 24" x 30". Courtesy of the artist and Salon 94, New York.

Page 173, 174, 175, 176, 177, 178: notebooks images © Richard Meyers: 1970-1988. Used by permission of Richard Meyers, courtesy of Fales Library and Special Collections, New York University Libraries.

Page 181: collage/painting by Joe Brainard: If Nancy Was the Santo Niño de Praga, 1972, mixed media on paper, 12" x 9 ". Colby College Museum of Art, gift of the Alex Katz Foundation, 20008.200. Used by permission of the Estate of Joe Brainard and courtesy of Tibor de Nagy Gallery, New York. As included in *The Nancy Book* (Los Angeles: Siglio, 2008) collection of the "If Nancy Was" series of Joe Brainard works.

Page 189: painting © Christopher Wool: She Smiles for the Camera I, 2005, enamel on linen, 104" x 78". Used by permission of Christopher Wool.

Page 191: photo © Christopher Wool: installation shot Gagosian Gallery L.A. show, 2006. Used by permission of Christopher Wool.

THANKS

Thanks most especially to Elyse Strongin of Neuwirth & Associates, who stuck by me so generously and skillfully through the crazily rushed, complex typesetting and formatting of this book.